# And on That Bombshell

# And on That Bombshell

## Richard Porter

First published in Great Britain in 2015
by Orion Books

1  3  5  7  9  10  8  6  4  2

The author and publisher are grateful to the following for permission
to reproduce photographs:
Section One: 1, 5 © Justine Sullivan; 2, 7, 9, 11, 13, 14, 15, 16 © Iain May; 3, 6, 8, 10
© John Lakey; 4, 12 © Richard Porter.
Section Two: 1, 12, 14 © Justine Sullivan; 2, 5, 6, 7, 8, 9, 16 © Richard Porter; 3, 4, 1,
11, 13, 15 © Iain May.
Section Three: 1, 2, 6, 13, 15, 16 © Richard Porter; 3 © Justin Leighton; 4, 5, 7, 8, 9,
11, 12, 14, 17 © Iain May.

A CIP catalogue record for this book
is available from the British Library.

ISBN (hardback): 978 1 4091 6473 9

ISBN (trade paperback): 978 1 4091 6474 6

Typeset by Born Group

Printed in Great Britain by Clays Ltd, St Ives plc

The Orion Publishing Group Ltd
Carmelite House
50 Victoria Embankment
London, EC4Y 0DZ
An Hachette UK company
www.orionbooks.co.uk

The Orion Publishing Group's policy is to use papers that
are natural, renewable and recyclable products and made
from wood grown in sustainable forests. The logging and
manufacturing processes are expected to conform to the
environmental regulations of the country of origin.

For Jules and Dylan

# *Introduction*

Hello. My name's Richard and for 13 years, 22 series and 175 episodes I was the script editor on what accidentally became the world's biggest car show.

When we started making the new format of *Top Gear*, beginning in 2002 with a pair of disastrous pilot episodes, we had no idea that our sincere but often inept efforts would become so popular around the world. All we wanted to do was create a car programme that wasn't like anything that had gone before. BBC2 told us that was ambition enough, and if we could get to three million viewers they'd be very pleased. By 2015 our combined television and iPlayer numbers were banging on the door of 10 million in the UK alone, and had topped 350 million viewers worldwide.

In the early days we were happy enough testing a medium-sized Mazda in the English countryside. By the end, we were making mini-movies featuring million-dollar supercars. At the beginning we'd cheerily take any minor celebrity guest we thought might be slightly interested in cars. By the 15th series, we were playing host to Tom Cruise. We shot the first few series on location without raising an eyebrow or attracting a crowd. A decade later, we had to hire security to repel the excitable crowds and it was the same whether we were filming in Monte Carlo or Macclesfield.

In the course of making the show we got chased by angry mobs, caused hysterical headlines in newspapers and almost killed one of our presenters. We also argued, bickered, made mistakes and had a lot of fun.

This book tries to give a little bit of insight into the deranged roller-coaster ride of the crappy BBC2 motoring show that became, according to *Guinness World Records*, the planet's most watched factual programme. Quite an achievement for a show that didn't have any facts in it.

This isn't an exhaustive history of *Top Gear* because I don't know anything about camera lenses, I can't remember the name of the song that was used as background in that sequence everyone likes and it escapes me for now why we never featured the Ferrari 458 Speciale.

On the other hand, I do remember who suggested we call our in-house racing driver The Stig, I can recall the time I had a furious argument with Jeremy and then got trapped behind a naan bread and I know which member of the team came up with the inspired yet idiotic idea for us to get a dog. So if you want that sort of thing, read on.

If not, don't worry, there's probably a repeat of *Top Gear* on telly.

# *Old Top Gear*

If you're very young or not interested in cars or you were sentenced to 28 years inside a Dutch prison back in 1974, you may not realise that *Top Gear* wasn't always a programme about three silly men arguing and falling over.

Once upon a time *Top Gear* was a sensible, magazine-style show in which fuel economy was assessed and classic traction engines were driven and almost nothing caught on fire. When it started in the late seventies it was presented by prim news doyenne Angela Rippon, shortly to be joined by beardy box-opening enthusiast Noel Edmonds. This is a useful thing to know if you're ever in a pub quiz and the question comes up, 'Who first presented *Top Gear*?' Don't be tempted to shout out 'Richard Hammond!' That would be wrong. Also, it's bad form to shout out stuff at pub quizzes.

Originally, *Top Gear* was broadcast only in the Birmingham region before it was promoted to national status and became a mainstay of the BBC2 schedule. Then Rippon went back to the news, Edmonds wandered off to have his late breakfast and the show settled into a steady rhythm of sensibleness under the reliable watch of solid, authoritative presenters, most notably William Woollard and Chris Goffey. Woollard was the raffishly-haired one who would loft a foot onto a car's bumper and stand there delivering information like an especially learned catalogue model. Goffey was the bearded one who sported chunky jumpers and seemed like the sort of solid chap who'd lend you his lawnmower, though woe betide you if you returned it in less than perfect order. There were other presenters of course – among them aquiline Frank Page and dads' favourite Sue Baker – but Woollard and Goffey were the figureheads, placing their hands firmly upon the wheel and carefully checking their mirrors before pulling off into another long and informative piece to camera.

As a kid in the 1980s, I loved *Top Gear*. It was varied and unashamedly a bit nerdy. Also, in a world before the internet, it told me things I hadn't heard before. Plus it was about cars and I liked cars a lot. Even today, hearing William Woollard solemnly intone his 'drive safely and goodnight' sign off gives me a little thrill as seven-year-old me thinks, *Oh good, that's the sound of* Top Gear. And then a little sadness, as seven-year-old me thinks, *Oh bollocks, that's the end of* Top Gear *for another week*. That was the programme throughout the eighties. Serious, sensible, and required viewing for a car-obsessed child.

In the nineties, however, things changed. Woollard and Goffey were quietly shuffled off and in their place came a roster of exciting new presenters. There was racing driver Tiff Needell, who drifted like a demon and spoke like something with teeth had got into his trousers. There was urbane car trader Quentin Willson, who had a nice line in silken metaphors and a wry smile which said see me after the show and I'll sell you this car at an excellent price. There was coquettish siren Vicki Butler-Henderson, husky of voice and deft of steering. And there was a well-spoken chap with an alarming Afro who had the wit and brilliance to change car television for ever. His name was Kingsley Flistwipe and unfortunately he was killed in a blimp accident just before his first *Top Gear* shoot. Which is when they hired a short-notice replacement called Jeremy Clarkson. I might have dreamt this last bit.

Anyway, *Top Gear* hit a golden patch in the 1990s as it became spikier and funnier and with a bit more bite. Not that you'd notice it if you watched an episode now, since it all looks very staid and someone is almost certainly at a steam rally, but it was a gentler time and people were still amazed by those T-shirts that change colour when you get sweaty. Jeremy led the charge to give *Top Gear* more attitude, whether it was driving a car four yards and then declaring the steering too heavy or refusing to drive a car at all simply because it was so dreary. His style was bold and noisy and most of all funny. Sometimes, Clarkson would appear in the same scene as Needell and Willson – perhaps at a motor show or capering around in their newly declared car of the year as Tiff embarked on an honest attempt to invert it – and they'd all say funny things and pull funny faces and seem like the gang you'd want to be part of. It was an unwitting prototype of what was to come. If you were a kid, or even just a bit childish, it was brilliant. I had loved *Top Gear* in the eighties, but I loved *Top Gear* in the nineties even more.

That said, I believe *Top Gear* presenters are like the actors playing James Bond or Doctor Who. In your heart, you can never break the sacred link with whoever was doing it in your early childhood. That's why I can't shake my fondness for the memory of Woollard looking earnestly into camera with one foot perched on the front tyre of a Rover 800 or

Goffey bristling from inside his cable knit as he grumbled about the headlamp switch placement on some new Datsun. They weren't funny or flippant or silly, but they weren't trying to be. They were proper broadcasters and they told you stuff.

Much though it might appear that new *Top Gear* had no real link to the past, we never forgot Woollard and Goffey on the 21st-century version of the show. That might seem a strange thing to claim, since at no point did we take an in-depth look at the workings of the Transport Research Laboratory or investigate a new type of anti-jackknifing tow hitch for caravans, yet the shadow of old *Top Gear* was cast over our work in one very specific way. Every so often we'd be watching edited footage of something especially idiotic we'd shot, or be standing on location waiting for a caravan full of jelly to explode, and one of us – usually Jeremy – would say, 'Uh-oh, this is going to make William Woollard VERY CROSS' or 'Oh dear, Chris Goffey is going to HATE this.'

And then in our minds we would picture the former presenters sitting in their homes – in my head they both had very nice oak-panelled rooms and wing-back chairs – wearily flicking onto *Top Gear*, even though they had told themselves they shouldn't, and hoping for once to hear some information about boot capacity or optional tilt/slide sunroofs only to find three utter buffoons looning around in beekeeper outfits or filling each other's gloveboxes with cake on what used to be THEIR programme; and their teeth would grind and their fists would clench and then, in a fit of despair, they would hurl the remote to the ground, frightening the flatulent Labrador by the fire.

I've no evidence that any of this happened. I'm pretty sure William Woollard and Chris Goffey, both very successful businessmen in their post-*Top Gear* careers, had much better things to be doing with their Sunday evenings. But if they did watch the show, I rather hoped that in fact they liked it or at least grudgingly respected what we'd done with it. Because in a way, without the legacy of old *Top Gear*, there wouldn't have been what followed.

# Matching Tie

You might remember Jon Bentley from old *Top Gear*. He was the well-spoken presenter with the energetic, infectious enthusiasm of an excellent uncle or favourite college professor. He later went on to apply his plummy glee for technical things to *The Gadget Show*. and once, for reasons too complicated to explain, followed me down London's Oxford Street intently observing me trying to buy a cheap mobile phone.

On *Top Gear*, however, the presenting job was just a sideline, since by day Jon was the programme's series editor. And because of this, he was able to give himself the mandate to pop up at the end of a Thursday evening's programme some time in late 1997 to announce that *Top Gear* was looking for researchers. Anyone interested should write in with a CV and three ideas for the show.

At the time I was working in the Wilmslow branch of Next. I didn't want to spend the rest of my days folding jumpers. I wanted to work on *Top Gear*. This unconventional job advertisement was so exciting I could barely breathe. As it turned out, the on-air ad broke several BBC rules on recruitment, as a result of which Bentley got a slap on the wrist along with a stern instruction to go away and put a proper ad in the paper. I didn't know this at the time. I just knew how to fold jumpers.

Unless *Top Gear* was branching out into a chain of mid-priced clothes shops, I was plainly unqualified for this position but I gave it a go nonetheless, agonising for hours until I had three ideas I thought good enough to send in. One suggested comparing brand-new cars with their direct ancestors from 30 years ago to see how far we'd come. Another had Quentin highlighting cars that would become used bargains in the future. The final one imagined Jeremy lurking in a hedge pretending to be one of those spy photographers who pap shots of secret new models before they're announced. It was 1997. The bar was a lot lower, editorially speaking.

My thoughts went into an envelope along with my CV, which I stuck at the back in the hope that the reader would be wowed by the ideas and fail to notice that my main employment experience was rearranging the sock display. I didn't mention my other skills which were: walking briskly around the shop holding a single item of clothing to give the impression of being busy; hiding in the stockroom to avoid having to deal with actual customers; and happily agreeing to see if we had a different size in stock but really using it as an excuse to go into the back for a quick sit down.

Many months went by. The on-air recruitment drive had been a bit more successful than they'd expected. Thousands of people had written in and even once they'd discounted the ones who refused to share their ideas, and the ones who couldn't count to three, and the ones who didn't know what a CV was, there were still a lot of applications to read. In the face of radio silence I just assumed that I'd been unsuccessful and went back to reordering the big cupboard where we kept the shoes.

It was quite a surprise when the BBC rang my parents' house and invited me for an interview. If you're ten you might be wondering why anyone would ring a building rather than a person, but it was 1997 and I didn't have a mobile. Another thing I didn't have was a car, so on the day of my interview I got the train to Birmingham wearing my best Next suit, a Next shirt ironed to the point of translucence and a pair of Next shoes buffed to a mirror finish. As a final touch, I rifled through my growing collection of Next ties and picked the one I thought most appropriate. It was bright yellow. There were two reasons for this. Firstly, bright ties were quite fashionable at the time. And secondly I thought it would make me stand out and I'd been told this was a good thing when applying for a job. By the same logic, when applying for other jobs I'd started sending out my CV on brightly coloured paper and once had the brilliant idea of sending an unsolicited request for work to an ad agency in which, for no readily apparent reason, I pretended to be asymmetrically-hairstyled Human League singer Phil Oakey. I think I might have been losing my mind. They never wrote back. When it came to the *Top Gear* interview, I had this vague notion that the bright tie might make me memorable. As in, 'God, do you remember that weird bloke in the awful tie? You know, the one who arrived at the interview and started asking if we wanted to sign up for the Next directory.'

Inadvertently, it turned out to be a good tactic. When I walked into the interview room at BBC Pebble Mill, the actual Jon Bentley off the telly was standing there. He was wearing the same tie as me.

'Oh, I like your tie,' he said.

'I like your tie too,' I replied.

'Yes! Ha haaaa!' he said. Things seemed to have got off to a good start.

The interview was conducted by Bentley, show producer John Wilcox (not wearing the same tie) and a nice lady from HR (ditto). The questions were firm but fair. One of them asked what I would do if I was asked to find a Lamborghini for filming.

Afterwards I regretted that my answer was, 'Ring Lamborghini'. It sounded like an idiotic response, verging on the sarcastic. It's only a while later that I found out that this really is what you do. Throughout *Top Gear* history, if you wanted to borrow a Lamborghini, you rang Lamborghini. And then maybe, if they said no, an owners' club or something. Without knowing, I'd accidentally given the right answer.

The rest of the interview seemed okay. Not as inadvertently successful as wearing the same tie as the most senior person in the room, but not too bad, all told. Buoyed by this success, mostly surrounding the tie, I met up with a mate in Birmingham afterwards and had a drink that turned into several drinks then we forgot to have dinner but did think perhaps another drink would be a corking idea. I'm mentioning this only as a way of explaining what happened next, which is that I got on my train back to the North West, began to feel a bit queasy and eventually had to run to one of the carriage doors, whack down the window and vomit out of it with great force and volume, which would have been fine except that we were pulling into Stafford station at the time.

I can only apologise if you were one of the people on that platform, maybe thinking, *Oh, look at that young man in his smart suit and vibrant tie, perhaps returning from some vital business in Birmingham or London and . . . OH MY GOD, HE'S MACHINE-GUNNING THE STATION WITH VOMIT!*

## Matching Tie

Some time after this, I got offered a position as a junior researcher on *Top Gear*. The money wasn't great, it required moving to Birmingham and I'd lose my attractive staff discount at Next, but none of this mattered. I'd got a job on my very favourite TV programme. I've never asked Jon Bentley this, but I'm pretty sure it was all down to the tie.

# An Exceptionally Large Face

BBC Pebble Mill in 1998 was a very jolly place to work. Not the building itself, which was a dreary sixties monolith with a small, gloomy reception area at the front and a bright, unused atrium where the lifts lived at the back, leading to the jocular suggestion that it had been built the wrong way round. But it was steeped in knowledge and full of friendly people who were willing to share it, which was useful to someone who'd just come from working in a shop and knew the square root of sod all.

Better yet, under the mildly bonkers stewardship of Jon Bentley, *Top Gear* seemed very happy to let someone with no experience have a crack at whatever they fancied. Not something complicated like working the cameras or operating a machine gun, obviously, but fine with letting you learn smaller stuff on the job. Within a few weeks of being there I'd been allowed to have a crack at writing a script (wonky, but passable), followed shortly by a stab at presenting (arms looked freakishly long, appeared to have terminal disease, generally hopeless) and, later, an attempt at directing (forgot to get vital shots, found editing rather boring, generally hopeless). There was also a bit of 'acting', as long as you accept that 'acting' means clowning about on camera pretending to be a car dealer or a punter or a bit of background interest. This carried on for some time until eventually the series producer told us that if we didn't stop titting around on screen every other bloody week he would have to enrol us in Equity.

The anything goes attitude was summed up in my first-ever credit in television, which was for an episode of spin-off show *The Car's the Star*, about Ladas. After unexpectedly writing the words and then even more unexpectedly appearing as a vagrant lying in some rubble on an abandoned industrial site in the East Midlands that was doubling for Mother Russia, I was listed at the end of the programme as 'scriptwriter and tramp'. I've never been more proud of a billing.

I liked the relaxed, have-a-go spirit of the Beeb's Birmingham branch office. I also liked the crackle and excitement of knowing that actual television was being made in the building, and with actual television came actual celebrities. I stood behind kids' news guru John Craven in the canteen. I heard former *Blue Peter* doyenne Sarah Greene tell a colleague it was 'pissing it down'. I watched with bemusement as hyperactive *Ready Steady Cook*-ist Ainsley Harriott inexplicably poked his head through our office door, went 'WAAAAH!' in the manner of a cooking lunatic and then ran off. It was brilliant.

Then there were the *Top Gear* presenters themselves. Quentin would pop in and with a knowing smirk tell you a story about buying an old Maserati for a song. Some days Tiff would appear, bouncing around and asking a million questions, like an intelligent, oversteering Tigger. Motorcycle man Steve Berry would arrive and pronounce the names of bike makers with such thick Lancastrian vowels it sounded like he was permanently consuming an enormous toffee. They were all exactly like they were on the TV, but funnier and friendlier and swearier.

Only Jeremy didn't show himself in the office during that first summer at Pebble Mill. He was off filming segments for an aquatic sub-show called *Waterworld*. This was a shame. Out of all the presenters, Clarkson was the one I most wanted to meet. Firstly, because he was that amusing bloke off the telly. Secondly, and more importantly for me, because I was a huge fan of his written work, ever since first reading his columns in *Performance Car* magazine, long before he ended up on screen. In print, he was one of the few car journalists who didn't get bogged down with mundane things like boot space and fuel economy, preferring to be interesting and entertaining, letting fly with deliberately contrary opinions which he backed up with flair and fifty million tons of exaggeration. Best of all, he was funny. Most car journalists didn't seem to have much sense of humour at all, whereas Clarkson peppered his pieces with gags and analogies and wonderful absurdities. He was unique and clever and having read him for years he was pretty much the entire reason I wanted one day to write about cars for a living.

You can imagine, then, my excitement when word went round the office that Jeremy had finished mucking about with boats and would be filming something on dry land that very week for which extra help was needed. Immediately I put myself forward to the director, an ebullient chap called Ewan Keil who had terrible trouble getting email past firewalls because his name contained the word 'wank'. Yes, he said, you can come along.

The gist of the shoot was this: A whole episode of *Waterworld* was being given over to Jeremy on board an

American aircraft carrier and it was decided that the show would be enhanced if some of the usual similes, metaphors and analogies were literally acted out. So he'd say, 'sleeping on this boat is like trying to sleep inside a lorry trailer while people bang on the outside with hammers, a man barks orders through a megaphone and a child practises violin next to your head' and then there would be a cutaway to Jeremy inside a lorry trailer with people banging on the outside with hammers, a man barking orders through a megaphone and a child prac . . . You get the idea.

So that's how we ended up standing on a disused airfield in Oxfordshire with a lorry, a tone-deaf child and a lot of hammers. There were various other props too, because there were several other set-ups, the filming of which was set to take all day. But the first thing we did was stand on the old runway, idly milling around. I was yet to realise that in the making of television there's a lot of milling around. It's why one of the most popular pastimes among people in television is smoking, simply because it gives you something to do while the crew fiddle with their lenses or the sound man says he can hear a small aeroplane somewhere within a 20-mile radius and we'll all have to wait five minutes for it to pass.

In this case, we milled about because we were waiting for Jeremy. I was excited. They say you should never meet your heroes and normally I'd agree. I could imagine myself going to extraordinary lengths to avoid talking to, say, David Bowie just in case the encounter turned out to be disappointing for me and downright embarrassing for him. But with Jeremy we both seemed to like cars and we both seemed to like words, so at least we'd have something in common. Also, technically we worked for the same place and it would be a bit odd to spend my new career studiously avoiding a particular colleague in case he turned out to be a twat.

Suddenly, a black Jaguar XJR appeared on the horizon and began cruising slowly towards us. In my mind, it approached through a shimmering heat haze, but though it was summer it was also Oxfordshire and I think this is pretty unlikely. The Jag rolled to a stop and from it stepped that familiar bloke off the television. The director went over with an energetic greeting and there was some chirpy back-and-forth during which Jeremy pointed out that one of the headlights on his XJ had come loose, leading to a brief routine about car makers knocking off early which he delivered in a funny Brummie accent, and everything was extremely cheery.

They say that some people have a star 'vibe', that they radiate something that makes them the centre of attention in any given situation, and even on a draughty old airfield Jeremy definitely had that. As soon as he got out of the car, the whole crew seemed to gravitate towards him and he became the totem at the centre of the shoot. As far as I could see, several things gave him that natural presence. Firstly, he was very tall. Secondly, he had a big personality, a loud voice and the perfectly timed comic chops of the seasoned anecdotist, which made him arrive at the head of his own bow wave of charisma. Thirdly, he had an exceptionally large face.

The first two things you could have guessed from watching Jeremy on television. But seeing him compressed onto your TV screen gave little sense that his entire head was like a 120 per cent model of itself. This, more than anything, was what really struck me upon first meeting Jeremy. Not literally. I was slightly mesmerised by the size of his face as we began our filming, mucking around inside the lorry trailer with the violining and the megaphone and all the various other metaphors made real.

During the day there was a break in filming and he sat next to me on the back of the lorry trailer. 'Where have you come from?' he asked. I told him I used to work in Next. 'Are all your clothes from Next?' he said, eyeing my shirt and trousers, which were indeed from Next. I told him that I was afraid they were. 'What about your shoes?' Yes, even my shoes were from Next. 'And is that a Next haircut . . .?' Up close, he was friendly and funny and everything I would have hoped for from the man who proved that car writing didn't have to be dull. He also had an exceptionally large face.

Later that day I noticed some other things about Jeremy that would prove to be constants throughout future iterations of *Top Gear*. Just because there was a script and a set-up didn't mean he wasn't constantly thinking about the editorial and ways to make it bigger, better and more amusing. In one scene he'd compared being launched off an aircraft carrier to sitting in a deck chair and then being hit by a lorry. As written, Clarkson would sit in the chair, say a few words and then a lorry would smash him out of the way. By using a locked-off shot – the camera in a fixed position on a tripod so the shots perfectly match – Jeremy's place could be taken by a dummy before the impact and a quick cut in the edit would make it appear that he'd been clobbered. On the spot, he came up with an additional idea. After the impact we should cut to a shot of the fast-moving lorry, with him clinging to the front, screaming. There was no provision to have a man dangling from the radiator grille of a massive truck but that didn't matter. Jeremy thought it was worth doing and he would simply 'hang on'. It's another thing I learned about him that day; he was uncommonly fearless. For the sake of adding something to the scene he was happy to spreadeagle himself on the front of a moving lorry, held in place by nothing more than a strong grip and some string. There was something very cool about a man who for the sake of his art was prepared to risk getting horrifically run over. It was impressive to watch him at work. Especially since he didn't fall into the path of his own joke.

As it happened, all of this filming turned out to be in vain. Back in the edit suite at Pebble Mill it was decided that the footage from the actual aircraft carrier was ample and interesting enough to sustain a whole programme without comedy cutaways and everything we'd shot, from the child violinist to the impromptu stunt work, was thrown away.

It didn't matter to me though, because the shoot had been another few feet up the steep learning curve of my new job in television. More than that, I'd finally met my car-writing idol. And he'd turned out to be a good bloke. A good bloke with an exceptionally large face.

# The Paddy Ashdown
# of Motoring

It was early 1999. All was quiet in the old *Top Gear* office, although we didn't call it by that name because it would have been weird, like someone in the trenches referring to 'the First World War'. So all was quiet in what was, at that point, simply the *Top Gear* office. I remember that it was quiet because when our series producer Chris Richards came off the phone looking slightly ashen he didn't have much of an audience with whom to share something earth-shattering – Jeremy was leaving the show. Those of us who were there received this news as you would that of someone dying. I think I said one word. That word was 'shit'.

Later, Jeremy would claim he threw in the towel because a Renault Clio had been delivered to his house, he couldn't think of a single thing to say about it and resigning was his only option. On the phone that day he hadn't mentioned any small French cars, but he did claim he'd heard Paddy Ashdown resigning as leader of the Liberal Democrats by saying he felt he'd taken it as far as he could and had decided that this sentiment applied to him too. In more recent times, Jeremy wrote a piece about giving up drinking and related it to the late Charles Kennedy. On this basis, he appears to be engaged in a slow-motion project to compare himself to every Lib Dem leader of recent times and I for one can't wait until 2031 to see what he can do with Sir Menzies Campbell.

Back at Pebble Mill we, like the Lib Dems, had a problem. *Top Gear* wasn't Jeremy's show but he was a huge part of it and it would be naïve to ignore how much of the programme's appeal in those heady and top-rated days came from the prospect that he would pop up and enliven a review of some dreary car with a metaphor about underpants or something. Nonetheless, as the news sank in we tried to put a brave face on it. The show was bigger than any one presenter, we said to ourselves. *Top Gear* can and will carry on. We have Quentin. We have Tiff. We have Vicki. We have Tony Mason for heaven's sake. Those steam rallies won't report themselves, you know. Deep down, though, I think we all feared that *Top Gear* had lost its biggest attraction. Yes, it could carry on and viewers would still watch, but it would be like going to the zoo knowing that their tiger had died.

One of our first jobs, post-Paddy Clarkson, was to find a new presenter or two. This was pretty much an ongoing task at *Top Gear* anyway. Not long after I'd started there Jon Bentley had told me to unearth some likely car journalists to screen-test and when the roster I'd found turned out to be people they'd already seen, or people they didn't want to see, Bentley insisted I had a go instead. We went down to the local park where he pointed a camcorder at me while I pretended that a small bush was actually a large Peugeot and entirely on the basis of this deliriously weird footage I was allowed to go away and make an item on car colours (which was too rubbish to broadcast) and then present a road test of a Subaru Legacy (which was also rubbish but eventually made it to air because the show was short an item one week and therefore desperate). After this Jon wisely realised he had not, as he hoped, found the new Clarkson. What he'd actually found was a man who betrayed the old adage about the camera adding pounds by looking thinner when viewed through the prism of television and with arms that seemed to be nine feet long, giving him the appearance of an anorexic octopus struggling to maintain eye contact with the camera. My presenting career was sensibly brought to an end. Besides, this was 1998 and at this point he still had the actual Clarkson.

When Jeremy left we looked again for fresh talent and invited a few people in for screen tests. One of them was a chap called James May. I admired James enormously for his clever and witty column in *CAR* magazine and for his clever and witty presenting on the Channel 4 car show, *Driven*. We liked *Driven* in the *Top Gear* office and everyone on the team watched it avidly. This was for two reasons. Firstly, because competition was healthy. And secondly because we secretly hoped that their show would be crap so that we could laugh about it and feel better about ourselves. Hence the howls of delighted laughter when we discovered that their branded lorry was always mysteriously driving on the wrong side of the road during their 'time exposed to danger' overtaking test because they'd had their logo painted on the wrong side of the trailer and couldn't afford to have it fixed.

On the day of the screen tests I made sure I was the one who met James at reception and since we were running behind schedule I took him up to the café on the first floor to distract him for a bit. Really, I just wanted to talk to him and find out if he was as funny and interesting as his *CAR* columns had led me to believe. With excitement, I offered him a tea or a coffee. He chose a coffee and then winced at the first sip. I apologised for the state of BBC coffee, as Ronnie Corbett and Terry Wogan had inadvertently taught us to do.

'Oh no, it's okay,' James replied. 'It's just that I don't really like coffee.'

That's no problem, I said eagerly, I can get you a tea if you'd prefer.

'No, no. You see, I love tea and I couldn't bear to have a bad cup of it,' James explained. 'That's why I asked for coffee.' I remember thinking he was a bit odd.

Later, James did a very good screen test, off the back of which he got a presenting job on *Top Gear*, where he proved himself to be an excellent person to work with and was actually as funny and interesting as I'd hoped. I never bought him a coffee again.

In our worst nightmares, post-Clarkson *Top Gear* would become a hollow shell of itself, watched by seven uninterested people. In reality, the show was fine. Producer Chris Richards compared it to running a football team: Yes, we'd lost our star striker, but we'd simply moved our other heavyweight players up front, brought in a talented player from Driven United and carried on as best we could.

Unfortunately, further up the Beeb food chain it was decided that things could be better. James May fulfilled the BBC's quota for people who had shaggy hair and were very nice, but not their quota for women. So they got rid of him and brought in Kate Humble, who fulfilled all three of those criteria. Kate was enormous fun to work with but making the show itself was becoming less of a joy. A new producer had been dropped in; some of the long-standing production team were shuffled off to other shows; it felt like management was meddling with our stuff. When it was suggested from on high that we should make an entire item in which we tested petrol-station sandwiches I decided that it wasn't the *Top Gear* I wanted to work on.

It was time to make like Paddy Ashdown and leave. I mean, *Top Gear*'s Paddy Ashdown. You'll note that even after resigning as leader of the Liberal Democrats the actual Paddy Ashdown remained very active within the party. I'm not sure what happened to that Jeremy Clarkson chap.

# We're Re-forming the Band

I left old *Top Gear* in summer 2000 and went to work for an online car seller run by a nice man who appeared to have misplaced his sideburns. I used to help write his speeches whenever he went to speak to rooms full of car dealers, all of whom hated him because he was trying to steal their lunch. When he wasn't around, the place was overseen by another chap who couldn't say words like 'problem', 'disaster' and 'massive cockup' but instead used to describe everything, no matter how catastrophic, as an 'issue'. I spent my days desperately trying to trick him into a situation in which he would discover severe troubles with a tissue, Vishnu or the Somalian city of Mogadishu but without much success. Compared to *Top Gear*, it was quite a boring place to work. After six months I handed in my notice and went to work for a new media company.

That was more interesting. It was 2001. There were lots of new media companies springing up. The one I worked for ticked all the boxes. Office in an old warehouse? Check. Table football in the office? You bet. Comfy seating area full of sofas and beanbags? Oh yeah. Hosing through a load of cash and going bust even before the massive fish tank had been delivered? Yes, that too. Bugger.

I was unemployed. The good thing about being a writer is that, like an actor claiming to be to be 'resting', you can stave off trips to the Job Centre and deflect worried questions from your parents by claiming to be 'freelance'. The freelance life suited me, especially the way it was unsullied by much in the way of work. At some point during this period of inactivity I signed up with a new internet provider and their package came with some free web space. It was still 2001. Having a website seemed like a fashionable thing to do so I set up a silly, badly made car thing called Sniff Petrol. It was meant to be satire in the mould of The Onion or Charlie Brooker's TV Go Home, though obviously not as good as either, since it was hamstrung by the simple fact that cars aren't inherently funny. I did my best to get around this snag by the simple expedient of making everything up, hence the first issue claimed that Volkswagen was about to launch a horse and F1 star Mika Hakkinen was to spice up his dull image by racing with a pair of underpants on his head. Things just carried on from there. I never put my name on the site so it was intriguingly anonymous and this, probably more than the actual drivel on the page, seemed to generate some interest. One of the newspapers mentioned the site. *Autocar* magazine ran a whole feature about it. It was given a hearty plug on the motoring page of a mid-range pornographical magazine, who then bust through the anonymity by asking for my name and address so they could send me two copies as keepsakes. Quite why they believed I'd need two I don't know. Perhaps they thought I'd like to give one to my parents. Why a mid-range bongo mag had a motoring page is another, equally puzzling matter. Anyway, it was nice that people seemed to be reading the site.

At the beginning of 2002 I got an email through the website from an old colleague. His name was Jeremy. I knew it was really him because the subject line was pure Clarkson. It said, 'READ THIS'. The message itself was very kind. After saying that Sniff Petrol was 'very, very funny', and taking an (incorrect) guess at who was behind it, he invited me to ring him. So I called up and outed myself, after which Jeremy promised to give the site a mention in his newspaper column, and that was that.

A few months later a Toyota PR man who had discovered my identity invited me to an informal car industry lunch for a select bunch of splendid old buggers. I didn't normally get invited to car-industry lunches, informal or otherwise, and it seemed rude to say no. We went to a Chinese restaurant in west London. Everyone seemed very affable. Then just as the crispy duck arrived so did Jeremy. He said a few hellos, raved about the book he was carrying and generally made the room a bit more entertaining, as was his wont. I caught his eye as he sat down. 'You're wearing a short-sleeved shirt,' he said, accusingly. Jeremy has several strange dislikes. Short-sleeved shirts is one of them. Then he got distracted by a possibly libellous story about another car writer and everyone carried on eating.

Since the room was full of journalists, I was rather expecting that lunch would ease us smoothly into a trip to the pub, from where we could fritter away the rest of the afternoon getting dog-dissolvingly pissed. But everyone else seemed to have other plans. I think some of them even involved doing work. As a newcomer, I felt I had misunderstood the terms and conditions of being a freelance writer.

As we prepared to leave the restaurant Jeremy sidled up to me. 'What are you doing now?' he asked. I said I was probably just going to go home. 'Do you want to share a cab back to Paddington?' he said. 'I've got something I want to talk to you about.'

I didn't actually need to go to Paddington station, but this seemed too intriguing to ignore so I pretended that I did and we hailed a taxi. As we bounced through west London, Jeremy explained that he and Andy Wilman were going to make a new car show for the BBC. I remembered Wilman from Pebble Mill. He was a mysterious and occasional presence in the *Top Gear* office and a mysterious and occasional presence on *Top Gear* itself, where he used to present amusing and unusual items in an endearingly scruffy style. Jeremy explained that the new show could have been called Carmageddon but there'd been a change of plan. Now it was going to be called *Top Gear*.

Just a few months earlier, old *Top Gear* had been 'rested' by the BBC and most of the on-screen talent had scarpered to Channel 5 to start *Fifth Gear*. The name was going begging so it was only logical that Jeremy and Andy would use it for their new, radically different car show and they wanted to talk to me about working on it. We like Sniff Petrol, Jeremy said, and we want that attitude in our programme. We want someone who thinks cars can be funny and doesn't take them too seriously. I was going to point out that the entire existence of Sniff Petrol was very much in debt to the man in the cab with me who thought cars could be funny and didn't take them too seriously, but that would have sounded so toadying we'd have both puked onto the flip-down seats.

We got to Paddington and went to the café on the station concourse. Jeremy said he often saw British land-speed recordist Richard Noble in this very spot and we speculated that he was just hanging around pointing at InterCity trains and saying, 'I've been faster than that'. After that we talked some rubbish about cars and television and Jeremy explained how he'd quit smoking. Then he realised he was going to miss his train home and got up to leave. 'Come in and see us,' he said by way of a parting shot. 'We need Sniff Petrol on this.' And with that he was gone.

On the Tube home I was delighted. It seemed as if I'd been tacitly offered a job. But then another thought crossed my mind. The smoking abstinence. The train home. This was all a cruel set-up and that man I'd just met was, quite plainly, a fake Jeremy. Quite a good one in many ways, but the details let it down. Imagine the actual Jeremy getting on a train while not smoking. It was absurd.

A few days later the real Andy Wilman rang and invited me into the BBC for a chat. It turned out the Jeremy I'd met was real after all. And he was really there when I went over to White City to meet Andy and Gary Hunter, the bullet-headed Scotsman the BBC had appointed executive producer, since they clearly didn't trust Wilman and Clarkson not to skyve off and smoke tabs behind the bike shed. We had an informal conversation. Andy was enthusiastic, Gary was visibly unimpressed, Jeremy made a superbly nerdy joke about building a test track on the roof of the building next door. Wilman said he'd be in touch soon and I went home to my moderate level of unemployment to await further instructions.

When the call came it wasn't from Wilman. It was a producer from Channel 4's *Driven* programme asking if I'd come in for a day of brainstorming as they attempted to reinvent their show. I was a bit broke, they offered actual cash money, naturally I went along. What we're planning to do, they said, is relocate the show to a studio, maybe with a track outside, and all the VTs will be introduced from this base. This was awkward. What they were setting out was almost exactly what Wilman had described to me as the plan for new *Top Gear*. In a rare show of professionalism I managed not to mention the Wilman plan to *Driven* or vice versa.

A few days later the Channel 4 people rang again and asked if I could do more work on the show. They seemed very keen and their show was populated with some very nice, very talented people. But it wasn't *Top Gear*. They were putting together a team to make another car show. Jeremy was re-forming the band.

In the nick of time, the late Andy Wilman rang and offered me a job. It took me a split second to say yes.

# Starting Up

It was early summer, 2002. *Top Gear* didn't even have its own office. Instead, a small team had been installed in some spare space within the BBC White City building, occupying an area left vacant by some long-forgotten production which appeared to have left in a hurry.

Andy Wilman sat in a small side office, along with our exec Gary and a fantastic producer called Kate Shiers, who called everyone a 'numpty' and made sure stuff got done. I found a space in the main office alongside our two researchers, Jim Wiseman and Rowly French. Jim went on to become a successful TV producer and Rowly became the creative director of the company that made the Top Gear Live shows. Both deserve massive credit for their input into the show in those early days.

Jim's fantastically daft sense of humour and boundless capacity for lateral thinking introduced a gleeful silliness and deranged ideas like jumping a bus over some motorcycles. Rowly's natural enthusiasm and love of smoky, skidding *Fast & Furious* shenanigans grounded the show with a simple, youthful love of mucking about with cars. When we got grannies doing doughnuts, that was the centre spot in the Venn diagram of their minds. But that was all to come. In the early days, we just needed to get the basics pinned down.

The studio was a given. So was the track. We'd make use of the studio by having a celebrity guest, and there would be a bit where we caught up on car news. For a while we talked about a weekly studio finale in which some sort of musical ensemble played us out with their version of the theme tune. One week it would be a string quartet, the next a school recorder group, the following week maybe Motörhead. We never actually asked Motörhead, but we were sure they would do it. I suspect we were thinking too much about the eighties student sitcom *The Young Ones*. I read somewhere that they booked bands every week because under BBC rules that turned them from a normal comedy programme (which meant a tiny budget) into a light entertainment show (which qualified for more lavish funding, allowing them to film segments on location and blow things up). No such political chicanery for *Top Gear*, we just reckoned that having a random musical ensemble to play us off air was a bit daft and therefore funny. Although many years later we would be moved from the factual department to BBC Entertainment after someone noticed that the programme had almost no facts in it.

Having a band on each week was probably the only thing we wanted to crib from *The Young Ones*. For the most part, we wanted to be more like the beloved Saturday morning staple *Tiswas*, perhaps with a dash of blokey nineties soccerfest *Fantasy Football League*. The sense of fun and anarchy from the former, the humour and beguiling passion of the latter. And also from that second show, a complete crib of the

'Statto' character, with our own in-house car nerd sitting in the corner and correcting Clarkson on minute details.

Other ideas came and went. We'd go to the pub with Jeremy and sit for hours trying to work out what we were trying to do, what we were trying to say and in what tone. Should we really insist that we didn't go overseas on sunny car launches and only tested things on our terms? Could we get away with calling our studio a 'bunker' when it was plainly nothing of the sort? Did we need to make a song and dance out of our lack of singing and dancing, thereby reminding everyone we weren't like every other TV show at the time and provided a place of sanctuary for people who liked cars? Tiny things were worried about enormously and unimportant things discussed with great importance. Sometimes it was hugely exciting and we buzzed at the prospect of doing something new. Other times it all seemed too difficult and pointless and we were consumed with Eeyore-ish gloom. Either way, it felt like there was a lot to get sorted. One of the major jobs on the massive 'to do' list was finding new presenters.

At some point in the planning stage, someone had come up with the bright idea of asking the public to send in audition tapes. It being 2002 these were, quite literally, tapes. As a result, the office was stuffed with vast, wobbling columns of VHS cassettes bearing bright-eyed submissions from eager hopefuls. Some were quite good. Some were not. My favourite was a chap who boldly announced that he was going to road-test the latest Lamborghini and then delivered a lengthy assessment of the car entirely from his sofa, miming the steering and the pedals. Between words, he made engine noises.

We invited some of the better applicants and a selection of more experienced presenters to screen tests in a studio just off the A40 in west London. In front of the cameras, each candidate was asked to talk us around a car and then sit behind a desk with Jeremy for a mock news segment.

We saw a lot of people. Some of them were very good and yet, somehow, not quite right. We weren't absolutely sure what we wanted, male or female, young or old, it didn't really matter. When someone was right, we knew that we'd know. At least, we hoped we would.

Jason definitely seemed right. He knew loads about cars and not just how they worked; his background in the trade gave him a deep understanding of what made them good buys, what went wrong with them and what sort of deal to expect. And he managed to impart his knowledge in an interesting way, overlaid with a cheery West Country charm. You'd have bought a car from him on the spot.

Richard arrived at another screen-test session in his old Porsche 911. It was a bit scruffy and it was left-hand drive, because you could buy them cheaper if the wheel was on the wrong side. That's how much he loved cars, and 911s in particular. He was so desperate to have one, he'd put up with a permanent pain in the arse at car-park ticket machines just to own one. We'd met before when he'd screen-tested for old *Top Gear* a couple of years earlier. In the final reckoning, it was a decision between Hammond, who had solid television experience, and car journalist Adrian Simpson, who was new to telly. I voted for Richard because he seemed ready to go. The producer went with Adrian because he felt it would be better to develop someone from scratch. When we met at the new *Top Gear* screen tests, I told Hammond that he almost got the job last time. 'Oh don't tell me THAT,' he wailed. This time around, he had a lot going for him. Not just that he was quick-witted and he clearly loved cars. There was also a sense that he really wanted this. His audition was great, especially when he started telling self-deprecating stories about his darkest days in local radio. When he left Wilman, Clarkson and I stood in the doorway of the studio scene dock watching him rattle away in his old Porsche. There was a pause. Jeremy spoke first. 'I liked him,' he said. We all did.

We watched the screen-test footage back in the office. There was a little bit of debate but in the end there was fairly easy agreement. We'd found our two presenters. Jason and Richard had got the jobs. We never did find our Statto. Come to think of it, Motörhead never played our theme tune either.

# The Bad Pilot

We spent the summer of 2002 worrying about this new, studio-based *Top Gear* and what it was supposed to be. Since we'd still need to shoot stuff on location, we hired some VT directors and gave them a space down the far end of the new office where they could gather and talk about directorish things like lenses and angles and who'd got the most elaborately fashionable lunch. In general, they were a very TV-director sort of bunch. A bit arty, a bit larger than life, talking in a way that made it clear words were only a device for describing pictures. Only one of them didn't quite fit into this mould. Nigel Simpkiss was an unassuming chap whose eyes burned with quiet intensity behind his wire-framed glasses. He didn't look like a typical director nor sound like one, but he turned out to be our secret weapon. All the directors turned in good material but Nigel did something exceptional. He made cars look dramatic, he made landscapes look epic, he made clouds scud across the sky, stop, and then fly back the way they'd come. I don't remember a single meeting where we said new *Top Gear* should be full of filmic grandeur, but Nigel did it

36

anyway and set a benchmark for the show that continued for the rest of its natural life.

It was Nigel who directed the very first item we shot for new *Top Gear*; a test of a strange French executive car called the Renault Vel Satis, which was filmed entirely on location in Swindon. I can't remember why. It was part of a general principle that we wouldn't test cars simply for testing's sake, we would take them somewhere and perhaps attempt to put them into some sort of context. I think Swindon was Jeremy's idea because it had a lot of business parks and the Vel Satis was what they'd call an executive car. I remember him asking me to look up some relevant information about the town that we could put in the script. For years afterwards, the desktop of my computer still contained a document called SWINDO-FACTS.

We gathered in the office one day to watch a finished cut of the film. It seemed pretty good. It was a test of a car, but with the added sense of doing something relevant with it, in this case touring the bizniz parks of a town which had given the world Diana Dors, Billie Piper and an unusually high teenage pregnancy rate. Researcher Jim Wiseman summed it up during one of Jeremy's pieces to camera. 'It's good to see him talking about cars on telly again, isn't it?' he said. It was.

Other VTs were in progress. Now we just had to sort out the studio bit of the show and for this we would film a pilot episode. This is pretty standard for a new TV format, just so you can check that everything works and debug all the bits that don't. So on a warm midsummer's day the entire team trekked down to the all-new *Top Gear* base on the site of a former British Aerospace factory near Dunsfold in Surrey, to see for the first time the studio set that had been built within a hangar formerly used to paint planes. It was a huge metal structure in a format theatre experts would recognise as 'in the round', with a small stage to one side, a gap at the bottom for the cameras to shoot through and the audience arranged on raised platforms around the rest of a circle, surrounding the floor space on which the new models from that week's show were parked.

A BBC safety person said it was dangerous to have cars with petrol in the tanks inside a building under hot studio lights. We successfully argued that heat doesn't normally make cars explode, otherwise an Arizona summer would look like the set of a Michael Bay film. Also, it seemed that the most dangerous thing to do with petrol was to syphon it out of cars and leave it lying around in cans at the back of the building, just near the place where people went to smoke.

Also entertaining them on that long and hot afternoon in our new studio were our star guest, ladies' favourite footballist David Ginola, the first appearance by the show's mysterious tame racing driver and the triumphant return to car telly of Jeremy Clarkson, joined by his two equally keen and knowledgeable co-hosts. We had been strictly instructed not to start cars inside the studio, a rule that Jeremy gleefully overturned by noisily revving a Pagani Zonda on set, to the amusement and slight suffocation of the audience. We went home tired but cheery. We had just made the first prototype of new *Top Gear*. The finished footage went off to the edit suite to be stitched together and a few days later it was ready for viewing. There was a buzz of excitement in the office as we shoved the VHS cassette into the machine and sat down to enjoy the first trial run of our brilliant new scheme to reinvent cars on television. No one said anything as the tape played. No one needed to. We'd all come to pretty much the same conclusion. It was crap.

There were, quite obviously, a number of problems. The set seemed oppressive and restricting. No one had thought that filming inside a powerfully lit metal box on a sunny day might have made things a bit hot, but it did. One of our ill-fated ideas was to have in the audience hardcore fans of whichever make of car was featured that week, and for the pilot these would be members of the Renault Owners' Club who, we claimed in the script, would get into a 'garlicky lather' over the contents of the show. Actually, the entire audience was in some kind of lather, garlicky or otherwise, at being made to stand for hours in a circular metal cage while we slowly attempted to roast them. And a hot, uncomfortable audience is an audience less inclined to clap or laugh along with whatever's happening in front of them.

The presenters fared no better, developing a visible and uncomfortable sheen through the proceedings, as did David Ginola. Another bad call on our part was to keep the guest on set the whole time so that they could give their thoughts on whatever was being discussed. Ginola seemed like a good booking for the pilot, being cool and sexy and interesting. Our insistence on keeping him around and making him talk about all manner of dull topics, including the British motorway network, effortlessly reduced all of these qualities to just short of zero and by the time he sighed and gave an impassioned speech about the problems of 'ze M6' all the women in the room decided they didn't fancy him as much after all.

To add extra awkwardness, Ginola mistakenly believed that he would be presenting the show in some ongoing capacity, perhaps because we'd kept him on set the whole time or perhaps because the French for 'Would you like to be a guest on our programme?' is very similar to the French for 'Would you like to come and present this new series?' We never found out. We had too many other things to worry about.

Another ingenious idea which the pilot exposed as flawed was the notion of wetting the track so that all lap times were equal, whether it rained or not. It turns out that while actual rain is absolutely brilliant at getting the track damp, a slowly circulating tanker lorry with a spray on the back is not. Thanks to the magic of evaporation, on a warm day all you end up with is a dry track with a few soggy patches. This impractical idea was binned. We'd just have to lap the star cars in whatever conditions prevailed on the day.

Then there was The Stig himself, or at least his triumphant introduction in front of the audience. The actual Stig had gone home at this point, so a chap from *Top Gear* magazine who was about the right size was shoved into the suit and told simply to walk slowly and dramatically through a cloud of dry ice onto the set. For some reason, he equated 'slowly and dramatically' with 'like a robot'. In the gallery, the director had pointedly told the floor manager to 'tell him to stop walking like a fucking robot!' but it was no good. Take after take, he creaked into view like a bad impression of C-3P0. And that creaky, unconvincing movement seemed to sum up many of the problems with the pilot. We thought we were making an exciting, free-wheeling, anarchic show. What we ended up with was a stuffy, stiff clunker featuring a weird robot racing driver and a slightly sweaty footballer.

When we handed in our homework to the BBC, they agreed. This was not right. It's okay, we said, we've got an idea of how we can fix it. Fine, said management, go away and have another go. And this time, try not to muck it up.

# The Even Worse Pilot

In a bid to correct the mistakes of the catastrophically cack first pilot, the first thing that had to go was the monstrous hangar-filling set. The designer said he could make some changes. Wilman answered this offer very firmly. 'Don't change it,' he said. 'Take it outside and burn it.' We didn't want the audience caged behind an elaborate steel structure, nor did we want the presenters stuck to their seats on their little stage area; we needed both to roam free on the studio floor. For our second trial run, the cars in the studio would be our set and nothing else.

Also on the subject of making everything feel less buttoned up, we binned the autocue. For the first pilot, all the links were read off the magic screen in front of the camera, allowing precious little freedom to ad lib and argue. Clearly this wasn't working, so the autocue was thrown onto the same mythical bonfire as the set. I was especially delighted about this. One thing I learned at the pilot is that autocue people don't like you touching their special autocue computer. I've been reminded of it again on other TV programmes since.

'Could I just type this in?' you ask.

'No!' the autocue people snap. 'This is a SPECIAL AUTOCUE COMPUTER.' Do not point out that it just looks like a normal laptop. This will not go down well. Just accept that if you want to make a change to the script on the screen you have to do it through the autocue person by reading out your changes, even if the autocue person is surprisingly slow at typing and wants you to spell every second word. Still, that particular scripting issue had gone away. No more complicated autocue.

Also on that note, no more complicated script at all, since it was reduced to a series of bullet points, with the idea that the presenters would have a vague sense of where to start and where to end up, but they would be winging it at all points in between. That should loosen things up nicely.

The BBC agreed to let us go back to Dunsfold and try all this out by making another pilot. We didn't need a star guest, although I'm sure we could have got David Ginola again since I'm not certain anyone had told him he wasn't a presenter on the show.

But there was no need, since this second trial run was just to see how the links worked, unfettered by anything as structural as a proper script and a few tons of ironwork.

The hangar looked very different this time around. When you build a proper TV set, it transforms a bleak, empty room. When you take that set away, what you get back is the bleak empty room. A couple of cars and two dozen bored-looking members of the public milling around them didn't really fill the space. Still, it was too late to add anything else now. We just started filming and hoped for the best.

For the chat out of the road test VT, it was decided that the presenters should go where the mood took them. If they wanted to run around the other side of the car or jump into the boot or begin licking the roof they should do so with abandon and a hand-held camera would follow them. Jeremy was very enthusiastic about this idea and encouraged the other two to do whatever they liked. Jason embraced this with gusto and while making a point about troublesome build quality on the featured Renaults he leapt into one of the cars and started pulling various bits of interior trim off with his bare hands, like a Kia-Ora-crazed Cornish toddler.

The cameramen did their best to keep up but TV cameras really need light, especially in a dark studio. The lights were not set up for random and unexpected moves like this so some of it was in shadow, some of it was very dark and some of it was pretty much just a murky soup with a large car dealer waving a piece of dashboard around inside it. Technically speaking, the whole thing was a terrible mess. And the words weren't much better than the pictures because, with only the loosest of scripts, conversations went on too long, or didn't make sense or had two people talking over each other. It was well meaning but quite distressingly amateurish.

Halfway through recording Richard and I went outside for a breather. Hammond looked at me with a plaintive expression. 'I don't want to do this,' he said quietly. He was right. It was chaos. And not a good sort of chaos. This was the rambling, badly lit sort of chaos that no one would want to watch. What the bloody hell had we been thinking? Trying to corral this show was like having a pet lion. Our first efforts had kept the lion on too tight a lead so it couldn't do its lion stuff. Now, in an overreaction to that, what we'd managed to do was let the lion off the leash altogether. Somebody was in danger of getting bitten and there was lion poo everywhere.

To compound my despondency on the day of recording, I had a stinking, snot-pouring cold. We were making visibly substandard television and on top of that I felt like crap. After persuading Richard not to quit the dream job that had turned into a nightmare, I wandered over to the production office, went into the unused celebrity dressing room, lay down on the small sofa and curled up into a tiny, tiny ball.

The footage we got from that second studio day was, unsurprisingly, not very good. A less polite way of describing it would be utter shite. It was too free-form and too shambolic. After the first wide-of-the-mark pilot we had somehow managed to seize our second chance and make something even worse. The VTs were fine, we reckoned we were generally on the right track with those. But the studio still needed work. We thought we could fix this by splitting the difference between pilot one and pilot two. We needed something between a huge set and no set at all, perhaps just a little stage with some chairs and a telly on it. We needed less than a full autocue script but more than a bullet point that said, 'talk about cars here'. With a bit of time we could definitely get this sorted. But there was no more time. It was September. The BBC had committed to new *Top Gear* and wanted it on air in mid-October. We could make pilot three but we would have to accept that pilot three would also be show one and would appear on television at the end of that very week. This was all very real now, and we hadn't got another chance to make a further balls-up. We took a deep breath and got ready to make our first series, using all the things we'd learned from the first two pilots. Mostly about what not to do.

Meanwhile, the tapes containing the two pilot shows were locked in a drawer, never to be seen again. Many years later, whenever the subject of long service on *Top Gear* came up in the office, James May would note that he had now done many years of active duty and surely that came with some perks of the inner sanctum. 'Have I done enough time to watch the pilots yet?' he'd ask hopefully. Clarkson, Hammond, Wilman and I would answer instantly and as one. The answer was no. The answer was always going to be no. No one has ever seen the terrible pilots again.

# *Series 1*

Despite the rancid shambles of our efforts in the studio to date, the first series of new *Top Gear* was committed to start in October 2002. All we could do was set a plan, which was to split the difference between the rigid borefest of the first pilot and the badly lit chaos of the second.

On the plus side, the VTs we'd been shooting in the late summer were looking pretty good. We just had to decide which one would start the very first show. When it came to decisions like this, Wilman and Clarkson often disappeared off into a corner to confer. Sometimes that corner would be in a pub. You wouldn't see them for a bit and then when Wilman arrived back in the office he would have some news. I think that's what happened in this case and the news he brought back was quite radical. The very first film in the very first episode of this brand-new *Top Gear* reboot wouldn't be a track test of a supercar or a shouty review of a hairy-necked BMW M car. It would be a very considered report on a Citroën van.

It seemed like an odd decision, but the logic was strong. First of all, it was exactly what people wouldn't expect. And this, in turn, would tell viewers that when watching new *Top Gear* they should expect other things they wouldn't expect.

Secondly, it made a bold statement about our confidence in our own opinions. If we say this car is good and worthy of your time, then you'd better believe that we're right. Once or twice the 'Delia Smith effect' was mentioned, a phenomenon based around the titular TV chef and her ability to wildly boost the popularity of any obscure foodstuff or utensil, simply because if she said it was good people believed her. *Top Gear* should carry the same weight in the car world, so if we said an odd-looking French commercial vehicle fitted with windows and extra seats was a bargain-priced alternative to a conventional family car then viewers should trust us. Besides, we weren't doing this for the sake of it; we really did like the strange Citroën van. It was called the Berlingo and it was endearingly unusual. It also had a tremendously comfortable ride.

It was a ballsy way to kick off our new endeavour but everyone agreed it was the right thing to do because it made a statement. And there would be a loud and smoky test of a Pagani Zonda in the same show, just in case people thought we'd gone nuts and turned into a programme for van enthusiasts. I remember the studio recording for that first show and the immense sense of the relief when it seemed to go quite well. The VTs felt strong, the links worked well, Harry Enfield was a fine and funny guest. After the mess of the pilots, this was a promising start. Obviously there were a few bugs to work out all the same. For some reason Jason wasn't in the news. The audience was extremely small and milled around in the background like awkward guests at the world's worst drinks party.

On a personal note, I didn't have a job title and was hastily bunged into the credits as 'script supervisor', which is a real position but not the one I occupied. Jeremy seemed to find this accidentally applied title hilarious, as if I stood around in a brown store coat holding a clipboard and checking each link contained enough verbs. From programme two onwards, I was labelled as script editor. There were other problems, but they were minor. In general, things went well. New *Top Gear* was up and running.

The first series passed in a busy, messy, stressy blur. Jay Kay tried his best to tip over the Liana. Lotus helped us to make a cool Lada. During a skit about rally spectating, I got to throw gravel at motorsport hero Richard Burns. Actually, it was a handful of Sugar Puffs. It turns out that breakfast cereal looks like gravel on television, but it doesn't hurt as much. There were other silly things, notably the grannies doing doughnuts, but there was also a lot of good, honest car reviewing.

If you want to find the bridge between old *Top Gear* with its sensible trousers and earnest appraisals of fuel consumption and new *Top Gear*, when it got big and silly and everything fell over, the first series is it. There was a very straight road test of a new Mazda, a review of some second-hand bargains and a studio segment in which two car designers were invited to talk at some length about how styling worked. But this was fine. We weren't setting out to make a crash, bang, wallop entertainment programme. We just wanted to make a car show for car nerds, lightly reinvented for the 21st century.

The evolution into something bigger, sillier and with broader appeal came later. Much else needed to evolve first. In the first series, the news segment seemed to roam all over the shop, sometimes popping up after the first VT, other times not appearing until later, at one point muscling itself up the running order to become the first item in the show, which rather killed the atmosphere and made the programme feel flat and featureless. We later learned that sometimes it's good to nail down some of the structural elements of a show and the news found its home after the first VT package.

The first series also featured a regular studio item in which Jason would run through some car-buying bargains he'd spotted that week and Richard would stand next to him, doing his level best to sound enthusiastic. We called it Used News, though it generally seemed to revolve around getting a few quid off a pre-registered Renault. Like the actual news, it gave us the chance to include some current information but it wasn't the most exciting item in the world, hence it became known in the office as Used Snooze. No matter where it came in the running order, we used to record it at the very end, at which point 12 of the 14 people in the audience would realise they had no interest in learning that they could get a non-metallic Megane for £9,995 and decide to leave. The entire production team would assemble on the studio floor to stop the place looking deserted while Andy Wilman blocked the exits and begged members of the public to stick around so that poor Jason wasn't slowly intoning his cheap Renault rundown to an empty room. During one recording I looked across at the hangar door to see Wilman fumbling for his wallet and offering people actual cash to stay. This item soldiered on into the second series and then was quietly killed off.

To the BBC's credit, they let us make our mistakes and refine our formula without hovering their hands over the kill switch. They did, however, keep a close eye on us, as if they imagined that without supervision we'd blow all the money on a yellow Lamborghini full of biscuits. The principal connection between the show and the bosses was an affable management type and former Radio 1 DJ called Andy Batten-Foster, who rocked a smart line in crisp suits and spoke like he was about to introduce a Tina Turner record. In *Top Gear*'s early years he was a regular presence in the office and a friendly bridge between the grown-up side and whatever it was we were up to. On one occasion he raised concerns that there were too many rude words in an episode of the show, leading to one of the strangest negotiations of my life.

'You can't have the bugger and two bastards,' Batten-Foster said firmly.

What if, I asked, we lost one of the bastards.

'Yea, that might work, but you'd have to give up the tit.'

I quite liked the tit, I said, could we ditch the bugger?

'I'm not sure about a tit and two bastards; just a bastard and a bugger is about as high as we can go.'

The swear bartering continued for some time, both of us carrying on as if we were debating the carving up of Berlin. I liked Andy. When the first series came to end in December 2002 we felt cautiously pleased with ourselves. During the planning of new *Top Gear* the BBC had asked for a show that could snare around three million viewers. If we could do that, we could justify our existence. The first series managed to fulfil that brief. After the final studio recording, just before the seasonal holiday, Jeremy grabbed the members of the team at opportune moments and quietly presented each of us with a couple of bottles of decent champagne as a thank you for our hard work. He seemed struck by the same feeling as the rest of us. Relief, mostly, and a strange sense that against all odds we'd just got away with it.

Unbeknownst to most of us, management weren't quite as happy. Yes, the show had turned out reasonably well but they felt that the presenting team wasn't working out. The timing was spectacularly cack-handed. Richard got a call to say that he might not be on the team next time round but that the bosses would let him know in the new year and, oh yea, have a merry Christmas. Jason also felt the cold steel of a BBC service revolver on the back of his neck. When management regrouped in early 2003, Hammond was given a stay of execution but poor Jason wasn't so lucky.

It was terribly sad and a little unfair. He'd never done TV before and was expected to arrive on the screen as a fully formed presenter. In retrospect, perhaps we should have given him more help to become better and to bring out more of his natural charisma. As it was, we were all so busy just trying to get this new show off the ground that we didn't have the time or spare brain capacity to lend him that support. It was a shame to see him go. He was a genuinely nice bloke.

With the next series scheduled to start in five months' time, there wasn't much space for being maudlin about the decision handed down from on high. We needed to find a new presenter. We needed to find James May. Someone was dispatched to wherever brown beer and old motorcycle carburettors live. It was time to make new *Top Gear* mk1½.

# Le Stig

I'm pretty sure it was Clarkson's idea. A lot of things were. The first time I went to meet him and Wilman, I recall him gleefully explaining that new *Top Gear* would have a mysterious in-house racing driver who never spoke and never showed their face. I remember thinking this wasn't a good idea. At the same meeting, they told me new *Top Gear* would be a car show based in a studio. I didn't think that would work either. If you want any betting tips for upcoming events, you know who not to ask.

I found the racing driver idea confusing. If he didn't take his helmet off, how would you get to know him? If he didn't speak, how would he tell us what the car was like? Jeremy had an answer for that. Racing drivers, he said, are boring. No one's interested in what they have to say, we only want to see them set lap times. This argument did make sense. You only have to watch the F1 coverage – where an endless procession of dullards drone on about how 'the guys' did a 'great job', before trudging off to a conference room to say joyless thanks for the sponsorship to a roomful of bankers and deodorant makers – to know that the average wheel jockey is at his best when he's got a crash helmet on and a car around him. You can develop massive affection for a driver upon seeing their talent within the car, and then lose a great deal of it when you hear them talk. I came up with a name for this phenomenon: Mansell's Syndrome.

So it was agreed, the driver wouldn't talk, he wouldn't reveal himself and he wouldn't use his real name. He would be known only as The Gimp. Through some suitably mysterious means, Wilman had found a man to do the job. We were never told his name. In fact, no one in the office knew who would be inside the suit. Andy said that if anyone leaked his name they would be fired. That's okay, we said, because we don't know it in the first place. Wilman gave this some thought. Alright, he said, if anyone even finds out his name, they'll be sacked. I'm not sure he was joking. I'm also not sure if he'd run this policy past HR.

Anyway, some time has passed now and so I think it's finally okay to reveal the name of the man who played the original Stig. It was Perry McCarthy. I know this will come as a shock to many of you as Perry himself never mentions it. Maybe he should.

Perry, not unreasonably, didn't like the idea of being called The Gimp because it was the name of the leather-wrapped, basement-trapped sex slave in the movie *Pulp Fiction*. When the BBC found out about the name, they weren't keen either. Allowing a prime time programme to remind people of Bruce Willis in a ball gag was the equivalent of permitting *Blue Peter* to introduce a new pet called Buggery the Cat.

In the run-up to the first pilot episode, we went for dinner one evening to discuss various knotty problems with the show, one of them being multiple objections to having a racing driver with a needlessly kinky name. The Beeb had issued an official instruction; you can't call him The Gimp, now go away and come up with a new name. Through a mouthful of steak, Jeremy had the answer; 'Wilman, remember what the new kids were called at school?' he asked. Wilman did. They were called stigs. What if the anonymous racing driver was called The Stig?

We mulled it over for a bit. It sounded strange, but quite good. Also, there was an old rally driver called Stig Blomqvist, so there was a tenuous motorsport connection. And, crucially, the name didn't have overt connections to having your arse fondled by a man called Zed. At least, I don't think so. I don't know what went on at Jeremy and Andy's school. But let's assume not. The Stig had a name. It was The Stig.

So we had a man to play the character, we had an acceptable name for the character, we had a little gag (shamelessly borrowed from the George Clooney movie *Three Kings*) in which the roar and fury of a car at full chat would contrast with eerily calm interior shots with easy-listening music dribbling from the stereo.

The man we didn't know was Perry threw himself into the role with gusto. He'd get changed into the outfit before he arrived at the track and would keep his crash helmet on throughout the day, no matter what. Watching him trying to eat was hilarious.

Eventually he developed a system where he'd sneak off behind the bins, slide his lid up just enough to reveal his mouth and quickly shove a sandwich into it while no one was looking. But even this dedication to security wasn't enough for the person we began to suspect was Perry but couldn't name for fear of dismissal. It was natural that during the day The Stig would need to talk to members of the production team, the presenters and the star guest. Clearly this could give away some clues to his identity if it wasn't managed correctly. But it was okay, the man we were increasingly sure was Perry had given this some thought and come up with a cunning plan, a clever piece of subterfuge, a diversionary technique so crafty the CIA themselves would surely want to analyse it and learn from its ingenuity: Whenever he spoke, he put on a French accent.

Perry is not French. Perry is quite far from being French. But every week when he arrived at the studio he would greet you from behind the smoked visor with a cheery, 'Allo!' If you had to ask him about, say, a car that hadn't performed as well as expected, he would explain that, 'ze 'andling, she is not good'. I never actually heard him say, 'Orheeorheeorhhh' while shrugging and fondling an onion but it wouldn't have surprised me if he had. Remarkably, the unconvincing subterfuge of an Essex man giving it the full Inspector Clouseau actually worked. Whisper went round the wider world that The Stig really was French.

Actually, lots of rumours circulated about The Stig. Some people claimed he was Alain Prost, probably because of that accent thing. Some people insisted he was Damon Hill, largely because the former world champion lived quite near Dunsfold and would have no trouble getting to the track to perform his duties. That made total sense because if there's one thing people look for in a racing driver above all else, it's punctuality. Internet forums were full of people claiming that their brother-in-law had met a bloke in a pub who knew someone who worked at McLaren and they'd spoken to someone at Silverstone who knew a geezer who ran a GT team who was married to this girl who overheard someone in an Ascari bomber jacket who definitely knew someone who'd told a friend that their next-door neighbour said without a doubt that it was Nigel Mansell.

This anonymous racing driver thing worked surprisingly well and we were very happy with the attention and intrigue this little gimmick had created. Perry was not so happy. He didn't like being anonymous and he didn't like being paid just four shillings a month plus all the crisps he could shovel under his crash helmet. He seemed to be getting less conscientious about maintaining his anonymity, to the point that sometimes he wasn't even bothering to be a rubbish Frenchman. By the second series, pretty much everyone on the team knew it was Perry inside the suit, though we still went through the motions of pretending we didn't. We were a bit disappointed that he was getting careless. When he registered The Stig as a trademark, the BBC commercial lawyers were a bit more than disappointed. They were quite cross. Some grown-up conversations happened. You can read Perry's side of things in his (extremely good) book. From our side, there came a day when it was official: We were going to kill off The Stig.

The Royal Navy had offered us an aircraft carrier to muck about on. We'd got an old Jaguar XJS we'd spanked up with nitrous injection which we didn't mind losing. Could we put the two together in some sort of Stig-killing, Jag-drowning, HMS *Invincible* idiocy? Amazingly, the navy types said yes. The XJS was craned onto the boat, we filmed it running up and down the deck and then stuck it arse first onto a powerful air cannon of the type they use to make cars do huge jumps in movies. With one push of a button and a loud bang it fired off the ramp at the end of the deck and plunged majestically into the sea. An elaborate and expensive airbag system had been installed inside so that it could be brought back to the surface. The elaborate and expensive airbag system didn't go off, but we'll gloss over that. The main thing is, The Stig was dead.

But not Perry, of course. Perry was still very much alive. It's a shame it didn't work out with him. He was funny and friendly and utterly fearless in the wet. The only thing he wasn't, I can say without fear of contradiction, was French.

# *Getting Into the Groove*

Before the second series, we screen-tested some possible new presenters in a tiny room behind the lifts at BBC White City. There were some good candidates but no one quite hit the spot like James May. He already knew Jeremy and Richard from the car journo circuit and they got on well. James bonded with Hammond over their mutual love of many things, including old cars and interesting motorcycles. He bonded with Jeremy over their mutual dislike of many things, including golf and people who say 'myself' when they mean 'me'. This strongly overlapping Venn diagram gave the three an instant chemistry you couldn't fake and made James a natural choice for the job. Plus, he had a sense of mischief which got him sacked from *Autocar* for putting a hidden message in a road test supplement, and he was hilariously candid about how his old Bentley was bankrupting him. We liked this second story so much it developed into his very first item for the show.

James blended seamlessly into the world of *Top Gear* and, aside from this personnel change, series 2 continued on from series 1. Cars were still tested, things were jumped over other things, we pursued an ongoing obsession with finding Britain's fastest [insert job here] until this finally disappeared up its own lap board with the quest to find Britain's fastest superhero which, we realised all too late, just produced a gathering of odd people in funny costumes, including a disgruntled Dalek handler who made us promise not to show the bit where it fell over. Richard inadvertently developed his own catchphrase when he shouted 'I am a driving god!' during a review of the Bowler Wildcat, James managed to get the German word for 'nipple' into a test of an old Triumph TR6, Jeremy drove a Vauxhall from the back seat.

Three months after series 2 ended, series 3 kicked off, as these things did back in the days when we made a chunky 19 shows in a year. The schedule was punishing but it also allowed the programme to develop a momentum and from it new *Top Gear* started to find its groove.

Television executives are forever squawking about 'wow factor' and 'water-cooler moments', by which they mean things that people talk about at work the next day. I don't remember either of those phrases being used in the *Top Gear* office and if they were the person responsible would have been asked to leave. What we did have, however, was a sense of what we sometimes referred to as 'pub currency', which on a small scale was a fascinating fact that people could wow their mates with over a pint and on a larger scale was an amazing thing we'd done which would cause people in boozers to ask their friends if they'd seen *Top Gear* this week.

The attempted destruction of a Toyota Hilux in series 3 was an early stab at the latter. The idea came from seeing news footage of battered Hiluxes used by rebel forces in war-torn countries and an old adage from Australia which said, 'Use a Land Rover if you want to go into the Outback, use a

Toyota if you want to come back'. We weren't even sure if our plan would work. We wanted to beat up the car very badly but for it to come back for more. There was always a strong risk that we'd simply destroy it, and prove nothing in the process. Nonetheless, we bought a stinky old Hilux diesel from a farmer, taking advice from people who knew about these things and who said a diesel would be easier to keep running, then set about trying to break it, armed only with a Toyota mechanic carrying a bag of tools and a can of WD-40 to get it going again. It was one of those films that turned out to be more successful and more memorable than we'd hoped for. No one was more shocked about this than we were. When the call came through that the Hilux had been fished out of the Bristol Channel and was running again, we were genuinely surprised. But surprise was part of what *Top Gear* should peddle. We reckoned we should be doing things you wouldn't see on any other British TV programme.

Jeremy's shrewd journalistic brain had long realised that a good way to get into an item was to ask a question. Can grannies do doughnuts? Which is the fastest religion? Is the Toyota Hilux really indestructible? By series 4, the scope and ambition of the questions started to get much bigger and yielded two films that would start to define what *Top Gear* would become. The first was the race to the south of France between an Aston Martin DB9 and public transport. Like many of the best ideas, it was rooted in a genuine, if slightly tenuous, piece of consumer reporting. Lots of people went on holiday to French places by the Med and perhaps they wondered if it was faster to drive or take the train. *Top Gear* would settle that debate. Jeremy would have plenty to talk about while reviewing a new car; putting Richard and James together would make an otherwise unexceptional rail journey more entertaining, as they giggled like kids on a school trip and bickered over James's refusal to run on television. It worked like a charm, even if the magic of editing made the end result seem a bit tighter than it really was. You can tell Jeremy had been waiting a while for the others to show up because in his final piece to camera he's plainly had a couple of large wines. Conversely, in the following series, the race to a ski resort was as close as it appeared on camera, which was testament to more careful planning and the meticulous back-timing that aimed to make the result too close to call on paper. The races were always run for real, but we got used to accusations of fakery and endlessly explaining that the arty shots of the car driving past the camera were gathered the following day as the film crew retraced the race route at a more leisurely pace to get the footage that would make it look nice.

The transcontinental race gave us a solid strand of material for several series. We dropped the ball with the one to Oslo since it necessitated a sleep break, which killed momentum, though this film did yield the rare sight of a TV presenter noisily vomiting on camera. I think we pulled it back with the Bugatti Veyron versus plane race from Italy to London and after that it felt like the sub-format needed to go off for a rest.

The other new invention of the fourth series was one that would endure for much longer. We'd never thought of putting all three presenters together in a VT before. Or maybe we had, but then had shied away from it because we thought the idea was they all hung around together in the studio and then went off to do their various VT things separately, or in twos if there was some heavy lifting involved. Lumping all three of them into one film might be a bit much and we were probably scared of seeming self-indulgent. Yea, I know. Jeremy, Richard and James running a radio station was still a long way off. At this point our fear of appearing pleased with ourselves was so strong there wasn't even any applause from the audience at the start of the show, never mind out of the VTs. That would have come across as far too backslapping. Clapping at the top of the show? But we haven't even done anything yet. Also, in those early days there were only 17 people in the audience and it would have sounded like someone had just hit a four at a village cricket match.

As a cautious experiment, we put Clarkson, Hammond and May together in order to investigate the suspicion that Britain was awash with perfectly serviceable yet almost worthless second-hand cars. It's an indicator of a formula yet to be worked out that part of the challenge was simply to drive to Manchester. No tricks, no gimmicks, just a 200-mile drive to see if the cars actually worked. In later years, we'd have been horrified at the lack of peril or chances for humiliation. It would have been 'Drive to Manchester with a car full of wasps' or 'Drive to Manchester without using any roads', but for this tentative trial of a new kind of film it was just a leisurely run up the M6. Nothing went wrong, no calamity befell anyone, the cars worked perfectly. The crash, bang, wallop came later when they were required to be driven into a wall. And by then the concept had been proved. Putting the presenters together worked. They were funny together. When they were put into competition, they argued and showed off and annoyed each other. You know what, we thought. We should do this more often.

A lot of television programmes are expected to hit the ground running and to become massive hits from the off. It's to the Beeb's credit that they let *Top Gear* quietly find its feet, bubbling away in the backwaters of BBC2, slowly expanding its appeal from a core audience of car nerds into something your mum wouldn't mind watching. It's a good job they did because it took a while. Series 1 wasn't great, series 2 was a little better. And, after three or four series, it finally felt like the show had found its groove. Although, truth be told, I don't think anyone imagined it would really catch on.

# Cars

We had to get hold of many things in order to make *Top Gear*. White coats, spare tyres, enormous plates of meat for some gag involving The Stig. But most of all, we had to get hold of cars. Despite the shouting and falling over and idiotic attempts to run an art gallery, we were a car show after all.

We needed all sorts of cars. Second-hand stuff for challenges. Old knackers to be turned into something else. Basic scrap that could be smashed and bashed by something else. And for track tests and road trips and so on there were brand-new cars.

In theory, this was the easy one. Most car manufacturers maintain a fleet of press demonstrators expressly for the purpose of appearing in magazines and on the television. You just had to ring the PR office and ask nicely. But this being *Top Gear* it didn't always work that way and before dialling any number you first had to think about how much we might have pissed them off. After a few series we pinned a 'loves us / hates us' chart to the office wall with the names of all the car makers on it, stuck to the side that equated to their current attitude towards our shenanigans and the things we'd said about their products.

Even with an advance warning, however, you couldn't be certain of how a friendly request might be met. I once rang Porsche, for example, to ask if we could have a 911 for something. 'I'm afraid that won't be possible,' replied the PR man tersely. 'The only one we have in that spec just punched a piston through the block after some idiots drove it on a beach and got sand in the engine.' Those idiots were us. Jaguar took a jauntier view of the ravaged XKR that returned from the same shoot, reasoning that the sandblasting was worth it for how cool the car looked on telly. Even so, they couldn't let the well-used car out into the real world so they took it back to the factory and crushed it.

A few years later Bentley were quite cross when Jeremy popped the back tyres on their Brooklands coupé during a track test. Then there was a mix-up somewhere down the chain; the promised Mulsanne wasn't ready for a trip to Albania, we used a tatty Yugo in its place, referred to it as a 'Bentley' throughout and relations became very frosty. But only for a bit. A peace summit was arranged, the word bygones was bandied around and next thing you know they were lending us a Continental GT which they cheerfully said we could take rallying. And as a bonus for them the car was so surprisingly unbroken afterwards that it had a second life as a hack on the factory engineering fleet.

For the most part, *Top Gear* maintained a cordial relationship with car makers and their PR people. I'm sure we made their lives utterly miserable as we sent back another demonstrator with bald tyres and a funny knocking noise from the suspension, but I don't think we were needless oafs about it; this was the collateral damage of making cars look cool on TV. To get a magazine photo of a sliding car, you can slither it three or four times around a corner and hopefully the job is done. To get the same effect on telly you do it again and again and again from different angles and at different speeds and with different numbers of doves or bouncy balls or explosions, depending on what the director has decreed. Privately they might have called us rude names and cursed our gearbox-bursting ways. Publicly, car makers were quite grown-up about this stuff. It helped that, as time went on, we could get their car in front of a few hundred million people around the world.

If there was ever a problem, it was that we wanted cars earlier than anyone else and for longer. Partly, this was down to filming schedules. And partly this was down to us being a bit of a shambles. We changed our minds a lot and we came up with new ideas at the last minute. Conversely, sometimes car makers had trouble getting cars ready in the agreed time. Andy Wilman took a robust view of such things. He once rang one of the nicest and most efficient press men in the business to express displeasure that a promised new model was no longer available at the right time. More specifically, his disappointment was couched in a range of quite strong words beginning with S and F and possibly C. The press man listened politely to all of this for several minutes before carefully choosing the moment to tell Wilman that he was on speaker in his car with his kids in the back.

This kind of thing was rare, however. Most of the time, we just asked nicely. Sometimes we didn't have to ask at all. Cars were actually offered to us. It was Toyota's PR man, for example, who suggested we had a fleet of preproduction Aygos to play football with, as long as he could have them back in reasonable nick. If you look up 'stoical' in the dictionary, there's just a picture of his face from the sidelines during the very first panel-bending sliding tackle. At least he'd had the presence of mind to disable the airbags.

We liked getting offered preproduction cars for the simple reason that, in this context, 'preproduction' usually meant 'you can smash it up'. They were cars from the tail end of the engineering process, destined to be crushed once their working life was done, and that meant we could give them a good send-off. Hence the jumping Ford Focus in this *Sweeney* film or the sawn-up Astra 'hire car' in the art-gallery piece.

It was rare that a car company completely refused to lend us a car. In fact, I can only think of one absolute flat refusal, and it was one we managed to turn to our advantage. In the dying days of MG Rover, the beleaguered Brummie company decided to sell a lightly rehashed version of an Indian small car called the Tata Indica, onto which it slapped some new bumpers and a badge that said CityRover. When we were putting together a list of new models to test for a forth-coming series, some would be a no-brainer, others we might ask to borrow for a few days to see if there was something to say about them. So we asked to have a go in a CityRover and the company said yes. It turned out to be a shockingly shit car with little to redeem it. It felt cheap, even though it wasn't, and it looked dismal. This second point was brought home to me when the editor of *Top Gear* magazine drove past as I was sitting in it at some traffic lights. He was openly pointing and laughing at me from the haughty heights of a Range Rover. The CityRover was crap, but that was good. Sometimes it was nice to review a truly awful car. It's more fun than writing a script about a brilliant one.

Unfortunately, between the time we sent the first demo back and the moment we asked for another one to film, Rover themselves seemed to have realised that their new small car was a rancid sack of cack. We'd rather not lend you another one, they said. It's just that we've got a new, improved version on the way and we think it would be better to wait for that. Well, we're filming quite soon, we said, and we'd rather just crack on. It didn't seem unreasonable. After all, they were still selling this car to punters and I doubt you'd hear a dealer saying best hang on until the improved model arrives, madam. In fact somewhere in Birmingham the company boss, a man called Kevin, told the PR man, another man called Kevin, that if this car was loaned to *Top Gear* for filming then a man called Kevin would be sacked. The first Kevin understood what the second Kevin was saying. There didn't seem to be much solidarity among Kevins.

*Top Gear* had never been refused a car before. Naturally, our childish response was to decide that James would test it anyway by going to a dealership with some hidden cameras and doing it in secret. If we'd have tried this in later years the dealer would have said, 'Oh look, it's that bloke off *Top Gear* inexplicably wearing a suspiciously bulky tie which has obviously got a camera in it'. Fortunately, this was 2004 and while the hidden cameras of the era weren't unnoticeable James May was. He'd only been on the show for a short while, the programme wasn't a massive hit and we were able to shoot an entire covert road test on a dealer test drive.

Perhaps because of this surprisingly successful buffoonery, I can't remember being refused another car after that. The closest we got was during our attempt to set up the definitive showdown between the McLaren P1, the Porsche 918 and Ferrari's LaFerrari, which descended into petty childishness worthy of *Top Gear* itself. McLaren said they thought Ferrari would cheat. Ferrari said they thought McLaren would cheat. Porsche seemed unbothered. McLaren said to get round the cheating aspect, all the cars must be from customers. Ferrari said that was unfeasible and all the cars must be from the factory. Porsche seemed unbothered. McLaren said the test couldn't be at the *Top Gear* track because they knew it well from testing there and their data said their car might be outgunned. Ferrari said that was fine. Porsche seemed unbothered. Finally, we arranged for a neutral location, with mutually agreeable sources of cars, and we seemed to have a showdown on our hands. McLaren were in. Ferrari were in. Oh, ah, this is awkward, said Porsche. We seem to have sold all our 918s. Leave it with us . . .

Further down the automotive food chain, borrowing new cars always involved a lot of phone calls, some of them after the event and starting with the words 'Now, um, don't be cross but . . .', yet it was rare to find anyone who wouldn't want to lend us a car, even if their teeth were gritted as they did. No wait, that's not strictly true. Once, many years back, a likeable American chap from a large company came to the office to talk through some things his company had coming up. Talk turned to a newly announced mid-range saloon of a type that was very important to the business. You'd think he'd be pushing it hard, but no. 'I don't wanna lend you one those,' the American man said loudly. 'I watch *Top Gear* with my kids and we wanna be entertained. Seeing one of those on the show would bore the ass off me.' We liked him a lot. He seemed to like us too. Despite the occasional mauling and misunderstanding, I think a reasonable chunk of the car industry did.

## Cars

The things *Top Gear* did with new cars might have been punishing and time consuming and sometimes required another vanload of tyres. But when it came to our treatment of new cars, I hope we never bored the ass off anyone.

# A Dwarf in a Suitcase

After a couple of years or so there came a point where *Top Gear* seemed to be working. This was a surprise, to us and to the BBC. Somehow three silly blokes messing around with cars had some audience appeal. Viewing figures were solid and creeping upwards. Beeb research said viewers liked what we did. We once received an especially brilliant bit of in-house surveying which said that the show was especially well received among young black men because they perceived Jeremy to be very much like them. Although we checked this out, he was definitely still a middle-aged white man.

In the face of an unexpected hit, the natural reaction is to copy it and attempts were made to mimic what was seen to be the successful formula of our show. Descriptive briefs for other programmes started flying around the place, name-checking *Top Gear* and almost always using words like 'edgy' and 'irreverent' to such a degree that your brain started to question what they meant. I don't remember sitting in a single meeting at *Top Gear* in which we decided to be 'edgy' or 'irreverent', but that was how the wider world of TV seemed to perceive us and they decided they wanted more of it. More edge and more irrev. Erence.

An edgerent and irrevery food programme was commissioned, packed full of edges and irreverentialness and featuring a format in which VT packages were anchored around a studio set-up in which presenters mucked about and mocked each other. To my mind it never quite worked because the on-screen talent used to say things like 'Oh you!' and 'I know what you're like!' in the manner of people pretending to be friends, while reading their piss-takes off a piece of card. They'd missed a crucial bit of *Top Gear* DNA, which was that when Jeremy called Richard an idiot and Richard called James a dullard they really meant it and the on-screen conversations were based on the conversations they had all the time in real-life places like the office or the pub.

Nonetheless, the Beeb thought it was a tremendous idea to invite the core of the *Top Gear* team to a series of brainstorming sessions and get us to share our thoughts on reinventing other long-running types of television. Typically this involved me, Andy Wilman and our researchers Rowly French and Jim Wiseman trudging up to the brainstorming development area upstairs which, we couldn't help noticing, was a lot nicer than our office and had one of those printable white boards that always seem quite magical, even if someone's just drawn a set of male genitals on it.

I'm ashamed to say we didn't take these sessions entirely seriously. We'd call them 'monkey tennis' meetings after Alan Partridge's most famously useless programme pitch, and we'd dare each other to blatantly pitch existing programmes with new names to see if anyone noticed. 'So this is a programme about the East enders who live in the East end of London and these East enders go to the pub with other East enders and they talk about the things that East enders worry about and do jobs that East enders do and the main thing is they're all East enders and I think it should be called Moaning Cockney Bastards.'

Inevitably we'd arrive a bit late and tumble into the room like crap Bash Street Kids to find it populated by two distinct groups of television professionals. There were enthusiastic types who thought we had loads of brilliant secrets we could share (which we probably couldn't) and grumpy people who resented being told they could learn things from a bunch of blithering idiots who were plainly winging it (which we probably were).

There really wasn't a lot we could tell them. We worked hard, we tried to come up with unusual and unpredictable ideas and we had a bunch of uncommonly gifted, editorially savvy presenters who got on with each other in real life. You could synthesise those first two points but you might struggle with the last. And, frankly, a lot of the time we didn't know what we were doing.

At some point we were asked to attend a brainstorming session aimed at reinventing the *Holiday* programme. I can't remember if the words 'edgy' and 'irreverent' were used for this one. Possibly not. It's hard to think of a show with less of either quality than *Holiday*, which seemed to consist mostly of reports that would conclude with a pleasantly spoken presenter sitting on a balcony claiming they'd discovered a little of the REAL [insert city or country] and then merrily raising a glass and saying 'Cheers!' There was nothing wrong with that because it was a programme that seemed to know its audience and was aware of what they wanted. Not everything on TV can be edgy and irreverent, otherwise you'd end up with weather presenters shouting, 'Listen up bitches!', after which the whole of middle England would spin off its axis and someone would get strangled with a tea towel.

Even so, the Beeb clearly thought that *Holiday* was in need of a rethink, which is how come Wilman, Wiseman, French and I came to be huddled in the corner of the surprisingly nice brainstorm room, trying to think of ideas which we could then present to the wider group of eager/resentful producers.

'What about exposing weaknesses in airport security?' Jim suggested. This sounded like a very hot topic and a good area to address. But how would we tackle this stout piece of consumer journalism? Jim had already thought of that. 'You know those security scanners?' he said. 'We put a suitcase through one of those scanners and see if anyone notices that it's got a dwarf in it.'

We liked this idea very much indeed. It confronted an important issue in an utterly daft way, and one that nobody else would have thought of. Put that in your weekend jaunt to Bruges and smoke it, Judith Chalmers on ITV's *Wish You Were Here*.

There were some other ideas I can't even remember, but we made the dwarf in a suitcase airport security test the centrepiece of our triumphant presentation to the group and awaited their grateful thanks . . .

'I'm sorry,' said someone on the other side of the room. 'You want to put a *dwarf* in a *suitcase*? And put the dwarf, *in a suitcase*, through a *security scanner*?' Perhaps we hadn't been clear. Yes, we said, that's *exactly* what we're suggesting. The room went very quiet. Someone else half-heartedly wrote 'dwarf' on the magic whiteboard.

Another producer piped up. 'I'm not sure that's . . . um . . . *safe*,' she said, wearing the bemused look of someone who suspects they're on a hidden camera show and is expecting Jeremy Beadle to pop out of a cupboard to tell them that they've won a Metro.

'No, it'll be fine,' Jim insisted. 'The dwarf might enjoy it.'
There was quite a long silence.

If I remember correctly, the meeting wrapped up quite soon
afterwards. It was around this time that we stopped getting
invited to brainstorm sessions for other programmes and were
left to get on with making *Top Gear*.

# *Tuesday*

Every weekly TV show has a routine. I could never shake the suspicion that other programmes probably had a better system and we were doing it all wrong. Even so, over the years *Top Gear* developed a pattern for those times when we were on air.

On Monday, the almost-finished VTs would be released from the edit, voice-over lines would be smoothed and refined and then that evening we'd meet the presenters at a studio to add their out-of-vision words to the pictures. On Wednesday we'd trek down to Dunsfold to record the show in the studio. On Thursday and Friday we'd prepare for the following week's show, or if we'd left our homework to the last minute as usual we'd shoot stuff for VTs later in the series.

Then there was Tuesday. This was the most frantic and shambolic day in our weekly routine, the day when we prepared the script, the news and the interview questions for the studio recording. Everyone was in the White City office that day and the place hummed with the busy business of getting ready to lay down the vital cement that went between vast slabs of VT.

On these Tuesdays the team would get in early and await the arrival of the presenters. James was usually first, wandering in with a motorcycle helmet under his arm and gratefully accepting the offer of a cup of tea. During the day he would consume over 200 more. Give or take a few.

Richard would arrive next, fresh from Herefordshire, having travelled into London very briskly on a motorbike or very slowly in a Land Rover. Then Jeremy would saunter in, scattering greetings to the assembled team, and the four of us would take up station in the scruffy meeting area at the very front of the office, where a solitary desk housed a computer that was fired up and ready to have writing done on it. Mandatory BBC software updates permitting. This machine will automatically restart in 2 minutes. This machine is about to restart. This machine does not like having an oafish TV presenter still jabbing at its keyboard shouting, 'Why is it doing THIS?'

In all the years of working on *Top Gear* I never mentioned this, but there was a major flaw with our office. It was the wrong way round. The editorial team sat up at the far end, as distant as possible from the meeting area where the writing took place, with the production management team in between. Every time there was an editorial question – How much does this car cost? How many BMW 5 Series were sold last year? When did they stop making the Toyota Picnic? – someone had to leg it down to the other end or shout loudly across the room. There was a lot of the latter, which gave the office a nice, buzzy, newsroom sort of feel but was also tremendously irritating for anyone trying to make a phone call underneath the flight path of bellowing. It was typical I suppose. Only *Top Gear* could create a seating plan for an office that was completely arse-about-face and then pig-headedly struggle through with it for years and years.

For many years, the desk upon which we wrote was also the wrong way round, idiotically arranged to face out into the room so that to sit down you had to squeeze between the desk itself and the wall behind, tripping over all the cables on the floor and running the perilous, file-losing gauntlet of pulling out the power lead. Finally, one Monday during series 19, I seized the initiative and turned the desk round so that it was pushed against the wall. The next day James arrived and cast his eye suspiciously around the room.

'Something's different here,' he said, warily.

Yea, I said, I've turned the desk round.

'Oh,' he replied. There was scepticism in his voice. Before I could explain my logic, Hammond turned up.

'What's going on here?' he asked, in the sort of voice people use when they fear impending disaster.

'Porter's turned the desk round,' May explained.

'Oh,' said Hammond. 'Is this wise?' A few minutes later Clarkson blustered in and stopped with alarm at the sight of the controversial new desk orientation.

'Someone's moved the desk,' he observed flatly.

Yes, I've turned it around.

'I can see,' he continued. 'Are you *sure* about this?'

We feared change. That's why, in general, the Tuesday routine was always the same. In the preceding days I would have bolted together a draft studio script using the rough introductions formulated for each VT, to which I'd then add all the bits I thought of as 'grouting'; writing a menu for the top of the show, a Stig 'some say . . .' set-up, a way to introduce the guest and so on.

The menu was a bone of contention. Andy Wilman believed it should be approached as if we were running a greengrocer's, putting our freshest and shiniest produce proudly on display at the front to draw in customers. Jeremy and I believed we should just muck about and make it extremely silly. This wasn't always the case, of course. In early series the menu was quite sensible, but after a few years we suspected that if people heard the theme tune and saw the titles they'd know what was coming and would avidly stick with us or turn off in disgust, and either way it didn't really matter whether the first menu items said, 'Tonight, a new supercar at full blast on the track' or 'Tonight, James May points at an otter'. I preferred the daft ones so the draft menus I wrote were usually quite stupid.

When the presenters assembled on a Tuesday morning, they'd start to go through the rough script on the screen while I stood back with clenched buttocks and rictus grin, hoping all my first-draft bits were going to hit the spot. If they elicited a chuckle we were on the right track. A full laugh meant it was definitely in the show. If Jeremy turned around, looked at me and went 'Hmm', it was probably back to the drawing board. If you're writing for other people, you can argue your corner and try to prevent them from drowning your kittens but the bottom line is this; they're the poor sods who have to go on TV and say this stuff.

So we'd spend some time writing and rewriting, trying out thoughts for the conclusions to films, debating where we wanted to go and what we wanted to discuss. Jeremy liked to work on the page, crafting the words carefully and buffing them to a fine shine. That's why he usually drove the computer. James would sit back pontificating and coming up with overarching thoughts, whimsical meanders and silly concepts to take a conversation somewhere new. Richard was the king of the one-liner, the person who would suddenly punch out the killer gag or the brilliant observation that would seal the whole link. It was good team work.

After a while of fiddling and fine tuning and then worrying that we were covering the wrong topics, which led to deleting the whole link and starting again, we would have a new, improved studio script and we could turn our attention to the papery slick of press releases, photographs and news cuttings on the floor, from which we would hash out topics for the news.

This was an important part of the day. It was also, basically, a shambles. The presenters would pluck likely-looking items from the items from around their feet and begin reading out segments or suggesting jokes, Jeremy ranting about some item from the paper, Richard getting excited about a new muscle car, James giggling over some badly worded claim about the sliding doors on a Fiat, and everyone talking over the top of each other. Since I was the only one with a notepad, I'd try to write some of this down. Once, many series ago, we thought another brain might help with the writing and I got in a friend of mine who's a very clever, very funny writer with years of experience, including regular gigs writing brainy things for the radio. After half a morning in the room going through the news he came up to me with a look of utter bemusement. 'How do you write anything out of that?' he asked. 'It's total chaos.'

It was, but from the chaos I'd go away with my notepad and type up the main points and the good bits so that we could knock them about on the page, slowly working towards a set of news stories, each made up of bullet points combining relevant information like power and price with the salient areas we wanted to hit and some of the one-liners that might have emerged from the shouting, bickering and sniggering in the room. I'm sure other TV shows had a better process for this sort of thing, but messy though it might have seemed, our system worked for us and was based to a large degree on four men in a room noisily trying to make each other laugh. Besides, there was never going to be a good moment to completely rethink the writing process. We got disorientated enough just from turning a desk around. Beyond the apparent disorganisation, though, there was a great deal of attention to detail once we got things down on the page. If you wanted to sum up writing on *Top Gear*, it was mostly about arguing whether 'raspberries' was a funnier word than 'hat'. That's the sort of fine-grain problem that would occupy an absurd amount of our time on a Tuesday and which was often solved by someone suggesting that actually the best word was 'vestibule'.

By mid-afternoon in our regular routine we'd have two scripts. The studio one, fully formed for straight down-the-camera links and with conversational elements plotted out. And the news script, which was bullet-pointed and a little more 'loose'. Then we'd call the entire team over to the shabby meeting area and they would sit on the tea-stained chairs and listen as the presenters read through the scripts. If they laughed at the jokes and didn't look suicidally bored during the other bits, we could cling to the vague hope that this was working.

If it wasn't, we'd begin the painful process of rewrites. If it was, Jeremy would stalk over to the other side of the office where, amidst stacks of old papers and the almost certain risk of tetanus, Andy Wilman would have started writing guest questions on his computer. Jeremy would begin bashing in his thoughts, again as bullet points and abstract thoughts rather than fully formed sentences, while Richard and James amused themselves looking at old motorbikes for sale online and our tireless script supervisor Liz turned our shabby Word documents into a properly formatted studio script.

Another quick canter through the words on the screen and then they'd be printed out for the presenters to take home. I suspect Richard and James were better at switching off after a long day of writing, disappearing off to May's garage to dismantle a carburettor or something while Jeremy went home to fret about the show, rereading the words and lying awake all night trying to refine a stubborn link that he was certain could be more concise or a junction between two separate conceits that he was convinced could be smoother.

The process of writing *Top Gear* seemed, and indeed was, quite noisy and silly and spluttering, but it also took a lot of work and a lot of revising and revisiting until the script was buffed to a sleek shine. That's why, in our long-standing routine, Tuesday was the most important day of the week.

# The Stars . . .

The whole, long-running, Star in a Reasonably Priced Car feature was constructed entirely around one man: Bryan Ferry. More specifically, it was built on the 'joke' of Bryan Ferry being forced to drive a cheap, low-spec car entirely at odds with his suave reputation. This was Andy Wilman's idea and when we were planning the very first shows we'd amuse ourselves at the incongruity of it. Bryan! Ferry! In a hatchback! He'll be wearing a dinner suit! But the car is crap! Bryan Ferry! Ha ha ha!

It could have been Bryan Ferry Is Forced to Go to Center Parcs or Bryan Ferry Attempts to Unblock a Particularly Manky Public Lavatory with His Bare Hands. Pretty much anything which might lead the former Roxy Music frontman to engage in an activity unbecoming of a sharp-suited, smoothly crooning legend.

Truth is, Ferry was perfect because of his easygoing cool but it could have been any high-ranking celebrity driving the misery spec shopping car in our minds. Trouble was, by the time we actually started to pull in full-house, all-the-medals

A-listers the feature was so familiar to viewers that the tenuous gag was lost. It wasn't incongruous to see Tom Cruise or Will Smith in an affordable family car because they were on *Top Gear*, and that's what *Top Gear* made them do.

When the programme started, however, getting proper Hollywood stars on the show was impossible. Securing any star at all was pretty tricky, and for good reason. As a celeb, doing a normal chat show didn't demand much effort. Turn up to studio in London, receive a quick dab of make-up, do a bit of chat on camera during which you tell a couple of solid stories and say something lovely about Dame Judi Dench, and by 10 p.m. you're back in your suite at The Dorchester for hot and cold running hookers and a refreshing glass of cocaine.

Or you could do *Top Gear*, in which case you'd have to be up at un-starry o'clock to be taken to a draughty airfield in the back end of Surrey where you would be welcomed into a foul smelling Portakabin and invited to try on a pre-used crash helmet then taken to a bleak taxiway, strapped into a medium-sized hatchback and shown the baffling, badly marked layout of a half-hearted race track by a man who never showed his face. After this you'd be sent back to the pungent Portakabin where you'd be given a plate of tepid food, then led to an aircraft hangar full of people in Subaru fleeces, which was either very hot if it was summer or very cold if it was winter, and pointed up onto a stage where a slightly rude man would mock various aspects of your career and/or clothes before torturing you with a slow reveal of your humiliating performance on the track. You can see why booking guests was sometimes difficult.

We got them nonetheless and most guests seemed to have a good time, despite the unusualness of what was required. Perhaps because of it. As the show got more established, we even had previous guests begging to come on again, typically because they wanted another crack at the lap. Hence the delights of Jay Kay, Lewis Hamilton and Simon Cowell, all fans of the show and all beyond happy to be there. This made the entire process a bit easier. If proper stars wanted to do it more than once, how bad could it be? Footballers and other sports people remained a tricky booking, mainly because their paymasters and nervous insurance brokers wouldn't allow them to do it, but film stars, telly legends and musicians were within reach. Some still said no of course, others did it just to plug their new film/book/range of dog hats, but many stars seemed genuinely keen.

You could get a feel for the degree of keenness in the pre-chat, a standard talk-show technique in which someone from the team has a phone conversation with the star a couple of days before and asks a few basic questions which, in our case, would give us a feel for stuff like car history, approach to driving, notable accidents and other things that might inform Jeremy's line of questioning. Down the line, some stars were excited, others a little wary. It could be a useful barometer of what to expect the following Wednesday. It was in the phone chat that Will Young gave an early hint of the disarming charm that made him such a surprise hit. It was while speaking to Wilman on his mobile that Jordan showed her ballsy pneumatic style wasn't an act. 'This car of yours,' she asked. 'Has it got a roll cage?' Wilman confirmed that it had. 'Good,' she replied in a matter-of-fact manner, ''cos it's going over.' She never managed it, despite her best intentions.

Lionel Richie, on the other hand, saw his previous hairstyles flash before his eyes when the bolts sheared through the Liana's wheel, sending him skittering into a field in a shower of sparks. Yet, sad to say, putting a proper singing legend in peril wasn't our greatest faux pas that day. Richie was our first big star from the US. We'd decided we couldn't ask him to relax in our usual mangy guest room so in an unusually lavish move we'd rented him a Winnebago of the kind a megastar would be used to, except rented from a company near Gatwick. It was only much later in the day, long after the former Commodore had been through his near-death experience in a small Suzuki and been invited to retire to these quarters to recover, that someone noticed the picture on the wall opposite the entrance and, therefore, the very first thing our American guest would have seen when he walked in. It was a lovingly rendered pen and ink drawing depicting the twin towers of the World Trade Center. This was 2004. Fortunately for us, Lionel Richie turned out to be one of the most laid-back and gracious stars we have ever had on the show. He was easy like some part of the week, I forget which.

We'd tried our best to make guests feel welcome and to acknowledge the effort they'd made in coming down to our inconveniently sited base. Sometimes this didn't get off to the best start. On a warm summer's day in 2003 we were sitting outside running through the studio links when an older gentleman wearing a cap, sunglasses and dad-tastic mobile phone holder on his belt approached our table. He looked like the kind of genial retiree who delivers press cars. Not now mate, we said firmly, we're rehearsing lines here.

'Well, it's just . . .' the man began.

No, seriously, we said, someone else can help you.

'Ah, you see, I'm . . .'

Without saying another word the man revealed his true identity, not by taking off his sunglasses but by flamboyantly removing his baseball cap to expose the distinctively hairless head of acting royalty. It was Sir Patrick Stewart. We were mortified. He was unfazed and deeply charming.

In fact, most guests were incredibly nice, especially given that we were demanding most of a day and some physical exertion, usually for free. We could often tell who were going to be the most likeable and excellent guests based on an imaginary scoring system in which celebs racked up extra points for certain behaviours. Guests could fail to score highly on this scale and still be fantastic, but if they notched up a good score here it was almost certain they would be remembered fondly by the team. Top points would be awarded if they:

1. **Drove themselves to the studio.** Turning down the offer of a chauffeured Merc to take them to Dunsfold spoke of a keenness and passion for cars that would bode well for their appearance on the show. And so it would prove to be with notable self-drivers including Chris Evans, Stephen Fry, Amy Macdonald, Simon Cowell and Jenson Button.
2. **Hung around afterwards.** Once the interview was done, all a star had to do was hand back the radio mike and they could jump in the car and head straight back to London. And, in fairness, some had other commitments and shouldn't be judged on the speed of their departure. But some of the most endearing celebs hung around to watch the rest of the show being recorded and then came to enjoy a past-its-sell-by pork pie and a warm glass of reasonably priced wine from our terrible after-show buffet. Sienna Miller was one of those. Stephen Fry too, though only on his first appearance. After his second he offered full and sincere apologies for a prior engagement, climbed into his London taxi and puttered off. Steve Coogan was so keen he spent the rest of the show standing in the audience with fellow car nerds. My favourite surprise was John Prescott, who had a right good dust-up with Jeremy on camera yet readily

stuck around afterwards and was to be found much later cheerily padding around our production office chatting to anyone and slurping from a massive mug of tea.

3. **Came with a minimal entourage.** Any star that turned up with a vast army of fluffers and feeders and hangers-on immediately seemed like they might be hard work. It wasn't always true, but there certainly seemed to be a correlation. That's why a minimal entourage was always respected, as was Roger Daltrey, who asked if he could bring a mate and then turned up with one of his oldest friends from Shepherd's Bush. I think he was a plasterer. Good blokes, the pair of them.

4. **Made themselves at home.** Our Dunsfold production building was a grubby and unhomely place, yet any star that cheerfully settled into it without a word was always going to be fine. Michael Fassbender, for example, who sauntered into the manky presenters' room and plonked himself on one of the tatty sofas for a chat as if he was round at a mate's house and about to fire up the PlayStation. Likewise, Blur's Alex James hung about afterwards playing us music off his laptop and Matt LeBlanc never wanted to leave, or at least not until we'd concluded a hyper-nerdic conversation about Porsche engines.

5. **Gave the impression they wanted to be there.** An amazing number of stars were fired up about coming to the track, about meeting The Stig and about being part of *Top Gear*. None more so than Tom Cruise, who shook off the cloud of pushers and preeners that follow a major star on a promo tour because he wanted to spend some time talking to Richard and James about old motorbikes.

I'm happy to report that only a few slebs disappointed in real life. There was the hardman actor who declared he wasn't hanging around in our 'pisshole' of a Portakabin and had to be taken to the local pub for lunch. There was the starlet whose people threatened to pull her from the show just before recording if Jeremy mentioned an aspect of her personal life which she'd previously seemed happy to discuss with the media. There was the popstress who turned up with an entourage that threatened to dwarf our production team. There was the comedian whose lack of humour could be blamed on jet lag and the comedian whose lack of humour could be blamed on him appearing to be a total arse. But most stars were really nice, despite being taken out of their comfort zone and into Surrey.

Star in a Reasonably Priced Car seemed to be a polarising item among viewers. Some found it an amusing diversion and a pleasant fourth voice on the show. Others thought it got in the way of the monster trucks jumping over exploding caravans and should be dropped. Yet without it, the show would have been harder to structure. Remove that hearty ten-minute slug of studio time in the middle of the show and VT would have shunted straight into VT, changing the pacing for the worse. Plus, what was the point in having a studio and a studio audience if we didn't have features that made use of them? More importantly, without Star in a Reasonably Priced Car we'd have missed some genuine moments of comedy, drama and excitement. Or, in the case of Sir Ranulph Fiennes, great dignity and warmth. The segment gave variety and a change in tone to the show and we liked having stars of all levels of brightness coming to our little home and giving their all, which is probably why Star in a Reasonably Priced Car stuck around.

We never did get Bryan Ferry to do it.

# . . . in a Reasonably Priced Car

Getting top celebrity guests onto *Top Gear* and then asking them to drive a cheap, low-powered car wasn't just a cack-handed stab at putting famous people into a situation that seemed beneath them. There was a practical aspect to it too. In a low-powered and deeply average car the guests with no skill could trundle about and not scare themselves, the ones with some ability could prove it by wringing every gram of ability from the sorry machine and anyone whose skill was overshadowed by their eye-bulging, white-knuckle fearlessness wouldn't have the power to get themselves into any real trouble. Although it was tempting to create a feature called Star in a Supercar, such a thing could have rapidly descended into Star Soils Their Pants, Star in a Very Tricky Insurance Claim and Star in a Tumbling Ball of Burning Wreckage.

Besides, it would be very difficult and expensive to get hold of a Lamborghini for our guests to hammer around the track every week. Whereas, in contrast, finding someone to lend us a cheapo car would be easy. Or so we thought. In 2002, before various also-ran car companies got good or gave up, there were lots of cars on the market that you might call reasonably priced. The phrasing was very specific. 'Reasonably priced' sounded euphemistic, like low-rent advertising copy in a local newspaper, and we thought that was funny. It also helped with the sales pitch to anyone we approached for a car. 'No wait, we're not saying you're cheap, we're saying you're good value . . . Hello? Hello?'

Despite our best efforts, nobody was interested. You'd think any company glumly peddling bare-minimum tin boxes as grey as a Mancunian Tuesday would like to get their stuff on telly. But no, they did not. A year earlier they'd been told *Top Gear* was dead. Now it was apparently coming back as something entirely different and they didn't know what, so they decided to play safe by turning us down. Or maybe they suspected that we'd say their car was crap. Every week. For ten weeks. And then for another series in the new year. The PR person who agreed to such a foolish thing might as well hand in their gun and badge on the day we got the keys.

Eventually, however, a nice man from Suzuki agreed to lend us something called a Liana. To do so, he had to put his job on the line. I'm not exaggerating. He told his bosses he thought it was a good idea and since they disagreed he promised that if it failed he would quietly leave the building. So, with the arrangement nervously made, the actual car turned up at the BBC offices in White City just before we filmed the pilot episode. Word went around that the Reasonably Priced Car was outside and Jeremy led a merry band of us downstairs to have a look. What we found was hilarious. The wheels looked tiny and withdrawn under the oversized body, like a thin man in an ill-fitting suit. The interior was no better, with a digital speedometer straight out of 1985 and an inexplicably huge ignition key that fitted awkwardly into a trouser pocket and threatened to pop a testicle every time you sat down. To make matters worse, the poor thing was painted the colour of an adult nappy. We howled with derisive laughter at this strange, gawky, odd little car. But in its defence it seemed to have quite a lot of standard equipment and it did cost just £9,995. It was, without doubt, 'reasonably priced'.

We didn't realise what a much-loved member of the team the Liana would become. Yes, it was funny-looking and a bit uncool, but it stood up to the celebs' lack of mechanical sympathy with fortitude and showed a quality as admirable in a car as it is in a person, or a small dog. It was plucky.

After Jay Kay appeared on the second-ever show with a driving style best described as 'exuberant', we belatedly had it fitted with a roll cage. When the hub bolts sheared straight through tortured steel, sending Lionel Richie spearing off the track in a shower of sparks, the wheels were beefed up. Apart from that, the amusing little blue saloon was bog standard. Eventually we got caught out once too often by a celeb who thought the clutch was there to be broken and asked Suzuki for a backup car. The nice PR man, still gainfully employed, had an easier time signing that off.

Car one continued to do all the donkey work. Every so often awestruck engineers would poke around it like doctors peering at the guts of the world's oldest man and declare the mileage on the clock to be equivalent to ten times that of a car in the real world. When we weren't on air Suzuki asked for the car back and would send it on tours of dealerships so eager punters could have their picture taken with it, just like a real star. We eagerly awaited the moment when it started demanding candles in its garage, claimed it only drank organic petrol and married a much younger model.

What actually happened, sadly, was semi-retirement. Much though we liked the Liana, after seven series the lap board was getting too full. Also, Suzuki had deleted it from their range and the nice PR man, though no longer fearing for his job, found it harder to justify sending us another mountain of tyres and spare clutches for a car you couldn't buy. So the Liana was put out to pasture, to be resurrected only when an F1 star came to the track.

Then we had to find a replacement, which was difficult because just four years after our first search there seemed to be fewer new cars that fell into the realm of reasonably priced. All was not lost, however, because as luck would have it General Motors had just performed a rebranding job on Korea's third-best car maker. Once known as Daewoo, from now on they'd be called Chevrolet, and we thought it seemed amusing to promise inattentive star guests a go in a Chevrolet, have them turn up expecting a Corvette and then lead them towards a dismal blue saloon. On that rather thin premise, we got ourselves a Lacetti. It was a bit faster than the Liana, but because it appeared to be pretending to be a proper car it was somehow not as charming. It lasted for seven series over three rather loveless years before we exploded a chimney on top of it. Well, on top of car one. Where car two went, I don't know. Or care.

Then the Kia Cee'd came along and despite Jeremy's insistence on saying its name in a daft way and trying to claim it was brown it was a much less comical car on account of being actually quite good. Likewise, the Astra that followed it. These were barely reasonably priced cars at all, at least not in the sense of having four electric windows and standard air-con for less than ten grand. Mind you, they weren't unreasonably priced either. They were just priced. You wanted some car, you handed over your cash, you got a five-door hatchback. It seemed like a fair transaction. Besides, the car world had moved on. Everything had lots of standard equipment and, in real terms, didn't cost much more than a few years ago. This is what we told ourselves when trying to find new track hacks for our stars.

Before we got the Astra we toyed with doing something a bit different. At one point we thought about a Toyota Prius (Pros – Hollywood celebs liked them. Cons – *Top Gear* didn't. Also, no manual gearbox) or a Mazda MX-5 (Pros – possibility of rear-wheel-drive slides. Cons – too small inside to accommodate roll cage, cameras and anyone over six foot) or even a Skoda Octavia vRS (Pros – lots of power. Cons – lots of power).

In the end, Jeremy insisted we should 'get something normal like an Astra or whatever that Toyota one is called' and it was Vauxhall that came up trumps. Then driving home from the office one day in early summer 2013, not long after we'd agreed on the Astra, I had a sudden thought that might bring back some of the incongruous quality we'd always wanted from the star car; why didn't we make it an Astra *estate*? The next day I suggested it to Wilman. Yes, it's a good idea, he said. But what was also a good idea was ordering two hatchbacks from Vauxhall several days earlier and asking them to pull out all the stops to get them built in time for inauguration at a celeb tea party in just a few weeks' time. He didn't actually say all that. He just said, 'It's too late'. I thought that was a shame because I reckoned it could be brilliant if some A-list Hollywood star wrestled their way around the track looking as if they were on their way to the municipal rubbish dump or were about to pop into Homebase for some shelves. I didn't actually say all that either. I just said, Oh bollocks.

So the Reasonably Priced Car ended pretty much as it had started, with a very normal-looking, slightly dreary car incongruously filled with the shimmering greatness of a top celebrity (or near offer). There is, however, a great Reasonably Priced Car that never was . . .

Sorry. Those dots there aren't because I've just passed out. They're meant to encourage you to read the next chapter where all will be revealed . . .

I've done it again. I'd just turn the page now if I were you.

# Good News!

Running gags can be good things, like a stamp on the loyalty card of people who stick with a TV show for the long haul. I don't think *Top Gear* ever really got into running gags, mostly because we were too disorganised to do them regularly, and if you don't then there isn't much point. A running gag isn't a running gag if every so often it stops and falls over or wanders off into a shop.

There were the Stig introductions and The Stig's wildly variable taste in music I suppose, but I'm not sure you'd call those proper running jokes. No, the only time we got even close was during the news segments of the 11th and 12th series with an idiotic riff that revolved around James exclaiming 'Good news!' and then imparting an extremely dull piece of information about a forthcoming Romanian car called the Dacia Sandero, to which Jeremy would give a one word reply of feigned delight and then immediately change the subject.

The routine came from the usual news-writing process of four blokes sitting in a room full of press releases reading out things and trying to make each other laugh. In this case,

James seized upon some bumf about a simple, small new car because James likes simple, small new cars and then, realising there wasn't much to say about it, caught the attention of the room by announcing good news before reading out a really tedious fact. It spiralled from there.

It wasn't even a proper running theme, though we tried to do one every week, since they sometimes got cut out in the edit, maybe for time reasons, maybe because that week's Sanderofact wasn't rubbish enough. It got to the point where May and I would comb Dacia press releases desperately hoping we'd find an especially arcane sentence about floor mats. I think we ended up getting a researcher to ring their press office and beg for more news.

Despite the irregular appearance of more GOOD NEWS! this thing escalated fast. The audience started tittering as soon as James made his excitable start to the joke. People were wearing GOOD NEWS! T-shirts. Viewers who'd been on holiday to places where Dacias were already on sale started sending James pictures of them. When we were putting together the *Big Book of Top Gear* annual for Christmas and realised we were two pages short, we just bunged in a picture of a Dacia Sandero opposite the massive words, GOOD NEWS! and this seemed to go down better than most of the other drivel I'd written for the rest of the book. It was all a bit weird. Nice, but weird. *Top Gear* had developed a sort of running joke and in the process had accidentally promoted James to the position of poster boy for cheap Romanian hatchbacks. The car wasn't even on sale in the UK yet and we'd somehow made it famous.

One day we got a phone call. It was a nice man from Dacia speaking in hushed tones. Just between us, he said, we've got a Sandero in the UK. This is all top secret, he went on, but it's at a top-secret location and we wondered if you'd like to come and have a top-secret look at it. I rang James. He said he was busy. There was a note of genuine disappointment in his voice when he realised he couldn't make it. I went alone to the top-secret location, which turned out to be a photographic studio in west London. There, in the middle of the floor, was the subject of so much GOOD NEWS! In some respects, it was a strange moment, like meeting someone you've only ever read about in newspapers or seen on television. In other, more realistic, respects it was like standing in a large, brightly lit room looking at a cheap Romanian hatchback.

The original Dacia Sandero was not the prettiest car, nor the most exciting and dynamic-looking. It sat very high on its springs which made it look tippy-toed and awkward. Basic items like the door mirrors and windscreen wipers appeared tacked on at the last minute. The doors closed shut with the unsophisticated clang of someone banging a baking tray against their head. But on the plus side it felt simple, sturdy and had a certain unpretentious charm. Most of all, when it went on sale in Britain at some point in the following year, it was going to be cheap. Or to put it another way, sold at a price that was reasonable. A reasonable price, if you will.

This hadn't escaped the notice of the nice man from Dacia who had a proposal for *Top Gear*: How would we like this to be the next Reasonably Priced Car? It didn't need much thought. We'd made so much of this funny little car that if we didn't have it hacking round the track in future series, driven by speed-crazed celebs, then we were missing a trick. Of course the Sandero should be our next star car, not only because the price was right but also because it had some of the knock-kneed, under-wheeled, unlikely hero appeal of the Suzuki Liana, all of which the current incumbent seemed to lack.

I agreed with the nice man from Dacia that we would talk again soon and headed back to the office to ring James. He was very interested to hear more about the Sandero. Over the next few weeks we kept talking to Dacia. They seemed to be as excited as us about the reasonably priced car thing. Since they were owned by Renault, they'd already arranged that the Sandero could have a top-spec roll cage and race seat installed by the people who prepared the cars for the Clio Cup race series. If we wanted, we could even have them track-prep the chassis and tweak up the engine. This we didn't want. The whole point of the Reasonably Priced Car was that it remained as much as possible in standard trim, heaving around in bends and wheezing up the straights. We were looking forward to seeing the Sandero in action, just as soon as Dacia put it on sale in Britain.

This is where things went awry. The economy tanked. Britain officially entered a recession. Renault decided that now was not the time to be spending a metric shitload of money on launching Dacia in the UK, never mind lending a couple of roll-caged cars to *Top Gear*. The Sandero was not going on sale in Britain for the foreseeable future. We were distraught. Ever since our stupid running joke had gained momentum it had felt like it was the Dacia Sandero's destiny to be our Reasonably Priced Car. This had to happen. We lobbied Renault long and hard to get us a pair of Sanderos from abroad so we could use those. The people in the British branch office tried hard to make this happen but their big fromages in Paris were having none of it. In the joyless world of suits and spreadsheets, spending money to get a car on a telly programme in a country where it wasn't sold made no sense. *Votre voiture à un prix raisonnable, c'est pas possible.* We'd tried our best to make it happen. We even looked at buying the cars ourselves, but no matter how reasonable the price this would seem like a bad use of budget when we ended up with two ragged left-hand-drive hatchbacks that we couldn't get parts for. The Sandero plan was dead. We wanted it, viewers expected it, but it just wasn't to be. You know what this was? It was not GOOD NEWS!

There is, however, a little postscript to this story because in 2013 Dacias finally went on sale in Britain, right around the time *Top Gear* was once again looking for a new Reasonably Priced Car. Surely this was the late-running destiny for the new, improved mark 2 Sandero? We borrowed one to try out and sent The Stig to lap it around the track. The results were a disappointment. Its handling was rather underwhelming and its performance, even with the top-spec turbocharged engine, was far from electrifying. In fact, it was slow. Really slow. So slow that the times it would post, even in the hands of an able celeb, would have been well down on those achieved by its Kia predecessor. It seemed appealing to install the Sandero in what felt like its rightful role, but not if the bar for stars was lowered. With heavy heart, we said thanks but no thanks to Dacia and eventually settled on an Astra. Maybe it didn't matter any more. After all, by now the running joke was years ago. Even so, it always seemed like at some point we should have the most reasonably priced of all cars as our celebrity track hack. It's a shame we never made it work. That would have been GOOD NEWS!

Great! Anyway . . .

# *Ideas*

Long before anything was written on the page, long before cars were found and locations were booked, long before Jeremy was blustering about shouting 'HAMMOND YOU IDIOT!' and James's trousers had caught fire and then fallen down and then caught fire again, there had to be the idea. Ideas were very important on *Top Gear* and we got through a lot of them.

Ideas came from all over the place. The production team were collectively and individually a rich source of new thoughts. Richard, James and Andy Wilman were good ideas people too. Jeremy, though, was a powerhouse, coming up with new thoughts or rejigging existing ones on a regular basis. We all pulled our weight on this front, but Clarkson never slept. He was the engine room at the heart of *Top Gear* ideas.

Having an idea alone wasn't enough, however. Something might seem superficially like a good thought but that was only the start. The idea would then find itself subject to a great deal of prodding and poking and the kind of questioning it might receive from a four-year-old. Why? Why? No, but *why*? Good

*Top Gear* ideas solved some perceived problem or answered some logical question, and if they weren't doing either of those things there had to be some other solid reason for doing whatever it was we had planned. The word 'grounded' was used a lot, meaning that an idea had to have at least its roots in some real world issue like ambulances or cheap cars or road chaos brought on by snow. At the very least, we needed this as a starting point to get the idea rolling, hooking the viewer and craving their attention for 20 minutes or so. Sometimes ideas started with a simple premise and then spiralled foolishly out of control, at which point Jeremy would declare them 'silly side up' and we'd go back to the place where, if it had been 1956, we'd have had a drawing board. Ultimately, with any idea we had to ask what's the point? And if there really wasn't one, that probably killed it.

In the very early days of new *Top Gear* it was a bit easier because we hadn't done much before. Car programmes up until that point had simply reviewed new models, looked at used car bargains and maybe gone to a traction engine rally. Anything we did beyond that would seem fresh and new. We got away with a lot more daftness simply because it was unexpected, although even then we were still answering vital questions like 'Can a bus jump over some motorcycles?' or 'Can your grandmother doughnut a Honda S2000?' You could almost call it consumer journalism. Although only if you had simply no idea what either of those words meant.

My very favourite lost item from those heady days of lateral thinking was one from our in-house master of unexpected ideas, researcher Jim Wiseman. 'I was wondering,' he said one day. 'Could a monkey drive a car?' We all laughed. It's a good question, we agreed, but don't you think it might struggle with clutch control? Jim looked at us like we were daft. 'No,' he said slowly, as if this was bloody obvious. 'It'll be an automatic.' We laughed some more, and it was agreed that this should definitely be on the show. There aren't many monkey suppliers in the phone book but there was a well-known monkey sanctuary place and they seemed to have monkeys coming out of their ears so Jim gave them a call. Strangely, they didn't share our enthusiasm for getting one of their inmates to drive a car. In fact, the lady on the phone seemed to take a dim view of the whole idea. Jim's attempts to convince her that the monkey might actually enjoy taking a spin in an automatic car didn't do anything to change her mind. They would not lend us a monkey. In fact, they were more emphatic than that: 'If I find out that you're attempting this,' the monkey lady said angrily, 'I will SHUT YOU DOWN.' That was the end of that one.

More normally, we were the ones who torpedoed our own ideas when exhaustive examination proved them to fall short. Even ideas that stood up to scrutiny sometimes needed a hefty tweak before filming began. In series 8, when the presenters tried to build a Caterham in less time than it took The Stig to drive from Surrey to the Knockhill race track in Scotland, that race originally wasn't against The Stig at all. It was against Jeremy's wife, Richard's wife and James's girlfriend, also attempting to build a kit car in the next garage. We'd had good fun when the presenters' mothers had helped us to assess small cars, so this seemed like a good follow-on.

But then a creeping doubt set in. We assumed that three intelligent, practical women would monster the car-making challenge and make the silly, shambolic men look stupid, but what if they didn't? What if it seemed like we'd set them up to look silly? What if it came across as rampant sexism? *Top Gear* was often accused of being sexist as it was. We used to be very sensitive about this. Someone would say we're sexist and we'd say show us an example of sexism on the show. Well, the typical response went, it's presented by three men. That's not sexist, we'd say, that's casting. If those three men said, 'Bloody women, can't drive, huh-huh!', well, that would be sexist. So we got cold feet about what might come across as a 1970s-spec battle of the sexes. A race against The Stig sounded more dynamic and interesting as a piece of television anyway, otherwise the whole thing would be shot inside two workshops.

Being prepared to rethink an idea was very important. The original and long-standing concept for the end of the Patagonia special was another one that got a severe revamp. We'd planned the finale of this film for months; the presenters would attempt to build the most southerly settlement in the world. It had seemed like a good ending and who knew, it might even get us into some record book or other. But somehow it just didn't feel quite satisfying enough. Yes, they could have capered about in the miserable rain and wind at the very tail of a continent as they tried to make a house and a shop and whatever else was needed to count as a small town, but once they'd done that, what then? You'd have had 15 or 20 minutes watching three buffoons badly erecting wooden huts and then seen the credits roll. Not a very exciting or worthwhile end to an epic journey. Some noble attempts were made to bolt on a proper ending, perhaps involving a triumphant town opening ceremony featuring a performance from a massively famous band, but really it was just trying to sprinkle rock glitter on a disappointing pile of poo. Besides, it's unlikely that someone like AC/DC would have gladly travelled to the very tip of Argentina to play a gig to three TV presenters in their crap new hamlet. We all knew it just wasn't quite right, but with the shoot looming we couldn't think of what to do. In the end our specials producer Chris Hale suggested we ditch the southernmost settlement idea and have a good old-fashioned game of car football, England versus Argentina. We could call it The End of the World Cup. This was a much better idea. It could be exciting and dynamic and, whatever the final score, we'd be ending on a bombshell. It's a bit of a shame that events conspired against us on that one.

Other ideas were not rejigged or rethought. Even after many hours of discussion and planning and hard work from the research team, we realised some part of them didn't add up and they were thrown entirely into the bin. One of the most promising was the notion we had sometime in 2009 that the presenters should run a petrol station. On the surface, this seemed to have everything we looked for in a *Top Gear* idea. It was something people could relate to, petrol stations had several failings the presenters felt they could attack and there was scope for ingenuity and idiocy all over the place. Jeremy would tackle those infuriating people who don't pull away from the pumps as soon as they get in their car, by giving them ten seconds and then releasing a wrecking ball from the ceiling to smash them out of the way. Richard would address the usual level of substandard catering by setting up an American-style hog roast on the forecourt. James would transform the usual shop into a welcoming, wood-panelled gentlemen's club and attempt to steal some of Hammond's business by selling top-quality pies. There would also be a high-speed car wash using insanely powerful fire hoses, an express lane staffed by an F1 crew who could change your tyres and brim your tank in a matter of seconds, and in a reflection of the *Top Gear* house stance on certain fuels diesel would be doubled in price and renamed 'loser juice', while the pump itself would be fitted with a PA system through which Jeremy could call anyone using it a 'cheapskate'. This all sounded very jolly and plans were made to find an old petrol station we could convert to our spec and then invite hapless punters to use.

This is where it started to get tricky. For some reason, it's not considered good form to have a whole pig roasting over a naked flame right next to the place where you dispense flammable liquid, safety experts do not look kindly on wrecking balls flailing about in the vicinity of the general public and the insurance people had a few issues with the smashing and soaking of other people's cars when all they came in for was a packet of Mentos and a newspaper. These problems could have been surmounted but the item had a rather larger issue at its heart; it was all well and good identifying problems with petrol stations and then addressing them, but where did the story end? We'd see the presenters' ideas in action, we'd see if they worked or not, and then what? Where was the finale, where was the big finish or triumphant conclusion? Ideally you'd have wanted something massive and it seemed inevitable that this would involve the entire place burning to the ground, which viewers would surely see a mile off. With heavy heart we realised we were setting up to make a protracted comedy sketch and little else. These were all amusing ideas, but they were better packaged in a magazine column than presented in an extremely complicated and expensive piece of television. The *Top Gear* petrol station idea was killed off. It was only by picking away at the idea that we finally worked out that to make it for television was daft. In the end it turned up as a lovely illustration in the 2010 *Big Book of Top Gear* Christmas annual. It worked quite well, and no one got crushed or set on fire.

The same thing happened in 2014 when we decided to reinvent the fire engine. The logic went like this; existing fire engines took too long to respond to emergencies because they were too big and too slow. If we made them smaller and faster, we could make them better. We had a lot of meetings about this one. We should build a tiny fire engine, we reckoned. But then there would be no room for all the ladders and hoses and burly men it needed to do its job. So we'd have to make it a bit bigger. But then it would have no advantage in traffic. So we'd make it smaller again. But then . . .

It went round in circles for many weeks before we realised that all we were doing was cueing up a load of jokes in which Richard Hammond zoomed about in a V8-powered Bedford Rascal with a bucket in it, signally failing to do the one job you want from a fire engine. With heavy heart we concluded that the ideal design for a fire engine is an existing fire engine. At that point, the idea was binned.

As the show went on, it got harder and harder to think of truly fresh ideas that would surprise an audience. Once you've navigated a pick-up truck across the English Channel and made a space shuttle from a Reliant Robin, viewers are probably comfortable with the idea that nothing is impossible. At the same time, that made the team more brutal and picky about every idea we had. Until you were actually committed and standing in a damp car park in the East Midlands ready to roll cameras, you always felt that any idea could feel the cool blow of the hatchet on the back of its neck. There was no room on *Top Gear* for persevering with an idea if it wasn't going to work. No wait, I've just remembered the India special. Alright, there was a little bit of room for persevering with an idea if it wasn't going to work. But, I hope, in general, not a lot.

# The Dog

It was normal between *Top Gear* series for the whole team to sit down and discuss ideas for the next block of programmes. A 'brainstorm', if you will.

The format for these sessions was simple; we would gather in a room and then Jeremy would start speaking. At some point we might break for a spot of lunch then we'd regather and Jeremy would continue speaking. The rest of us might chip in now and again but generally, since he was the tallest, his voice was the loudest and he had the most ideas, Jeremy would speak. Because I had a notepad and I'm quite a fast writer, I would try to scribble down everything that was said and type it up later into something comprehensible. This was how we started the planning process, which enabled us to fill in the gaps on the massive whiteboard in the office upon which each series was mapped. Or, as more normally happened, part fill it and then panic midway through the series when we realised we were one item short.

Normally these early brainstorm meetings would take place in our manky office, since everyone was usually there anyway and at lunchtime it was only a short walk to the canteen. But when, in early 2006, we sat down to plan series 8, someone must have been reading a management book or something because it was decided that our 'brainstorm' should be 'off site' and to that end we booked a room in a swanky central London private members' club. Normally we wouldn't have been so lavish but this move was justified because that evening we were moving to another room in the swanky central London private members' club to have a belated and modest celebration for the International Emmy we'd won a couple of months earlier.

So there we were in the swanky club, idly passing round various sheets of suggestions and thinking ahead to plundering the £7.50 the BBC had put behind the bar as a token of thanks for our award-winning ways. Then Jeremy arrived and began speaking. The speaking went on for most of the day as we batted ideas back and forth and mostly listened to what he had to say. Finally, sometime in the late afternoon and with the prospect of a subsidised thimble of booze getting ever closer, Jeremy appeared to have grown tired of speaking. He turned to James May, who was lounging on a sofa in the manner of a man who has stopped listening and started daydreaming about old motorcycles.

'James,' Clarkson said briskly. 'Have YOU got any ideas to discuss?'

'Well, yes,' May replied, without missing a beat. 'I was wondering if we could get a dog . . .'

Never has a room been in such instant and unanimous agreement. This sounded like a brilliant idea. *Blue Peter* had a dog. *Doctor Who* had a dog. Sort of. Why shouldn't *Top Gear* have a dog? I can't remember a single other idea that came out of that meeting in the swanky central London club.

Perhaps there weren't any. All I can remember is that James suggested we get a dog and everyone agreed that we should get a dog so that was that; we got a dog.

Normally if a TV show decided such a thing they'd have to hire a suitable mutt from a reassuringly expensive company in the business of supplying animals to TV shows, but *Top Gear* was more fortunate because Richard Hammond had spotted a small corner of his house that wasn't infested with creatures and was already thinking of finding another dog to fill it. His latest pet would become our new star. A few weeks later the Hammonds adopted a Labradoodle puppy which the office decided should be called Top Gear Dog. At home she was simply Teegee.

We were very pleased with ourselves. Getting a dog was exactly the sort of thing we liked to do, simply because it was childish and idiotic and separated us from other high-profile BBC programmes. *Songs of Praise* didn't have a dog. Nor did the *Ten O'clock News*. And nor, for that matter, did *Watchdog*, and they of all people had the perfect excuse. Whereas here we were, a car show with an inexplicable in-house dog.

Top Gear Dog's arrival couldn't have been better timed either, because series 8 marked some big changes for the show. We had a new studio, we had new titles, we had a very well-known DJ/producer reworking the theme music. And now, on top of all that, we had a dog. All of these things were to become a stout reminder of why *Top Gear* was a liability at the controls of its own destiny.

The 'much bigger' studio turned out to feel 'much smaller' once we'd filled it with cars on stands and giant Airfix kit replicas. The new titles featured animated silhouettes of the presenters which made them look deranged and gave Jeremy an inexplicable quiff which flapped around in the animated wind. The updated theme tune was so completely revamped that it didn't really sound like the *Top Gear* music at all. Still, at least we had the dog. We liked the dog. BBC building services weren't so keen and told Hammond he couldn't bring her into our London office unless he suddenly turned out to be blind. Someone filled in some forms and had her reclassified as on-screen talent, which made that issue go away.

Then it was just a matter of sorting out the other problems brought on by our own hopeless attempts to reinvent things. The studio problem was fixed by getting rid of some of the set dressing. A mysterious stranger helped out by stealing the alloy wheels off the big Airfix kits. The titles were tweaked so that no one looked like a terrible Elvis impersonator. Someone rang the well-known DJ/producer to tell him that his work was very nice but we'd forgotten to mention that it should sound like the *Top Gear* theme tune and since it didn't we probably couldn't use it on *Top Gear*.

Problems solved, jobs done, and we still had a dog. Not just any dog, either. As it turned out, what we had was the least suitable dog in the world. The first problem was that she hated being in cars. In fact, they made her sick, often all over James May. The second problem was that she was almost completely inert. Not all the time, oh dear me no. During rehearsals in an empty studio she'd caper around all over the place, chasing rolled up bits of paper torn from the back of scripts. But as soon as you put her in front of an audience or a camera or both, she instantly went to sleep. If you watch back her appearances in that eighth series you can see Hammond practically having to drag her onto the set like some hairy, car-sick narcoleptic.

There was a third problem too. We'd got a dog in a fit of excitement at behaving like the 1970s children's programme we secretly believed we were, but we hadn't thought beyond that. And now we simply didn't know what to do with her. After all, she was only a dog. A lovely, good-natured dog but completely incapable of doing anything on the show beyond lying in shot like a lumpy rug and making a dreadful mess of car interiors.

We soldiered on for series 8 pretending that this was still a good idea and then quietly let it drop, allowing Teegee to go back to a normal life with the Hammond family, where she remains to this day. Like a lot of things on *Top Gear*, it had seemed like a good idea right up until the moment when we realised it wasn't.

Oddly enough, people still asked about the dog long after she had retired from television. Very occasionally she would even receive a piece of fan mail through the post, years after her last appearance. Top Gear Dog had a remarkably enduring fan base for what was basically a very sweet, very fluffy but completely and utterly stupid idea.

# Cars 2

We got through a lot of old cars on *Top Gear*. Some of them were simply old scrappers to be dinged, shot at or crushed, and getting those was easy. Scrapyards are full of such things and you could find some really presentable stuff in the queue for the crushing machine. It wasn't like the early days of top hosp drama *Casualty* when a bloke playing a company director or high-ranking pilot would say a cheery goodbye to his wife before getting into a rotten, worthless, 15-year-old Cortina and you'd think, well, this character is plainly going to have a car accident.

Even during the life of *Top Gear*, scrap cars seemed to reach higher standards as rustproofing got better and electronics got more complicated, so ageing cars looked good as new but could be felled for the sake of a fault with an expensive ECU.

In earlier times, cars to be used as expendable props were MOT-failed former minicabs like the bunch we got in for the home-made limos shoot, along with an 'evasive driving expert' who tried to demonstrate a dramatic and highly effective escape manoeuvre but simply drove dismally into the car in front. That sequence got edited out. Mostly because the presenters were laughing too much to speak.

By the time we got to shooting a tribute to Peugeots in summer 2014, we could fill the car park of an Oxfordshire garden centre with death row metal so pristine and recent that I remember double-checking with one of the producers that this was definitely the area where we could hit stuff. Even then it seemed implausible that we weren't about to clobber someone's actual Laguna while they were inside browsing the chrysanthemums.

If sourcing scrap was easy, getting hold of a very specific old car was a little harder. In summer 2008, while shooting a story about communist-era cars on the old Greenham Common airbase, we set fire to a Morris Marina under the premise that we'd turned it into a brazier. I drove the Marina in question before it was torched and it was pretty dismal. Also, James May insisted that it made me look like a rural vicar. So there was no great sadness when it became engulfed in flames.

Unfortunately, the massed Marina lovers of Britain didn't share this casual attitude to the destruction of their favourite car and wrote furious things about *Top Gear* on the internet and in letters to the office. Our response was, I'm not going to pretend otherwise, utterly childish. In essence, we decided that if they were annoyed then the solution was to annoy them some more. Another Marina was bought, and then a piano was dropped on it. The Marinaists were incandescent with rage. So we did it again a while later. And then again. Leading lights in the Marina movement put out a stern warning to all fellow enthusiasts to be extra careful when selling a car in case the buyer was a researcher from *Top Gear*. At some point during this very puerile attempt to annoy Morris people we got an email from someone complaining not about Marina destruction but about one of the pianos we'd dropped, saying it appeared to be quite a rare and interesting model. Perversely, we were quite mortified about this.

The hardest bit of old crock sourcing was finding very specific hero cars for those three presenter challenges where things were bought for buttons and subjected to a series of tests. At the very start, this wasn't so complicated. For the £100 cars challenge Jeremy's wife spotted his old Volvo at the back of a dealer's yard while having the family XC90 serviced. It had been taken in part exchange, it had no real value, scrap-metal prices were in the doldrums, it would probably get junked. At Jeremy's behest, she went back and offered them a quid for it. Richard and James found their cars by scouting the internet looking for old crap, which they spent a lot of their time doing anyway. A researcher went to collect May's Audi and when it turned up at the office James was so excited that a load of us piled into it and he drove round to the local car wash to have it made shiny. It was only much later that we began to suspect that what he'd actually bought and then spent seven quid on having cleaned was not one but two Audis, though only half of each.

Presenter self-sourcing wasn't going to work for much longer. For one thing, car traders weren't stupid and prices would become mysteriously higher if a bloke on the telly rang up to enquire about something. So we worked out a new system which enabled us to maintain a degree of anonymity. Whenever a challenge was agreed, each presenter would be invited to choose the car they thought best equipped to take it on. A researcher would look for examples of that car for sale online and then go back to the presenter, regretfully telling him something like, 'Sorry, Jeremy, but you can't get a Nissan GT-R for £900', so perhaps he should think again.

Whatever their realistic choice was, a list of likely examples would be put together and the presenter would choose one they liked. Then a member of the team would buy it, have it checked over by a tame mechanic and arrange for presenter and car to be united so they could gaze upon its majesty and get to know all the faults they would later pretend it did not have. It was a heart-warming moment when the presenters got excited to see their cars in the metal for the first time. May only lived up the road and he'd often come racing to the office to inspect whatever it was he'd chosen. Hammond too was a terrible sucker for old cars and often wanted to buy them off the production when filming was done. Jeremy's wife once wearily told me he couldn't come to the phone because his Mitsubishi Starion had just arrived and he'd gone off for a play in it.

In principle, this process worked well. In reality there were always snags, like the only affordable example being in Aberdeen/pieces/a river, but the grit and dedication of the *Top Gear* research team was usually able to make the presenters' cheap car dreams come true. And with a free set of spare floor mats thrown in.

The next challenge was keeping these cars running so we could film them. They'd get checked over beforehand to make sure they weren't death traps and in the early days we'd just set off and hope for the best, although in *Top Gear*'s case 'best' ideally included a certain amount of trouble because that gave us good material. Unfortunately, what the average old car does most of all is overheat and after a while that ceases to be good television and simply becomes a pain in the arse. Standing beside a Majorcan highway with Richard Hammond and a dwarf called Brian watching steam pouring from a crap old Lanchester very rapidly ceased to be amusing somewhere around the 15th time it happened. By then we'd taken to having the AA on speed dial or a friendly mechanic following us so that repetitive niggles could be dealt with quickly, rather than having to watch Jeremy blundering about trying to remove the expansion cap with a cricket bat.

Once we'd finished filming the VT and the trio of old crocks had appeared in the studio for the links, we used to have a problem. They were often in less than brilliant condition. They generally weren't worth very much and yet we couldn't flog them for fear of strident headlines proclaiming 'TOP GEAR SOLD ME A DEATHTRAP'. So the cars just hung around, cluttering up the place. In the end, the £100 cars were donated to the local fire brigade who cut them up during rescue training. Most other stuff simply ended up in a sad boneyard on the far fringes of the Dunsfold site. The S-class country cottage escaped this for quite some time because its battery went flat and its stupid concrete floor made it too heavy to push, so it sat outside the production office getting in the way. Everything else was dumped among the weeds, out of sight and out of mind.

Eventually some nice people from Beaulieu, Britain's least spellable car museum, stepped in and agreed to take our old crap which they would put on display in a special *Top Gear* exhibit. As such, they must have been delighted when the show stopped because it meant some respite from receiving regular consignments of battered, oil-piddling crap off the telly.

Not everything went to the museum, however. The presenters would spend so long with a lot of these cars they'd develop a weird form of Stockholm syndrome and insist on buying them from the production afterwards. Jeremy did that with his Sprite from the Majorcan rally film. James did the same with his Citroën Ami, although he couldn't think of anything to do with it and lent it back to Beaulieu. Hammond now owns his MGB from the classics film at the very end of the end. James wanted the bright green Datsun 120Y that featured in the British Leyland film but then got into a bidding war with one of the camera crew.

If you want to see some of the other cars from the show, head down to the museum. Don't bother looking for the Porsche 928, Ford Mustang or Lotus Esprit though. They're still in Argentina. Long story.

# The Stig Too

After two series, Perry McCarthy ceased to be the black Stig. At the beginning of series 3, we killed him off. The black Stig, that is, not Perry. The BBC said that would be unacceptable, and also illegal. Since The Stig as a character was in his infancy, it was decided to mark the change by making him a different colour and nothing made the contrast with a black suit as well as a white one. It was only later we realised that the new Stig was very hard to keep clean. Every so often you'd see a shot of him on the show and he'd be visibly grubby. On reflection, a nice dark grey or navy blue would have reduced our dry cleaning bill but it was too late for that. The bigger challenge was finding a driver to fill the new suit, ideally someone quick and gifted and not prone to spontaneously removing their crash helmet while shouting 'TA-DAAAAAA!'

In late summer 2003, Andy Wilman set up a top-secret test session at a top-secret location with a top-secret roster of hand-picked drivers. Actually, it was at Dunsfold and everyone in the office knew when it was happening, but we were explicitly told we couldn't come and watch. Out of this rigorous session in which a scruffy man with a note-book invited various hot-shot wheelmen to lap a couple of cars while he timed them, Wilman found our new Stig. And though this will almost certainly come as a shock to you I can exclusively reveal that it was Ben Collins. I know you'll be surprised to hear this because for some reason Ben has never mentioned his time as the tame racing driver. If you'd like to know more about Ben, why not follow him on Twitter at @BenCollinsStig or read his latest book, *How To Drive: The Ultimate Guide, from the Man Who Was the Stig.*

Ben was brilliant. His driving was good, of course, and he had a brutish, Mansell-esque quality to him on the track, but there were other things that made him such a superb Stig. In the very early days, The Stig was just a driver. But then we decided to get him out of the car and put him in the real world, building on some of the character we'd tried to establish with the silly, 'some say . . .' studio introductions. Ben completely got this and his body language in the suit was spot on. The surly arm folding, the businesslike walk, the slight cock of the head or the intimidating turn of the helmet that showed he was aware of what was going on but was almost certainly not interested. At the risk of sounding like a right old luvvie, Ben made the character his own. He had a terrific understanding for what The Stig did and, perhaps more importantly, what he didn't do.

At one point we developed this outlandish plan to build on The Stig's growing profile by entering him into an actual car race. Not just any car race, either. We wanted to get him into the legendary 24 Hours of Le Mans endurance event. Wilman and I went to see Aston Martin team boss David Richards, who was very affable and very up for this wheeze, although I noticed that he put his hands in his suit trouser pockets while sitting down and this so distracted me I found it really hard to concentrate for the rest of the meeting. From what I remember, they seemed to know full well who was in the suit and they were happy to have The Stig as one of the three drivers taking turns in the car. He'd keep his suit on at all times and the team would play along. It was only later that Wilman and I spotted a problem. We'd set up The Stig as the fastest driver on the planet and for as long as he remained within Top Gear Land, it would never have been proven otherwise. Once he went out into the real world and mixed with other racing drivers, though, what if his times were beaten? That rather undermined the heroic and invincible nature of the character. Also, the organising authorities in France wouldn't let him enter as 'The Stig' even if he agreed to put on a Perry-style outrageouooooos accent and that meant a greater risk of his real name getting out. With regret, and our hands very much not in our pockets while sitting down, we had to bin the idea. The Stig could do many things but he couldn't be seen as anything but infallible and he couldn't give his name away.

As it was, the internet was always awash with rumours of multiple Stigs and various outlandish stories of other big-name drivers who'd occupied the suit. Most of this was utter horse-wash. F1 teams tended to want only their paid drivers inside their cars in order to protect their secrets but otherwise we insisted as much as possible on using Ben because he was The Stig. In fact the really amazing story, less reported online, was how much we made use of him when there wasn't even any driving required. The Stig on public transport across London? That was Ben. The Stig having a fight with some scouts? That was Ben too. He was a professional racing driver who was suddenly required to be an actor, but one of those out-of-work sort of actors that ends up inside the Mickey costume at Disneyland. And he did the performance stuff brilliantly. We only realised how good he was when he was gone. When Stig 3 came along we got a professional choreographer to give the poor bewildered bloke some lessons in posture and movement, just to get him ready for Stigness, in the hope of matching the high bar that had been set by his predecessor.

For 13 series and almost seven years, Ben occupied the role of The Stig with aplomb. Frankly, I'm amazed he managed it that long. It can't have been easy to live inside one of the most recognisable and well-known characters in the world and not be able to do a damn thing about it. It seemed inevitable that something had to give. And of course eventually it did. I came into the office one day, sat down at my desk and waited the usual 30–40 minutes for my top-notch BBC-spec computer to warm up.

As the machine whirred and whined and insisted it needed another 17 software updates, Wilman sidled over. 'Ben's written a book,' he said. My reaction was the same as everyone else's: He's done WHAT? Ben was a racing driver. We didn't even know he could read. What the bloody hell was he playing at?

We were baffled, and a bit put out. He was The Stig. He'd been The Stig for ages. What had suddenly got into him? The grown-ups at BBC Worldwide were even more disgruntled about this, since they had warehouses full of branded stuff that related to a mysterious superhero whose whole character revolved around his anonymity. No one wants to buy a pencil case depicting a man from Bristol in a costume.

Wilman started turning up at the office in a suit. The normal, irritatingly jocular response to such a thing on a man

May, Clarkson and Hammond in a jocular mood after a day's filming, 2005.

Filming the ill-fated and never-seen Pontiac Solstice test in California, September 2005.

James and the author at Dunsfold, 2006.

Jeremy hard at work on a studio script in the *Top Gear* office.

Keyboard legend Rick Wakeman studies Justin Hawkins's chops during the celebrity track day, April 2006.

The Stig admires the result of a rare mistake after crashing the Koenigsegg, May 2006.

The celebrity green room at the *Top Gear* studio in all its dismal glory.

The presenters and *Top Gear* dog outside the studio, about to record the first show of series eight, May 2006.

James pauses to receive a visit from the sound recordist during the first amphibious challenge.

The presenters about to do an outdoor script read-through on a nice day in summer 2006. That's the author leaning on the table and producer Alex Renton behind him.

James filming the Winter Olympics special.

The Stig seems to have developed a strange nose. That's producer Grant Wardrop on the right.

Captain Slow, about to let Sir Jackie Stewart show him how it's done.

In the Alps training for the polar special, 2007.

Richard delivers an unusual piece to camera during the polar special.

Jeremy pretends to be the cameraman. Actual cameraman Ben Joiner is behind him.

not normally seen in formal clothes is 'What time are you in court, huh-huh?!' Except that in this case, he really was due in court. The High Court, in fact, where the Beeb tried to block publication of Ben's book. It didn't work.

In the *Top Gear* office, we didn't care so much about the squawking of the legal eagles, we were just shocked that Ben had done this. He was one of the team. This felt like he'd let us down. When, some months later, we filmed a road trip in America and the presenters took turns to fire guns at Stig cut-outs, Hammond grinned while yelling about being 'shot in the back', but his words were a decent approximation of the mood in the camp at the time.

Also, with Ben very publicly out of the white suit, we faced the arse ache of finding a new Stig. Obviously, in an ideal world we needed someone who was a demon in a car but, just to be on the safe side this time, a blithering illiterate in front of a Word document. Wilman arranged one of his secret track auditions to find a new driver. The bloke he picked was superb. Fast, discreet, no interest whatsoever in speaking to major publishing houses.

Then there was the question of whether Stig could be regenerated in a different colour and the vexed issue of how we introduced him into our world, especially given that Ben's departure couldn't have been more newsworthy if we'd glued it to Cheryl Cole's sideboob. The colour change was hotly debated. On the one hand, it made sense for a fresh Stig to be a new colour. On the other hand, a lot had happened since black Stig became white Stig. The current colour of The Stig was bordering on the iconic and it seemed perverse to chuck that away. This was a tough one. Every so often, someone from the commercial side of the *Top Gear* operation would nervously approach Wilman to ask if a decision had been made, their fingers ready to speed-dial the toy factories in China and tell them not to pour the white plastic into the moulds. In the end, Wilman ruled that Stig should remain his recognisable white.

Now we just had to work out how to introduce a new Stig who looked just like the old one. We had ages until the next series but there were Top Gear Live shows coming up and Stig always featured in those. In the end, we spent a day in the countryside shooting a stupid VT called 'Stig farm', which claimed that we had some rural smallholding full of Stigs in all colours and we just had to pick a new one from good stock. If you saw that film being played into the various arenas during that live tour you might have noticed that some of the multicoloured Stigs were wearing painter's overalls and crap pretend crash helmets. It didn't matter, it just got us round that particular snag until we could think of some daft explanation for where the new (but still white) Stig came from. Then someone suggested that since the upcoming Middle East special was planned to end in Jerusalem, what if we found a baby Jesus Stig in a lowly stable and claimed this was the birth of the new tame racing driver? There's still some debate about who actually came up with this mildly blasphemous idea, but suffice to say it probably wasn't the Archbishop of Canterbury.

Problems solved. Stig back on track. But this didn't conceal how sad we felt that Ben had departed the way he did. When he signed his publishing deal we thought he'd been a wazzock, but he was still our wazzock. Some time passed. Ben's book became a best-seller. Lines of communication were reopened. He ended up appearing in a film Hammond made about amputee servicemen forming a rally team. Ben and *Top Gear* were officially friends again. You could sometimes bump into him at car races and it was always good to catch up. I sent him an email recently to tell him I was writing this book. His reply was classic racing driver: 'Make me sound faster.'

The moment when we all started speaking again was a wonderful one because *Top Gear* is a pretty tight-knit unit and we don't like to lose a long-serving soldier, even if they've shot themselves in the foot. After all his time on the show, Ben wasn't just a great Stig; he was part of the family.

And anyway, what sort of idiot writes a book about working on *Top Gear*?

# *The Accident*

Every so often the presenters used to pop into the *Top Gear* office unannounced. This was especially true of Richard and James because they made other programmes for the BBC and were often in the building, so they'd pop by to have idle conversations about cars and buzz around Andy Wilman's desk while he was trying to reply to complaint letters, firing him ideas for films and deliberately trying to annoy him. It was during one of these impromptu sessions that Hammond first mentioned his idea. 'I want to drive fast,' he said. 'Really fucking fast.' There was no more to it than that. No clever question, no contrived set-up, just a TV presenter attempting to move as quickly across land as he possibly could. Wilman stopped searching for another way to write 'I'm very sorry' and started paying attention. There was an elegant simplicity to this idea. If that's what Hammond wanted to do then he should go away and do it.

A jet-powered dragster was found. The jet bit was the important thing. It was basically a massive fighter-plane engine on wheels and everything else was just along for the ride. A suitable airfield location was booked and it was arranged to give Hammond a bit of training in league with a racing driver called Ben Collins who was not The Stig, oh dear me no, what gave you that idea? We always had safety cover for any *Top Gear* track test but our researcher Grant Wardrop decided to step it up on this occasion and found a proper, top-level motorsport spec safety crew who would be on the scene in case anything went wrong. This would be a wise, and spookily prophetic, decision.

I wasn't on the shoot that day at Elvington in North Yorkshire. We were busy preparing for the next series and I was working on a planned strand about great car adverts. Another of our researchers, Debs McCarthy, and I had driven up to one of those slightly depressing businessmen's hotels in the Midlands to meet a retired ad guru whose brains we could pick. He turned out to be a fascinating bloke, or at least I think he was. It was hard to be sure since our meeting took place in the hotel bar and his voice was the exact frequency of background noise. We were driving back to London when Debs got the call. Richard's had an accident in the jet car. There was no more information than that.

When we arrived back at the office in the early evening, the mood was sombre. All we knew was that he'd gone for one last run, lost control and the car had flipped. Wilman had left for Yorkshire immediately. We sat around waiting for more news. When it didn't come, everyone reluctantly drifted home.

I'd arranged to go for a drink in my local with an old colleague. He bounded in full of cheer. He hadn't heard. It was all over the news by now. At 10 o'clock we watched the coverage of the accident on the pub telly. They had no more to tell than I already knew. Richard Hammond had crashed a jet-powered car, he'd been taken to hospital by air ambulance, he was alive but the extent of his injuries wasn't known. Across London, Jeremy and James were separately dashing towards their cars to drive north. I left my phone on all night but no more news came.

The next morning the *Top Gear* team sat around the office struggling to concentrate and feeling a bit useless. We started getting calls from newspapers and radio stations. In an attempt to do something worthwhile, I printed the BBC press office number on several pieces of paper and stuck them around the office so that anyone fielding a call would be able to remind the journalist on the line where to direct their questions. It was a token attempt to be helpful and it occupied a few minutes of an agonisingly long and distressingly quiet morning. By mid-afternoon I'd had enough. The BBC had instructed that no further staff were to head up to Leeds. But I wasn't staff, I was freelance and I had the keys to a supercharged Jaguar XKR. I was due to be at a wedding in Harrogate that Saturday so I decided to travel to Yorkshire a couple of days early. The Beeb couldn't stop me doing that.

I bombed it home, grabbed my suit and some spare clothes then hit the M1 at a lick. When I got to Leeds that night, Andy Wilman and Grant Wardrop were back at their hotel, sitting at the bar and wearing the haunted stares of sleepless people with a lot on their minds. They were pleased to see me, though I don't know what I thought I could do to help, short of gumming the BBC press office number to the walls of the room. We made a feeble attempt to eat dinner and spoke in cautious whispers in case anyone overheard our discussions. The press were all over this one now. In the end we all turned in for another fitful and restless night.

The next morning I shared a cab from the hotel with our series producer Pat Doyle. I got dropped at the hospital, he went on to the local police station to turn in the raw footage from the jet-car shoot, as instructed. The hospital had given us a little room in the bowels of the building and a few of us gathered there, pacing about not really knowing what to do. Wilman asked me to liaise with the press office in London. There was a lot of nonsense in the morning's papers and it was deeply frustrating to read untruths presented as news. I remember imploring the head of press to put out a statement denying some of this absolute bollocks. He very wisely declined on the basis that you can't put out a statement every single time a news outlet gets something wrong, otherwise you'd be churning out press releases every hour and they'd become meaningless. That's why he was the head of press and I wasn't.

James and I went outside for a cigarette. At the front of the hospital a frenzied pack of photographers and news crews threatened to block the entire entrance. We snuck out the back entrance and stood untroubled in full view of the street, laughing at the missed opportunity for a plucky pap to get a shot of Hammond's TV colleague having a crafty fag. We spent a lot of that Friday pacing around the secret back bits of the hospital. Later, when it started to rain, we sheltered gloomily under a hidden bit of overhanging roof until a cheery medic in a cagoule came over and said if we wanted to smoke we were welcome to do so in the doctors' lounge. We couldn't work out if this was a trap.

James had to head back to London later but he was told he could see Richard again, so we dashed to a newsagent to buy a copy of *Auto Trader* with which they could play their favourite game: picking out the rusty old crocks they'd like to buy. I didn't ask to go in with James. It seemed wrong to intrude. May wandered out a while later and came to say goodbye to the rest of us. We asked how Hammond was doing. 'Yea, he's okay,' May said, mustering some cheer. 'You know, still a twat.' We all smiled weakly.

After May left we milled around, fielding phone calls and feeling a bit useless again. Richard's wife, his parents and his brothers passed by, moving briskly through the corridors with the stoicism the best families find at times like these.

By early evening Grant and I were sitting restlessly in a waiting area toying with the idea of heading back to the hotel when one of Richard's brothers appeared. 'I've told him you're down here,' he said. 'And he's asked to see you.'

We trooped upstairs and filed cautiously into the room, not quite knowing what we were going to find. What we found was Richard Hammond sitting up in bed with a broad smile and a jaunty 'Hello, boys', as if he'd just popped in to have the doctors deal with an irksome wart. His face was a bit banged up and he was attached to all manner of tubes and wires but he was awake, he was talking, he was very much alive. It was almost bizarre. We tried to be upbeat in that way you do when visiting someone in hospital, noting the immense speed at which he'd crashed and doing a good impression of being impressed by this.

Hammond sat forward. 'Have you got any fags?' he whispered. I said that I probably had. 'Great,' he said. 'Can we go for one?' Ignoring the cat's cradle of plumbing and wiring around him, he began getting out of bed. A nurse came in and told him he was going nowhere, in that cheerily no-nonsense way that is the preserve of the medical profession. She looked at Grant and me like we were causing trouble. We took our cue and left. It was strange to see Richard so upbeat. He seemed okay. He seemed normal. We had no idea what really lay beneath the cheerful exterior.

The next day I went to my friends' wedding in Harrogate. It was a nice bash. At the end of the night, after a little too much Scotch, I was trying to tell someone what had happened to Hammond and found myself unexpectedly getting a bit weepy. It didn't matter that he seemed okay, it was the fact that the accident had happened in the first place and what that could have meant. Richard was part of the original gang. We'd been through it all. The disastrous pilots, the tricky first series, the growing success and confidence of the programme, but it was more than that. Away from the show, there were the hours whiled away talking nonsense about cars, the participation in the inter-BBC rounders match that had seen *Top Gear* field the only team with one of their actual presenters in it, the boozy nights out in which we'd pushed him to the front of queues and used him like some sort of live-action VIP pass. We hadn't nearly killed one of our presenters; we'd nearly killed a mate.

*Top Gear* hung in limbo waiting to see if Richard was well enough to return to work. One day Clarkson, Wilman and I went up to an anonymous meeting room and sat with a couple of management people to watch the footage of the accident. I knew what had happened, but seeing it for the first time was a vile and visceral experience that brought a sickened knot to my throat. Jesus, the poor sod really was lucky to be alive. Not only alive, but planning to go back to the day job that had almost finished him off.

You can read a much better and more accurate account of what Richard went through after his accident by reading his book, *On the Edge*. As a team, we didn't know the half of it at the time. When he came back to work Hammond managed to put a brave face on the turmoil within. On occasion he might seem a bit withdrawn, like he had left the room even when he was still there, but for the most part he seemed lively, funny and the same as he'd always been. He'd always had this uncanny ability to memorise words. You'd show him a link, he'd go on camera and deliver it perfectly, you'd wonder if it was working, you'd put your heads together to have a little rethink and then he'd instantly go back on camera and nail the new words in one take. He never lost that skill, which is remarkable considering the battering his brain had taken. We spent a long time wondering how to deal with his triumphant return. Clearly what had happened was huge and there was no place for utter flippancy, yet it simply wasn't the *Top Gear* style to be soppy or sappy or words like that. The presenters had this ongoing joke that if one of them really did die, this would be announced on the show and then followed immediately by the word 'Anyway . . .' What we had to deal with now was not actual death, but it was something close. Also, more to the point, we had to deal with real feelings, and that wasn't very easy for such a mannish ensemble. Even so, we struggled through, dealing with the emotional element by not being emotional and letting that gut-wrenching footage of the accident leave the biggest impression.

After that, the strongest legacy of the accident for *Top Gear* itself was the effect it had on our viewing figures, bumping them into the big league where they stayed thereafter. We'd like to imagine that this could have happened anyway but the attention that the crash drew to Richard and the show definitely had an effect. But that doesn't make the awfulness of the whole experience anywhere close to worth it. Some things are more important.

*Top Gear* liked being the centre of attention for doing daft things, but that meant firing a Mazda full of custard at the moon or something. It really shouldn't include harming one of our own.

# Imperial Leyland

Like a long-running band, *Top Gear* went through several phases during its life. The well-worn path went a bit like this: Start with the obscure, nerdy, hardcore fan years. Then into the unexpected success era. Follow that with the age of ridiculousness when audiences are huge but fans and critics seem to tire of your bloated ridiculousness. And then slip into the part-of-the-furniture period when you'd be missed if you went and even critics at the *Guardian* grudgingly admit that they like what you do.

But there's another era in there, fitting neatly between unexpected success and preposterous pomp. It's the phase you might call the imperial years when the show, like a large band, has found a strong run of form and a large audience and it feels like it can do no wrong. This period, though fragile and short-lived, is the best of all. You know what you're meant to be doing, you're having a good time doing it and you still seem fresh and interesting to the ever-swelling ranks of fans.

When you work on a show for a long time it can be hard to distinguish between series because the whole thing blurs into one massive blob of work. Watching back an episode of *Top Gear*, I would struggle to tell you precisely when it was shown. Only the length and style of Richard Hammond's hair, acting like the rings of a tree, might provide some idea of age. Or, if it's a really early show, the fact that Jeremy looks like a 28-year-old impersonation of himself.

But if I had to pick favourite VTs from this vast 13-year blur, one of them would be the British Leyland film from series 10. There are two reasons for this. Firstly, because it's from the imperial *Top Gear* era, when we seemed to be on a run of good form. And secondly, because I really like shit seventies cars. Also, the making of this item met pretty much all of the textbook requirements for a successful *Top Gear* shoot, as follows.

1. **Trudging around the Midlands.** *Top Gear* filmed all over the world, but there was something comforting about any shoot that involved two or three days of loafing around in the middle bit of Britain. Perhaps it was something to do with the ghost of old *Top Gear*, which seemed to make everything within 30 miles of its Pebble Mill base, sometimes travelling only as far as the Bristol Road right by the office and shooting a new car driving up and down there for as long as it took. Also, the Midlands was far enough from our London base to require an overnight stay, which meant the camaraderie of staying in a dubious, BBC-booked hotel and having a drink in the bar, but close enough to make getting home less than a chore. For the BL film we trudged magnificently around all that the West Midlands has to offer, which is mostly places where cars used to be made but aren't today.

2. **The cars were good, but also bad.** In any *Top Gear* film involving three old cars, I liked it when the models chosen by

Jeremy, Richard and James were different shapes and sizes, giving the whole thing a slightly comical and mismatched appearance. A bit like the presenters themselves. On this score, the BL film worked well, what with the contrast between Clarkson's rakish Rover SD1, Hammond's upright Dolomite and May's none-more-seventies wedge of Princess. These films also worked best when the presenters could mount a total and unswerving defence of their choice, which they did, having taken their cars home and got to know them before filming started. On the way to the meeting point, I passed May in his Princess on the M40. It had an alarming lean to one side and he was doing 63 mph in the inside lane, but he looked like a man cheerfully and completely at peace with his world. Also in these films, we liked the old cars to have faults, because that gave us something to do and to argue about, but nothing too major that delayed filming. When Hammond's Triumph let go before we'd even left the start location, that was fantastic. Especially since the cars were surprisingly dependable after that. As an aside, Rover SD1 doors don't normally just fall off, not unless an oaf has fiddled with them.

3. **James got lost.** A not uncommon occurrence on *Top Gear* shoots. Or indeed, anywhere. Put it this way; when we used to record voice-over in the labyrinthine building next to our office, Jeremy and Richard could be left to find their own way to the recording studio because they'd been there many times before. Someone had to be sent to accompany James. On the BL shoot we were ambling through the Midlands filming the star cars with cameras mounted in the back of Range Rovers. Unfortunately, we were also near the place in Warwickshire where the Range Rover was designed and developed. There are, as you might expect, a lot of them

on the surrounding roads. At a large roundabout, James got briefly split from the tracking car in front and then made up the distance and latched onto the back of a blue Range Rover. The wrong blue Range Rover. Unfortunately he didn't spot this, even though it had no cameraman in the boot and its tailgate was closed. He followed it for several miles before we rang to find out where the bloody hell he'd got to.

4. **Sunburn.** It's a little-known fact that television shoots generate their own microclimates, managing for no readily apparent reason to be significantly colder or hotter than the surrounding area. It can be a balmy and mild spring day in the rest of the country and yet the precise spot where the film crew are standing will be bitterly cold and whipped by the icy blast of an arctic squall. That's why the North Face clothing company is entirely kept afloat by the patronage of all television crews. Conversely, it can be a mild autumnal Tuesday for everyone in Britain, the kind of day you'd be advised to take a stout jacket on any trip outdoors, and yet in the exact spot where TV is being made the sun will pierce the milky ceiling of cloud and cause everyone under its glare to receive third-degree skin burns. I don't know how this happens, it just does. It's certainly why I spent half an hour standing on the scruffy patch of land where the Longbridge West Works used to be and came away the colour of a humiliated tomato.

5. **Real people, really annoyed.** A section of the BL item was filmed at the MIRA test track in Warwickshire, which was appropriate since keen geeks will note that before Leyland built its own proving ground at Gaydon this was the place where much of their car development was incompleted. Off camera, the MIRA people were unamused by Richard

Hammond's Triumph Dolomite rolling down a small hill and hitting one of their signs. Also, I don't think they found it very hilarious that in the finished programme we inaugurated the ongoing *Top Gear* gag in which a location was described as 'top secret' and then its address was given out in slightly too much detail. But a *Top Gear* shoot wasn't complete unless someone had to say sorry for something, a job often given to ace series producer Alex Renton, since he was polite and charming and among his many talents apologising was near the top.

6. **Car enthusiasts, also annoyed.** Although *Top Gear* started out as a car show, even in its new format, as we zoomed off into the clouds of light entertainment, some people who really liked cars became very grumpy and peevish about what had happened to 'their' show, although they still seemed to watch it every week so they could complain about it on the internet. No *Top Gear* film would have been complete without this background hum of disgruntlement, and when the BL film was transmitted hardcore British cars fans seemed quite angry about the ruination of three 'perfectly good' classics, thereby fulfilling this requirement. In particular, their annoyance seemed to stem from the final sequence in which the cars were filled with water. Now I like British Leyland cars, probably a bit too much, but I'm not ashamed to admit that this was my idea, although I basically nicked it from one of Jeremy's Christmas DVDs. In my defence, these were not rare cars and not especially fine examples. Plus, the Dolomite was later rescued by our tame mechanic to be restored and turned into a seventies touring car replica, while the Rover and the Princess were taken to the Beaulieu museum where people can go and look at them. Ironically, they're probably some of the

most valuable examples of their kind because they've been on telly. Luckily, they aren't for sale. But if you do want a Dolomite Sprint, a Rover 3500 or a Princess 2200HL, there are usually several available in the classifieds. That's why I didn't feel too guilty about mucking up the ones we bought. Especially since I thought the final film was a nice celebration of their charms; and that's why it's always been one of my very favourite *Top Gear* things. Also, because it's a good example of a programme at the top of its game and firing on all cylinders in a way British Leyland cars often didn't.

By way of a reminder that this was our imperial era, the BL film came in the same series as the Peel P50, a lightweight super-cars road trip, the second amphibious cars film, the Botswana special and the time we entered a 24-hour race in a car with ARSE BISCUITS written down the side. It was a run of shows we were very proud of and it achieved a level of variety and quality we perhaps never matched. I'm not saying it was all downhill after that but the following series did contain Top Gear Stuntman. So maybe a little bit downhill. Sorry about that.

# *The Cool Wall*

There are lots of TV chefs. There are plenty of TV gardeners. TV property experts are now so plentiful you hardly need flip channels more than once to come across someone helping a couple who want a brand-new Victorian second-floor semi-detached terraced bungalow conversion close to Banbury but within 20 minutes of Ulan Bator.

Yet if you ask anyone to name a TV car expert, they'll say Jeremy Clarkson. Other television car experts are available – not least Richard Hammond and James May – but for 25 years Clarkson has dominated his field in a way no television cooker, planter or south-facing patio botherer has managed.

There's a reason for this: Jeremy was the first specialist in his field of broadcasting to realise that he didn't have to be nerdy and technical. Of course, secretly he has a nerdy and technical side which allows him to reel off the exact make, model and size of the tyres fitted to the Mk1 Volkswagen Golf GTI, but he keeps this ability well concealed.

Placed carefully in front of it is an uncanny understanding of what normal people care about. It's not piston strokes and gear ratios; the average viewer just wants to know if a car is fast, how much it costs and whether it's cool. And from this last point emerged The Cool Wall. In many ways this long-running feature was a stroke of genius, brilliantly tapping in to the way people actually think about cars and discuss them with their mates. It didn't even matter that it was utterly preposterous and that *Top Gear* was presenting itself as the ultimate arbiter of coolness via the medium of a little chap in a leather waistcoat and a tall man dressed like a trendy geography teacher. The point is, The Cool Wall was the nation's pub debates made real and it became a very popular part of the programme. I hated it.

For one thing, I hated trying to write it. This involved getting together a list of recently announced cars and then working through them, trying to think of relevant jokes and amusing ways to explain their coolness or lack of it. It was fiddly and time-consuming and you knew most of it would be cut out in the edit. Also, in the first instance of drafting some suggestions, it required an earnest attempt to second-guess the moving target of Jeremy Clarkson's opinions. Richard was a bit easier. His idea of true cool was old Land Rovers and Morgans and he readily accepted that his main job during any Cool Wall segment was to be the bloke on the other side of the net in an ongoing tennis match of bickering.

I'd present my first thoughts to Clarkson and Hammond and then we'd bash them back and forth until we had a definitive list of cars, with something pertinent to say about each of them Sometimes Jeremy would come up with a brilliantly obtuse reason why a car was cool or an equally perverse explanation for why it wasn't. The main point was to have a good few gags that explained each decision. The Cool Wall was many things: a debating point, a good way to take up studio time, a perfect basis for a series of fridge magnets. But most of all it was a prime example of what TV critic A.A. Gill once called 'an aircraft carrier for gags'. As each picture of a car was held up on camera it was the go-sign for another squadron of incoming one-liners, and hopefully at least one of them would drop gracefully onto the deck of HMS *Hilarity*.

The only thing I hated more than writing The Cool Wall was watching it being recorded. During the news segment the presenters would have a bullet-pointed list of basic facts and a few choice observations on the table in front of them. With The Cool Wall they were standing up and holding the pictures of cars, so they couldn't also have a piece of paper to hand. We used to hide a sheet of reminders in the pile of tyres the set designer had plonked underneath the wall to make it look more interesting but for the most part once Jeremy and Richard were out there, they were on their own. As the script editor, that made me nervous. Whenever we did this segment I used to sit in the gallery with my arse clenched so tightly someone had to crowbar a swivel chair out of it afterwards.

Sometimes they remembered all the stuff we'd come up with in the office. Sometimes they came up with new, better things off the cuff. The one constant was that the entire thing seemed to teeter on the edge of chaos. Jeremy liked to get the audience involved, thundering off into the crowd to solicit opinions and then telling the people who'd shared them they were wrong. This just added to the freewheeling, out-of-control nature of the entire sequence.

We'd record for twenty or thirty minutes, which would be cut down into four or five minutes of television. This was no small job in itself. With the news, tiny cuts could be made to tighten a line or cut out a duff gag and no one would notice because the presenters sat in one place. With The Cool Wall they were constantly moving about. Get too busy with the editing scissors and the whole thing could have looked like stop-frame animation. And just to complete the continuity nightmare, each presenter was holding a big stack of pictures which would magically change in size on TV. Cutting it together was a tough job.

Preparing for it got harder too as Clarkson came up with ever more elaborate ways in which to confound Hammond's efforts to put cars in the 'wrong place' on the board, culminating in the brutal use of a chainsaw. There were a lot of BBC health and safety forms to fill in for that one. I know, I know. What is the country coming to when you can't simply cram a few hundred people into a room and then let a hyperactive manchild flail about with a live chainsaw?

Eventually, The Cool Wall fell out of favour. This wasn't deliberate, it's just that our VTs seemed to get longer and more ambitious, slowly killing the need to fill a few minutes of the show with a cheap studio item. It made one last appearance in 2011 and then became relegated to a sad piece of set dressing, looming in the back of shot with the sadly neglected air of a derelict kids' swing no one had the heart to throw away. If you'd looked more closely you'd have noticed that most of the cars on it weren't even made any more.

And then, just when we thought it was dead, the Wall threatened to rise again. The tenth and final show of series 22 was looking a bit light, content-wise. The only thing coming up even shorter was the budget. What we needed was a cost-effective piece of studio nonsense to fill a few minutes. The Cool Wall was coming back. Oh Jesus, we thought. We'll have to get dozens of new photos printed up on foam board with little bits of Velcro on the back and then repopulate the bloody board with cars that aren't obsolete. With heavy heart, I started drawing up a list of new models and scribbling down a few thoughts on jokes we could make about them. In the office there was a palpable sense of resignation at the return of a segment we thought had died some time around series 16.

And then, as we know, the show came to a sudden, spluttering end and we didn't have to revive a long-lost studio segment after all. So at least there was some good news. The Cool Wall was once a popular part of the show and it seemed to delight much of the audience, either because it tapped into the real appeal of cars or because they liked the absurdity of a silly man in saggy-arsed denim telling them what was cool. Either way, it served its purpose over the years. But if I see that stupid wall again, I'll take the chainsaw to it myself.

# NASCAR Sucks

There was an unspoken rule on *Top Gear* which was so unspoken I don't think we could bear to admit it to ourselves. It said that the regular features we planned would most likely turn out to be useless whereas the big ideas that became successful were almost certainly accidental. It was hard to acknowledge this because what could you do with that information? Start planning to do things accidentally?

You can see the fruits of this theory in carefully planned but never-loved features like Barn Or Bin and the utter toss-fest of Top Gear Stuntman. And conversely, the 2006 attempt to make a normal-sized VT out of an American road trip, which spiralled out of control, earned a whole show all to itself and spawned the idea of the annual *Top Gear* special, completely by accident.

There are a couple of things people seem to remember from that inadvertent special. The first is the cow on the roof of a Camaro. Jeremy came up with this one in the field, possibly literally, and since there weren't any dead cows lying around he rang the office back home and one of our researchers hammered the phones into the night until he found a nearby farmer with a recently mooing corpse we could use. I often thought *Top Gear* had the most talented and dedicated production team in television and there's your proof: our people could source locate a stinking, bloated, rotten, disgusting cow corpse from 4,000 miles away.

The second thing the American road trip is remembered for is the slogans daubed down the cars. I'm delighted to boast that this was my idea. In fact, it was my idea from long before the US road trip came about and it formed the backbone of something called The Texas Smartcar Challenge, in which a presenter was required to drive a tiny, bright pink car covered in jauntily liberal slogans across the Lone Star State to see how far they could get before a lynching occurred. This idea was well received in the office but fraught with complications. We'd need to ship the Smart over there, and have it wrapped in pink, and we'd have to fly in our crews from the UK, and it all started to sound like a lot of time, expense and effort just to get someone's head kicked in. So the idea went away.

It came back to me when we started planning an American road trip and our intended route appeared to take in some places where 'liberal' is basically a swear word. I mentioned the slogans part of my Smart idea in a meeting. People seemed to like it. 'So basically, you want us to be killed?' said Hammond with mock indignation. No, no, no, I'm sure it'll be fine, I insisted.

Since the idea seemed to be a goer, I wrote some suggested slogans on strips of paper, divided these up among three envelopes with the presenters' names on them and waved everyone off to the airport. Around this time I'd started a long-distance relationship with someone in Los Angeles. If you live in London and start seeing someone in, say, Sheffield then you can meet halfway. In Leicester, for example.

Or Kettering. Not places known for their romance, but at least they're driveable. If you're dating someone in Los Angeles, the halfway meeting point is New York, which is rather harder to reach in a car. Instead, I took some time off while half the team was heading to Florida and got on a plane to JFK.

I spent a few days dandering around Manhattan and heard not a word from our Southern states road-trip shoot. Then one afternoon we went for a drink with a friend called Tracey, who's from the American south. We're actually filming in the south at the moment, I said breezily. Yes, it's all terribly amusing, I went on, we're writing slogans down our cars and driving them through Alabama. Tracey looked aghast. 'You're doing *what*?' she spat. No, no, it's fine, I laughed. We're just messing around, I'm sure it'll just be a little bit awkward or something.

'Trust me,' she continued in that casually aggressive tone New York obliges its inhabitants to perfect. 'I'm from down there, I know those people. They. Will. Fucking. Kill. You.' Oh dear me no, I said, trying to maintain an upbeat tone. I'm sure it'll all be fine.

Shortly afterwards my phone rang. Several times in fact. I can't remember the specifics of what was said, but the words 'properly angry' and 'bloody scary' might have been used and I think Jeremy possibly claimed they were 'almost literally killed'. A woman had shouted at them. Some angry men had turned up. The atmosphere had turned sour. In the resulting panic, Wilman had jumped into the wrong crew car as it scarpered, leaving another team sitting on the increasingly menacing forecourt staring at the empty seat in the back and assuming its occupant had been kidnapped. God, that sounds extremely frightening I thought, as I sat in a New York bar preparing to order another cocktail.

The reaction to this sequence when it was broadcast in early 2007 was pretty extraordinary. Some ultrafans on the internet minutely dissected it and concluded that some of the sounds made by objects hitting cars seemed dubbed on, thereby proving that all the locals in the scene were actors and the entire thing was fake. I'll let you into a secret: sometimes in TV sounds have to be enhanced in post-production because microphones don't always record things with the clarity and volume you would like, especially when they're attached to or being operated by people who are fearing for their lives. I can certainly promise that at no point did one of our researchers call up an Alabama am-dram society and demand that they provide us with a job lot of their most toothless simpletons.

Some Americans didn't seem to like this scene either and took particular exception to the idea of pompous British bastards coming to the nether parts of their great nation expressly to poke the inhabitants with a stick until they bared their teeth. On that score I suppose we were a bit guilty but I don't think we ever imagined our foolish plan would actually get such a visceral reaction. I certainly never imagined that some idiotic things I'd invented in an office in London could be daubed down three cars to such dramatic effect. Secretly, I was quite thrilled. Obviously, it's easy to be thrilled when you're 1,000 miles upcountry with your face in a bucket of mojito. Even so, it was quite remarkable. It was one of several times when a dumb, throwaway idea on *Top Gear* turned into something unexpectedly memorable. I'm only slightly ashamed to admit that it's one of the proudest moments of my career.

# *Becoming Huge*

Many years ago, one of *Top Gear*'s researchers had an email auto signature that boasted about our audience figures. They were pretty healthy in the UK and getting stronger around the world. We didn't know how strong exactly since a lot of our international audience seemed to be downloading the show illegally and hooky bit-torrent sites aren't famed for their diligent reporting of audience figures. Because of this, our researcher took a guess at what our total number of viewers might be. He started at something impressive but plausible like 50 million. Get away with you, some of us scoffed, there's no way it can be that many. Ah, but it could be, our researcher replied. In fact, it could be 100 million, we just don't know. No one does. As if to prove his point, he amended his auto signature to claim a global audience of 100 million. If you're going to claim that, someone said, why not go all out and make it 150 million, eh? So he did. And from that point on, every so often somebody would dare the researcher to add a few more million to the total, making it an increasingly ridiculous number. This game ended when he reached a figure he thought sounded so absurd he couldn't go any higher. It was 350 million. That was just daft and *Top Gear* would never attract an audience of that size. Apart from a few years later, when it did.

I'm still not sure how this happened. When new *Top Gear* started in 2002 we were told that if our funny little car show could draw an audience of three million during its weekly showing on BBC2, it would justify its existence. Thirteen years later, we had more than twice that number of viewers in the UK alone, never mind the monster worldwide number that still sounded like some sort of in-office piss-take.

The thing is, when your programme becomes that massive it doesn't happen overnight. You don't arrive at the office one day to find a note asking if you could crack on with the next series because someone's run some numbers and it turns out the whole world is watching. *Top Gear*'s growth into a planet-straddling behemoth happened very gradually and very naturally. I'm loath to use the word 'organic' because it sounds like I'm trying to sell you expensive vegetables but that's pretty much what it was. Obviously Richard's accident in 2006 saw our UK audience take a sudden step up, but otherwise you could probably plot *Top Gear*'s increasing popularity at home and abroad by drawing a fairly steady line on a piece of graph paper.

The effect of growing popularity on the production team was, in a very real sense, sod all. Every so often we'd get word of some new numbers or someone would come by and tell us we were now Latvia's top-rated show with 'gear' in the title, but it was hard to comprehend what this meant. So we just got on with making the show as we always had, in the same old manky office in the same old manky way. Viewing figures were always nice to know because, after all, no one wants to work on a show that no one's watching, but they never quite seemed real. It's like being told how far different planets are from the sun. The numbers are too huge for the tiny mind to comprehend. On this basis, perhaps Professor Brian Cox is exceptionally good at taking viewing figures on board. I know I'm not, and I don't think the rest of the *Top Gear* team were either.

Anyway, what could we do with this information? We were never asked to pander to an international audience, nor did we feel inclined to, because we were first and foremost a British show, funded to a great degree by British licence-fee payers. Besides, the global audience had continued to expand while we kept talking about 'boots' and 'bonnets' and 'the outskirts of Ipswich' and no one had turned off. It would seem strange and patronising if we suddenly made attempts to be blandly international. The only exception to this was in 2005 when we repackaged a load of VTs for transmission in North America and re-recorded all studio links for them with a smattering of localised words and references. I kept having to ring an actual American to check that these weren't bollocks. 'What's bollocks?' they said. You can imagine that our efforts weren't very convincing.

For international audiences there was, however, a worldwide version of the programme. In the early days this consisted of a brutal half-hour edit designed for one of those international BBC channels that seems to be piped exclusively into hotels. Cutting out precisely half the show meant someone going into the edit suite and pretty much flailing around with an axe until many parts of each programme were gone. The finished products were a clunky tribute to the art of butchery. I saw one once in, predictably, an overseas hotel. It was an episode from the first series in which Jeremy did a film, Richard did a film and then the show was over. Poor Jason didn't get a look in, except at the end when he suddenly popped up next to the other two waving goodbye. If you'd never seen the show before, and at this stage you assume most people hadn't, you'd think there's that tall chap and there's that small chap but who on earth is that smiling portly gentleman bidding me goodbye? Perhaps he's the show mascot.

In later years the worldwide editions got better. In fact, the version taken by most overseas channels was the same show, perhaps with a little bit of nipping and tucking to allow for transmission on commercial stations and with generic music replacing original tracks that couldn't be licensed for use outside the UK. And of course in some countries they dubbed the presenters into another language which was done locally and was out of our hands, though we always prayed that we'd come across a version in which one of the presenters had been given an incredibly squeaky voice for no readily apparent reason. A BBC World Service programme once arranged for Jeremy to meet the man who did his voice in Iran. Not in a squeaky way, sadly. It was, in fact, a very sweet bit of radio. The Iranian guy used to get recognised just for being the voice of Jeremy.

Of course, this was nothing compared to how people reacted to the actual Jeremy, and indeed the actual Richard and the actual James, and the changing reaction to the presenters over the years was one of the stoutest indicators of *Top Gear*'s success. While viewing figures seemed meaningless because you couldn't see hundreds of millions of people watching your show, you could vividly see how people got giddy over the presenters walking into a pub or a petrol station or Peterborough. The way people interacted with them was really quite extraordinary.

If you saw Brad Pitt in a restaurant you'd lean towards whoever you were with and hiss, 'Brad Pitt is over there . . . don't look . . . I said DON'T look.' What you wouldn't do is go over to Brad Pitt, slap him on the back and immediately engage him in jaunty conversation because you do not know Brad Pitt, you have not met Brad Pitt before and Brad Pitt is not your friend. Unless you're George Clooney, in which case ignore this paragraph.

With the *Top Gear* presenters, however, not knowing them didn't seem to matter. Viewers had seen them on TV dozens of times and unlike Brad Pitt they were not playing a part or adopting a character, they were themselves. So people thought they knew them and, by extension, that they had licence to approach them as if they were old mates. And this was one of the first indicators that the programme had somehow dug into people's brains.

Jeremy got the brunt of this overly chummy onslaught from well-meaning fans, having been famous for longer. Conversely, when some cheery bloke got in his face as he tried to eat and insisted on telling him some unsolicited motoring fact: 'Alright Jezza! I've got a Calibra, whaddaya think?' Jeremy, by dint of his on-screen persona, was able to be dismissive.

'I feel sorry for you.' And they would go away happy.

'He's dead funny that Jezza, said something dead funny about me car, like he does on telly.'

Hammond and May were less fortunate, being saddled with reputations for being less outspoken and crushed by the weight of their real-life politeness. It must have been difficult. Total strangers would march up to Richard and pointedly tell him that he was short. You wouldn't approach a stranger on the street and make some remark about their stature but people didn't see Hammond as a stranger, they saw him as their mate Rich off the telly. James rarely got insulted like this, but he did seem to be a magnet for aeroplane bores, all of whom wanted to take issue with something he'd said in a newspaper column about the Lancaster bomber or suchlike.

As the show gained traction, the presenters' profiles just got bigger and bigger, stretching beyond the car nerds we'd set out to entertain. In 2006 Richard Hammond won a readers' poll in *Heat* magazine. The poll was for 'weird crush'. The following year he was upgraded and entered their normal crush chart instead. Although I don't think they use the word normal. His place at the top of the 2007 weird crush ranking was taken by James, and the following year by Jeremy. In the office, we didn't have a crush on the presenters but we definitely found this increasingly weird.

Hanging around with the three of them got stranger too. In the early series, we'd go to the pub after studio writing day and chat through the script for the following day's recording. That would have seemed unthinkable in later years when there would have been a good chance the people at the next table would have been listening in and then writing about it on the internet. To spend time in the company of the presenters as the show got really big was to get a strange sense of what it might be like to become invisible. You'd be talking to them in a car park when someone would barge you out of the way in order to tell Jeremy about their Civic Type-R or to shout 'midget' at Richard before demanding his autograph or to spend seven minutes trying to take a photograph of James next to their wife before admitting they had no idea how to use the camera they were holding, as demonstrated by the 15 shots they'd just taken of their own eye.

Filming in Britain started to become tricky because crowds would gather wherever we went. We started having to get security to come along with us on location. It must have looked terribly self-important but it became necessary, not least to sort out some crowd control, without which you'd have had eager fans cheerfully standing in the middle of a dual carriageway and a bloke called Gaz in a tracksuit walking in halfway though a piece to camera to tell Jezza about his Sierra Cosworth.

Over time, the ability of a *Top Gear* shoot to draw a crowd spread overseas too. It was another indicator of the show's growing reach. Once we could film all day in, say, France and no one would give une shit. There came a point where that changed and suddenly we'd be in some foreign land with a reasonable impression of Beatlemania happening outside the hotel.

It was at moments like this when we'd realise that maybe the numbers weren't wrong. Maybe people really were watching this poky little BBC2 motoring show and not on BBC2 itself but in places where you couldn't get BBC2. It never failed to bemuse us because, in our heads, we were a BBC2 sort of programme. We were obscure, niche, still a bit nerdy. Even transmission on BBC1 would have been a lofty ambition, never mind on dozens of different channels around the world and drawing the kind of numbers only proper TV shows enjoyed.

All this was very odd because in the middle of it we were still much the same team making the same programme out of the same shabby office. The only things that changed were the email auto signatures. To everyone's surprise, they got more truthful.

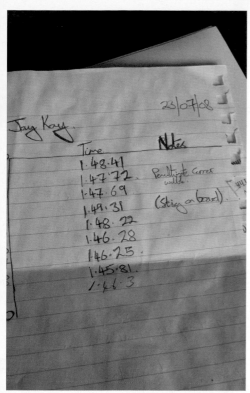

The highly scientific way lap times were recorded. This is Jay Kay's record-setting run in the Lacetti from July 2008.

Jeremy and James pretend to be on strike around a Marina 'brazier' during filming of the Communist cars film, autumn 2008.

Jeremy during filming of the Vietnam special, enjoying a rare moment of not being on a scooter.

James on a train in Vietnam, apparently unamused.

The homemade police cars, stashed in the car park at the studio. The big red thing lurking behind the trees on the right is the never-seen Unfunny Bus.

During filming of the making a car ad feature, Jeremy dangles from a cherry picker. Obviously.

Andy Wilman, Jeremy and Jeremy's alarming shirt outside the studio just before recording the first programme of series 13, June 2009.

Shenanigans with a massive raft on the Amazon, October 2009. It took so long to get the cars off, it went dark and they had to have another go the next day.

Admiring creepy crawlies in the Amazon rain forest.

Jeremy in an unusually quiet mood up a Bolivian mountain.

Hammond gets the controls to the camera tracking vehicle.

Bill Bailey jams with Jeremy and Richard at the celebrity track day to welcome the Kia Cee'd Reasonably Priced Car, June 2010.

The toppling Reliant Robin goes into a canal. That's Jeremy's crash helmet mounted on the headrest, rather than Jeremy himself in the car.

Cameron Diaz and Tom Cruise set about The Stig, July 2010.

Camera assistant Chris Dunford and cameraman Ben Joiner filming the India special.

In Downing Street filming the opening link for the India special, December 2011.

# *An Act of Charity*

The bona fide rock star was doing his best to sing the part, even though the thudding, clattering drums from behind him were plainly not in time, until finally he could sing no more. Something else had thrown him. 'I'm sorry,' he said across the empty studio. 'I just can't get this bit.' He waved towards the lyrics written up on large boards and being held aloft in his eyeline for this rehearsal. The band stopped playing. The drummer smashed one final, arrhythmic and unnecessary cymbal splash and then dropped one of his sticks. Something wasn't right, and it wasn't just the gaping flaw in the rhythm section. Eventually somebody spotted the problem. No wonder the singer couldn't get it right. The person who'd written out the lyrics on the cheat boards had missed out an entire line. The drummer dropped his sticks again. This was all going tremendously well.

As you'd expect from a public service organisation full of well-meaning people, the BBC did a lot for charity. There was *Sport Relief* and *Comic Relief* and *Children in Need* and, as a result, working in a BBC building meant forgetting this stuff at your peril and then wandering into work one Friday to find your desk had been replaced by Pudsey Bear sitting in a bath full of beans.

We were often quite busy on *Top Gear*, usually as a result of having left our homework to the last minute, and we had little truck with all the enforced jollity and zaniness and competitions to see how many newsreaders you could fit in your mouth at once. There's a special place in hell for people who say, 'If I put some money in your Strictly themed bucket will you stop covering me in glitter and piss off?' Well, that's where Team Top Gear will be.

Naturally, whenever one of these charity events was on the horizon, the Beeb liked to get all of its high-profile programmes involved. Weather reporters would make music videos, period drama characters would be dropped into soap operas, the corporation's Middle East correspondent would be forced to front a new kids' show called Orla Guerin's Puppet Vestibule. I might have imagined some of this. As befitted our collective curmudgeonly attitude to this generous merrymaking, *Top Gear* would refuse to take part in any of these things because Andy Wilman would tell anyone who asked to get lost. He might have put it in slightly more professional language, but that was the gist of what he said.

It's not that *Top Gear* was uncharitable. We often gave away autographed items for fund-raising auctions and had a long-standing relationship with the Make-A-Wish Foundation, which regularly saw terminally ill children granted their dream of a lap with The Stig. It's just that we were normally struggling to find enough time to make our own programme, never mind get involved in other people's.

Finally, in 2007, we could hold out no more. Some extremely senior people within *Comic Relief* asked very nicely if we could create one of their self-contained shows in which two disparate BBC programmes were merged and since we both had Top in the title it was suggested that Gear merged with Of The Pops.

Jeremy, being quite into music, was very keen on this. His listening taste caused me great pain. This was because a) a lot of it was interminable prog rock featuring ludicrous song titles and ghastly five-hour flute solos and b) his *Desert Island Discs* choices included two of my favourite songs in the world – 'Heroes' and 'Make Me Smile' ('Come Up and See Me'), since you ask – and he was the only other grown man I knew who had 'Rush Hour' by Jane Wiedlin on his iPod. In other words, our tastes weren't so dissimilar, and that concerned me, mainly because of point a) and a fear of developing an enthusiasm for quadruple albums called things like *A Pocketful of Silences*.

Proclaiming himself to be some sort of music expert, Clarkson threw himself into Top Gear of the Pops and there were many heated debates about who we should have on the show. Jeremy wanted a 'modern' rap artist so that he could loudly not enjoy them and then a band that he actually liked, so he could. The search began for people who fitted these criteria and who were prepared to visit a crappy hangar in Surrey on a Sunday evening. The search ended when we found Lethal Bizzle and Supergrass.

They were joined by McFly, because *Top of the Pops* always had a boyband on it, and Travis, because they had a single out and that would make things current. Then the really ambitious idea; the show would close with a number by the Top Gear of the Pops house band, the backbone of which would be the presenters themselves. Two-thirds of this was of no concern. James had a degree in music and liked to relax by tinkling about on his piano at home. Richard had played bass for years and was blessed with nimble fingers, a keen sense of rhythm and the effortless ability to adopt the cool, neutral, middle-distance playing stare commonly known as 'bass face'. Yet this idea came not from them but from Jeremy, who was a drummer. Or rather, who was a man who'd had seven drum lessons.

We'd booked to record this show on a Sunday and *Comic Relief* was due to go out on the following Friday. That meant if we made a total cockup of things, there wasn't time to try again. With this in mind, it was decided that the 'band' should have some practice. Wilman got a mate who was a proper musical director to come down and act as sergeant major while a guitarist, an extra keyboardist and three backing singers were booked to bolster the sound. The day before the recording we gathered in a disused building on the far side of Dunsfold for band practice. As the proper musos tuned their instruments and Jeremy flailed at his drum kit like Keith Moon swatting wasps, a familiar rock face appeared at the window. It was Justin Hawkins, friend of the show and lead singer of The Darkness, who had agreed to come down and take on what 1950s sleeve-note writers would call 'vocal chores'.

Jeremy had picked the song – Billy Ocean's 'Red Light Spells Danger' – because it had a relatively simple drum pattern. Also, Billy Ocean used to work at the Ford factory in Dagenham, so there was a tenuous car connection, not including the lyrical and possibly overcautious message about traffic lights. May shuffled behind his keyboard, Hammond put on his bass, Hawkins grabbed a microphone and off we went, wonky timekeeping notwithstanding.

The professional musicians were, naturally, note-perfect, but Richard and James more than held their own. Even Jeremy wasn't totally hopeless, just as long as he remembered to count out loud and think of literally nothing else while he whumped his sticks against the skins. In between running through the song, Hammond idly jammed with the pro guitarist, May tapped out little classical melodies on his synth and Hawkins grabbed the nearest free instrument and hammered out well-known tunes with irritating ability. As evening fell, the backing singers had to leave for a gig and I took over on what I think they call BVs, mainly mumbling near the mic and banging a tambourine against my leg. I don't know how the pros do that. By the middle of the second chorus it really hurts. We left our scruffy rehearsal space that night believing that we could actually do this and it wouldn't sound too bad.

The next day was show day. And it was predictably the sort of controlled chaos that *Top Gear* naturally managed to generate. The final parts of two large stages were being built where cars normally sat in the studio. An encampment of Winnebagos was set up on the fringes of the track so our various guests had somewhere to tune their rock-star guitars and put on their extra-tight rock-star trousers. Our celebrity booker raced around the place, pinging off the limiter with a mixture of excitement and nerves at the arrival of so many proper slebs at once. In the studio, the hopeless rehearsal of the house band thudded onwards, dubious drumming, missing lyrics and all.

Evening arrived. We were, in so many ways, out of our comfort zone/depth/heads on strong coffee. But it was too late for that now. And remember, it was all for a good cause. Against expectation, the recording was one of the most enjoyable things ever to happen in the *Top Gear* studio. It felt novel and exciting and there was the thrill of teetering on the brink of everything going wrong even if, mercifully, it didn't.

Lethal Bizzle was very gracious, even when Jeremy unplugged his PA and then referred to him by a name I'd mentioned earlier as a joke, not an actual thing to say on television: 'Jizzy Tissue'. McFly had agreed to write a song during the show and handled it beautifully, even when we blindsided them with a challenge to get the words 'sofa', 'Hyundai' and 'administration' into the lyrics. Supergrass kicked the bottom out of Richard III, helped by Adrian Edmondson on guitar and not helped at all by Jeremy releasing dry ice and pigeons onto the stage. Even the closing performance from the Top Gear of the Pops house band was a triumph of optimism and good vibes over a weirdly variable tempo. Watch it back and you can see two men (Richard and James) really enjoying themselves. And another man (Jeremy) really concentrating.

It was an idiotic and throwaway bit of television but it was fun to make and hopefully not total agony to watch. I think it went well. Probably a bit too well. Top Gear of the Pops had two knock-on effects. The first was that the presenters got into the idea of being a band and would commandeer instruments in local bars as they careered around the world on their TG Live tours, almost certainly causing great pain and distress to other patrons. The second effect was that the band re-formed itself for a miserably self-indulgent sequence during the terrible India special, for which I can only apologise.

Actually, there was a third piece of fallout from our charity special. To our horror, they asked us to make another one.

# *Another Act of Charity*

*Comic Relief* had unexpectedly enjoyed our charitable efforts and the following year we had *Sport Relief* on the phone. As before, they wanted us to take on the duties of another programme and I think it was Jeremy who suggested we meld ourselves with *Ground Force*. In light of what had happened at Top Gear of the Pops, this was a canny move. We'd proven ourselves perfectly reasonable at hosting a music programme. Even our attempts to form a house band had skirted the fringes of the listenable. We needed to put ourselves into a realm we didn't really understand and weren't especially interested in. Gardening sounded about right. Even with the outdoorsy and countrified presence of Hammond on the team, we didn't really know what we were doing and that was seen as a good thing. Bumbling about and coming up with things that seemed like good ideas and attempting to reinvent landscaping was to be *Top Gear* territory; as fertile as, I don't know, whatever that brown stuff that comes in massive bags from garden centres is called.

From this, Top Garden Ground Gear Force was born. No wait, someone said, that doesn't make sense because neither of those programmes has the word 'garden' in the title. Oh shit, someone else replied, we've already ordered the branded jackets for the presenters. That's why the jackets were wrong. Not at the top of the list of things that were wrong with this programme, but they were wrong nonetheless.

The modus operandi of the original *Ground Force* programme was that cheery hibiscus border enthusiast Alan Titchmarsh and his team would sneak into someone's garden while they were out and completely revamp it, racing against the clock to get it done before the target returned home to react with joy at the miraculous and delightful transformation. For our version of the show we'd do the same, but since it was for *Sport Relief* the garden would belong to a top sports personality. Finally, news came back to us that the lucky recipient of our unique makeover skills would be Olympic rowing hero Sir Steve Redgrave. His wife had okayed this but the legendary oar wrangler was none the wiser and would be called away to important meetings all day in order that we could improve the view from his kitchen window. Oh, by the way, the *Sport Relief* people added, he's very proud of his garden.

We met at dawn in a lay-by near Sir Steve Redgrave's house. Everyone was wearing tracksuits bought from Shepherd's Bush market the day before and we'd got a small lorry ineptly emblazoned with the logo of our new hybrid programme. As the sky lightened over Buckinghamshire the signal came through that Sir Steve Redgrave had left the house and the coast was clear for Operation TGGF.

The badly dressed army of the entire *Top Gear* production team entered Sir Steve Redgrave's garden, which turned out to be a pretty simple affair, made up of a large lawn and some trees. Oh, we could definitely liven up this place, we thought. Sir Steve Redgrave's wife appeared at the front door and greeted us with great cheer. Someone asked the inevitable: Do you think Sir Steve Redgrave will be okay with this? 'Oh no, he hates surprises,' she said breezily, and went back into the house.

So it began. I suspect that on the real *Ground Force* show, as indeed in any large-scale garden-remodelling effort, there would be a project manager who would co-ordinate efforts so that pointless holes were not dug in pristine grass, large and heavy rocks were not plonked in the wrong place and huge lorries were not backed onto soft ground and beached in extremely inconvenient places. We did not have a project manager. We had Jeremy in a cheap jacket with the wrong programme title on the back, marching about with a shotgun. It was semirural bedlam.

Hammond tipped his digger over. James spent most of his time on a shed. A man caught on fire. Obviously not a real man; it was a stuntman. You can't just go around setting fire to men. The BBC health and safety people are quite strict about that.

One of the gags we'd come up with in the office was that we'd play parping brass band music throughout the show, just as they did on the real *Ground Force* programme, then reveal that this was being played by a real brass band, following the presenters around the garden. In recording breaks, Jeremy got them to play requests and became quite misty-eyed as the mournful sound of Yorkshire drifted across the increasingly ruined Home Counties landscape. The whole thing started to feel like a fun day out from the office. We had to be reminded that we were working against the clock and that this was all for a greater purpose than simply finding out what happens if you drop a rugby post on a shed.

Hammond got pushed to the front when it came to doing the serious, charitable pieces to camera, firstly because he had the basic decency to realise that television presenters were in a position of power and should do this stuff to make a difference and secondly because he was the best at doing the sincere voice you need to cue up an appeal film. In this case, it led him to solemnly intone one of my favourite things ever to have come from his mouth and the single greatest intro to a charity film in history: 'Now before we go any further, it's time for a quick reminder of why Jeremy has just shot a tape measure.' Except he didn't say 'Jeremy', he said 'Alan', because we were pretending to be *Ground Force*. To that end, James May wasn't wearing a bra.

As the afternoon wore on various pieces of preordained idiocy occurred, there were some unforeseen calamities and then the shout went up that Sir Steve Redgrave was on his way up the drive. Everyone ran and hid. You can see what happened next on the finished show. Sir Steve Redgrave was quite cross. Not acting a bit cross or pretending for the telly a bit cross; actual, real-life a bit cross. The atmosphere in Sir Steve Redgrave's garden became very chilly. Except near the shed, which was on fire.

Sir Steve Redgrave went inside Sir Steve Redgrave's house and shut Sir Steve Redgrave's front door firmly behind him. We didn't know what to do next. This didn't happen on the real *Ground Force* show. Sir Steve Redgrave's parents were in on the whole garden makeover thing and had come round to see his reaction when he got home. Sir Steve Redgrave's mum went inside to have a word with her son, Sir Steve Redgrave. Jeremy crept in afterwards to apologise and assure him that it was all for a good cause and a team of actual gardening experts was on hand to smooth out some of the rough edges.

Sir Steve Redgrave came back out of his house a little bit less cross and patiently listened while Jeremy talked him through some of our landscape 'improvements'. Then we switched the cameras off, quick-thinking Wilman gave Sir Steve Redgrave some cash to take his family out for dinner and we began clearing up the worst of the mess. As Sir Steve Redgrave drove the Sir Steve Redgrave family away in Sir Steve Redgrave's car, you could tell he was still a bit cross. He must have really liked that garden as it was.

I was at Television Centre on *Sport Relief* night. Richard was anchoring some of the evening's live show and I was on hand for script assist. When our Top Gear Ground Force special was introduced I went down to the green room to watch it going out on TV. Sir Steve Redgrave was there with Sir Steve Redgrave's family. Sir Steve Redgrave's wife sat on a sofa chuckling along at the programme. Sir Steve Redgrave's children lay on the floor, hooting with delight at seeing their house on the telly. Sir actual Steve Redgrave stood at the back of the room, still looking a bit cross. It was hard not to think that *Top Gear* had done a bad thing. Normally our incompetence and idiocy in the name of comedy lived within our little world and affected only our little gang. Now they'd spilled out into someone else's world and made it worse.

In our defence, Sir Steve Redgrave's garden was put back the way it had been when we found it, though admittedly this took a while longer than expected, thanks to the scattergun scale and flammability of our hopeless makeover. Also in our defence, we did our bit to raise a load of money for good causes.

Even so, that was the last time *Top Gear* got asked to make a charity special. Or to meet Sir Steve Redgrave.

# Some Say . . .

In headier times the *Top Gear* production office was a cheery place, full of the jocular, back-and-forth verbal tennis that tedious bores like to call 'banter'. In particular, we had a great fondness for what you might call a 'riff', in which someone starts a gag and everyone escalates it in that way that keeps men bonded together without having to do anything as horrifying as talking about feelings. And it was from this tendency to amuse ourselves that the 'some say . . .' Stig intros were born.

It was 2005 and we were working on the sixth series of the show. On the whole, things were going quite well for *Top Gear*. So well, in fact, that efforts were being made to develop a US version of the programme. Andy Wilman and I were in our scruffy corner of the office discussing this flattering development in a not-especially-serious way. 'What are they going to make of The Stig over there?' asked Wilman. 'I heard . . .' he continued in a preposterous, below-the-Mason-Dixon-line accent, '. . . that he's a CIA robot experiment what has gone wrong.'

I spat imaginary tobacco into an invisible spittoon. 'I heard he done got lasers for eyes,' I said, like an insultingly feeble tribute to Uncle Jessie. 'And if you looks at 'em, they done burns through your brain.' And on it went, probably for the rest of the afternoon. In fact, the riff wouldn't die. Every so often, and triggered by nothing, someone would start it up again, assuming the deep-fried Southern accent to claim that their cousin reckoned The Stig was a government assassin or was made of space shuttle stuff or somethin'.

Normally, titting around in the office stayed in the office for the very good reason that, as you might have noticed, it's not very funny unless you're there. But this one wouldn't go away and when we started writing links for the first show of the next series it seeped into the script. Up until that point, The Stig had been introduced with a series of ghastly puns: 'It's time to introduce the GTI to the STI . . . G' and so on. By the time we got to the wanton awfulness of 'Mitsu-Stig-i' it was high time we tortured the audience in a whole new way and the mythical claims of Southern state conspiracy crazies seemed like a good starting point. All we needed to do was switch 'I heard . . .' for the broader 'Some say . . .', which gave the claims a certain vagueness, underlining that each statement was a curious rumour which *Top Gear* could neither confirm nor deny. Right from the start The Stig was always meant to be a man of mystery, and this seemed to fit well with this conceit. Although, obviously, it was also total bollocks.

I liked the new Stig introductions immensely, largely because I clung to this notion that The Stig was more than just a mute bloke in a crash helmet who appeared briefly to do a lap of the track. To my mind, he had a full character, which was enigmatic, unusual and exceptionally strange. So I wrote a load of introductions to reflect this, the main point of them being that he lived in an extremely odd way and did exceedingly odd things. Over time they evolved so that The Stig became weirder and weirder. I liked the weirdness a lot, especially intros that suggested he had a full-size tattoo of his face on his face, kept a photo of his wallet in his wallet or was in some way caught in a nonsensical logic loop of his own making. Every so often Jeremy would warn that things were getting too bizarre and it was time to pull it back. I used to protest, countering that oddness was part of the whole Stig character. Also, the pattern we settled on tempered the abject stupidity of the first line with a topical gag in the second. Some weeks that was a gift because something funny or controversial was in the headlines and The Stig could be dropped into a world of celebrity or politics he was plainly ill-equipped for, and some weeks it was a right arse ache because the news was full of war, death and pestilence, none of which could be considered fertile ground for introducing a man in a shit racing suit driving round in circles at high speed.

Still, it was a good challenge and my aim was always to have a fully formed intro in the draft script when the presenters came in for our Tuesday writing session, the day before studio recording. If I'd hit the spot, Jeremy would read it, give an amused snort and move on. If the intro wasn't strong enough there'd be a mumbling noise before he'd swivel around in his chair with the words, 'I'm not sure about this . . .' Then we'd sit around trying to think of something new, during which Clarkson would charge through some path-of-least-resistance options involving genitals, since they always amused the studio audience, May would get caught up in a brilliantly over-complicated odyssey into Stig's taste in crisps and Hammond would remind us of the embarrassment inherent in a trip to a hauntingly cold, silent place available only to TV presenters standing in front of live audiences which he called 'the unfunny moon'. Then we'd decide to claim that The Stig once punched Princess Anne and move on.

I enjoyed this weird world we created around The Stig. He was single-minded, stubborn and comically petulant. Specifically, in my head at least, he was a mixture of Kimi Raikkonen, the keyboard player from Pet Shop Boys and a 15-year-old boy forced to go on holiday with his parents. I used to get quite defensive about other people messing with his on-screen persona and we started to police how The Stig was used to promote the programme or associated commercial things. This was actually quite easy. In general, you just said no to everything. No, The Stig wouldn't be interested in soft drinks. No, The Stig wouldn't wave to the camera. No, The Stig wouldn't put on a funny hat. Less was more. One day *Newsnight* made a feeble item about a pub opening in a motorway service station and got a man in a crap knock-off Stig suit to go up to the bar and attempt to drink a pint. We were furious about this. They hadn't asked permission and this was just the sort of thing The Stig wouldn't do. I suggested we take revenge by inventing someone called 'Jeremy Spaxman' who was a heroin addict and a murderer, just to see how they liked having one of their lead characters misportrayed, the rude bastards. We could monkey about with what The Stig did or didn't do, but other people could not.

Likewise, I thought only we could write 'some say . . .' lines since it was our riff to begin with. Of course, by the same token they were ours to kill off and if anyone was going to come up with a new way to introduce The Stig, I thought it should be us. After a while I wondered if they were getting a bit tedious so in between series I had a bit of a think and worked out this new introduction thing based around a triple rhyme. 'He's slick, he's quick, he's often covered in sick . . . It's The Stig.' That sort of thing. 'He's speedy, he's needy, he's in love with Cheryl Tweedy.' That was another one. Then I realised we'd need loads of them to keep it going and it all sounded not only far too difficult but also even more annoying. So I kept it to myself and quietly dumped the rhymes into the folder of crap ideas. Besides, I think people had got used to the way we did it and maybe even quite liked it.

Some say we came up with a distinctive and enduring way to introduce The Stig pretty much by accident and could never think of a better way to do it. And they'd be right. Probably.

Executive producer Andy Wilman inexplicably dressed like a street thug amidst the chaos of the *Top Gear* office.

The presenters outside the studio, apparently pretending to be a boy band, just before recording the third episode of series 18, February 2012.

Cameraman Iain May assumes the classic filming position in the boot of a Range Rover.

Some say he was a bit cold ... The Stig filming a Ferrari FF and Bentley Continental GT within the Arctic Circle.

Jeremy, James and new friends during filming of the Nile special in 2012.

Filming for the hover van film outside the *Top Gear* Penistone Engineering Workshop in South Yorkshire, May 2013. Note the 'accidental' sign split.

The 'Audi Do That' high-speed tracking car used to get many of the dynamic shots on the airfield.

The presenters demonstrating a typically contrasting approach to dress code, about to start filming the Burma special in 2013.

Jeremy and a friend relax by the River Kok, Burma.

Cameraman Iain May films Richard and James at a Burmese truck stop.

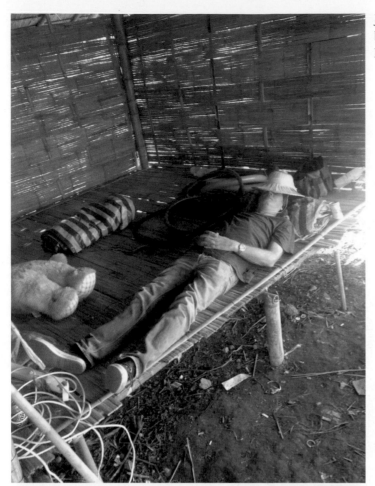

James has a nap during bridge-building in Burma.

James and Jeremy during a break in filming, checking Twitter probably.

Dawn over The Mall before the Best of British finale shoot. Note Andy Wilman in shot, wielding the precious measuring stick.

Jeremy filming against a green screen for the international rescue sequence in the ambulances film, July 2014.

In the manky 'dining room' at the studio production office, about to shoot the opening links for the Patagonia special, December 2014.

In the deserted *Top Gear* office, the planning whiteboard still showing the films for what would be the very last series, June 2015.

The presenters and the author outside the studio, about to film the second programme of series 22, January 2015.

# *Wilman*

Andy Wilman was a strange man to work with. Sometimes he would sneak up behind our balding producer and pretend to play his head like a bongo. Often he would sidle towards your desk at lunchtime like a shabby fox and steal food from you without asking. If you sat next to him in the gallery during studio recordings, he would use any lull in the action to draw rude diagrams on your script. When he was in a cheery mood he would sing a revolting song of his own invention about the effect a piece of good news was having on his nether regions. He was a deeply annoying man. Fortunately, he was also a genius.

While Clarkson, Hammond and May formed a perfect triangle on screen, Wilman was the clever and talented off-screen force that made it all happen. I was going to describe him as the fourth Beatle but I realise that would make him Ringo Starr. He wasn't even the best drummer in *Top Gear*. But if it's a Beatles analogy you want, then Andy was George Martin or perhaps Brian Epstein. He was the hidden force behind the public face of the whole endeavour and without him it wouldn't have been so successful.

As the programme became more of a globe-rogering behe-moth he would be acknowledged as such in newspaper articles and he even developed his own groupies, usually *Top Gear* megafans who would approach him on the studio floor as if in the presence of a minor deity. It was strange to watch this adoration around a bloke I once saw eating discarded Chinese takeaway out of an edit suite dustbin.

I first met Wilman when he worked on old *Top Gear*. He was a sometime producer and presenter, combining this with his day job on *Top Gear* magazine. As such, he was only an occasional presence in the office, breezing in and out at random, and this made him seem quite mysterious. He specialised in strange and unusual items for the show and no matter what he wore he always looked scruffy on camera, and indeed in real life. In light of this, a colleague and I hatched a plan for him to start a report by emerging unexpectedly from a rubble-filled skip wearing a tattered dinner suit, without once referencing either. We never had the guts to suggest it to him. In one item Wilman dispensed with clothes altogether by reporting a classic car show for nudists entirely in the buff in what was, without contest, the weirdest and most alarming piece in old *Top Gear* history.

I never really knew Wilman that well when we worked at Pebble Mill. I remember he once bought me a pint in the shabby scout hut known as the BBC Club but we never socialised and after a while he stopped turning up in the office altogether, having been told his presenting services were no longer needed. I didn't see him again until he rang and asked if I'd come in for a chat about the reinvention of *Top Gear*. Around that time, I'd had a few people asking if I could write stuff for them, 'like on your website'. Wilman was the only one who said he didn't want stuff exactly like on my website, he wanted the mind behind the website to apply itself to his television programme. He was the only person I'd spoken to who enjoyed the website but could see beyond simply mimicking its content because he was, as I discovered, a very clever bloke. And he used that cleverness to become the pulsating brain of *Top Gear*.

That's not to undersell the whole production team and the massive talent in the office but even that could be traced back to Wilman. He was the one who picked new people when we needed them and had an uncanny knack of sensing who'd fit in well. He was always pretty tuned in to that sort of thing.

He was, in fact, pretty tuned in to most things. Apart from choosing new clothes and working a computer, both of which appeared to be an ongoing struggle. In every other field, however, the most annoying thing about Wilman was how often he was right. On editorial matters he had remarkable skill and judgement, and this also applied to the wider world. One of the reasons he was so good with people was that he knew exactly the right tone to strike. Sometimes soft and charming, sometimes like a sweary bull in a china shop. Either way, pitched with care and precision to get the right result.

I once got into an argument on the phone with a man from a small sports car company, whose PR person had just told him that Hammond had pronounced the company's name incorrectly during the previous day's studio recording. Why, I asked, didn't your chap say something at the time, eh? The sports car company man skirted this issue and focused on becoming quite angry that we wouldn't cut out the offending segment entirely, all because of the fluffed vowel sound. I told him this was impossible since it would leave an ugly jump cut in a link. The man was increasingly irate. I referred him to Wilman. When someone is very, very cross it can be too easy to get very, very cross as well and then a full-blown argument breaks out. But Wilman is smarter than that. He could have been defensive, haughty or dismissive. He could have told the man to bugger off. But Wilman chose to be jaunty. Professional and helpful, yes, but mostly jaunty. And it's extremely hard to remain angry with someone who is being jaunty. I'm sure we can sort this, he suggested. Perhaps by plucking the correct vowel sound from another link and dropping it into the right place in post-production. Then he started listing words from which such a sound could be taken. The list became increasingly absurd. I think the sports car company man completely gave up on being furious by the last suggestion, which was 'vagina'.

It was a typical moment from a very atypical executive producer. While many execs sit in ermine robes inside glass-walled offices and delegate everything except going for long lunches, Andy wasn't like that. He certainly didn't wear ermine robes, and if he did they'd have been like his normal clothes, ripped and covered in soup stains. Sometimes he'd set off the tramp-like effect by hauling his tatty notebooks and paper-work around in an old carrier bag, even if he was going to an important meeting. I think some of it was deliberate, to make the point that he wasn't a lickspittle executive from the BBC sausage machine. And part of it was simply because he's an incredibly scruffy man. Years ago we were invited to an awards ceremony and in a grotesque error of judgement I asked Wilman what to wear. He said a suit and tie would be fine. Indeed, that was what he was intending to wear. The pair of us walked into the venue looking like Rodney and Del Boy on their way to a court appearance. It was immediately apparent that crumpled suits were very much not okay. It was a black tie event. To make matters worse, the first person we saw as we stood in the lobby was our old and deeply urbane colleague Quentin Willson, armed with the wry eyebrow he kept cocked and ready for such moments. 'And this,' he smirked, 'is why you *always* read to the bottom of an invitation.'

Wilman avoided other producer-ish airs too, camping out with the rest of us on the office floor, behind a desk covered in unimaginable chaos and several well-known diseases. This was partly because he liked to keep an eye on his troops and partly because he liked to lead by example. If things needed sorting, he'd make calls, write the emails and muck in to make things happen. Never was this more true than in the editing process for the show. We had a brilliant team of video editors working with our supremely talented directors and all manner of supporting roles to make sure the show was cut with the precision and elegance we demanded. They could have got on with this in isolation but Wilman was always there as ringmaster, bouncing between the suites, masterminding the whole thing with an innate sense of story and a beady eye for detail. On long nights in the edit facility he worked every comedy moment to milk the naturally oafish, stupid and pedantic sides of Jeremy, Richard and James respectively. But he was also the man who saved them from their worst excesses, taking out the moments when Jeremy became spluttering and over the top, carefully editing around times when Richard was too much of a chiddy-chaddy TV presenter, hacking away at the footage in which James became bogged down in his own lengthy thoughts. He ruled the edit with a rod of iron. A rod of iron that was bent and covered in soup stains.

Of course he couldn't have done it without the people around him, but he chose those people wisely and he remained at the heart of the operation. He'd disappear into the edit for weeks on end but pop up in the office when you least expected it, even if it was simply to keep an eye on the unspoken office code which severely censured apostrophe misuse, took a zero-tolerance stance on reflexive pronoun abuse and considered that using the word 'season' instead of 'series' was a sackable offence. I was with him on all of these points. We shared a similar outlook on many things. I particularly liked his sense of silliness. On my last birthday, for example, he gave me a vast selection of random tat from a pound shop. Conversely, when I got married his wedding present was incredibly generous. That was Wilman all over. Daft and funny when it was appropriate, serious and even a little touching when it mattered.

He was capable of being stubborn and grumpy and he was brilliant at pretending he couldn't hear his phone when he didn't want to speak to you. But he was also kind and warm and funny. Most of all, he was charming. You could be in a furious mood with him for overriding your great idea, for ignoring your thoughtful feedback or for simply eating half your lunch when your back was turned, yet it was hard to remain annoyed with him when he turned on the charm.

Last time I saw Andy, I was waiting for him outside a pub in central London in a crowd of early evening drinkers. He spotted me across the road and attracted my attention by shouting COOOO-EEEE, simply because he knew I'd find it embarrassing. Then he shared his recent fitness tips while leaning on a wheelie bin drinking a pint of lager, smirking at his own absurdity. And that was pretty much Andy Wilman. The silly, scruffy, funny man at the very heart of our silly, scruffy, funny show.

# *The Specials*

After blithering into the idea of making an annual special, we
had to confront the yearly issue of deciding where to go. In the
early days this was easy. We'd simply head to a country Jeremy
had recently visited on holiday. Hence Botswana and Vietnam.
But then Jeremy stopped going to interesting places and started
taking his holidays in the Caribbean, which immediately put
the kybosh on that one. Tonight we spend two weeks driving
round and round Barbados may have sounded very nice, but
not especially challenging.

This is when we moved to the second method of selecting
the location for the special, which was maps. We liked a
map on *Top Gear*. Even in the age of Google Earth and the
many interactive mapping delights of the internet, the office
was still a temple to the papery and hard-to-fold art of
the cartographer. Whenever any ambitious shoot was being
planned, a map would be pinned to the wall and covered
with little scribbles and stickers so the team could get their
heads around the scale and direction of the intended journey
while another would be laid out on a table so we could

squint and stare at it as if it was 1943 and we were planning another nighttime run over the Ruhr Valley from behind a set of enormous moustaches.

For the specials, we might put up a map of the world and then jab randomly at places we hadn't been before. Jeremy would often lead the charge on this one, peering keenly at sections of the globe previously untroubled by *Top Gear*, tapping a finger against them and turning to the researchers with the words, 'What's there?' Sometimes the answer would be, 'the world's largest and least interesting zinc mine'. Other times it would be something more promising like 'the death road'.

From such a starting point, one or two of the team would start looking into this region more deeply, trying to see if there was a logical journey to make across it and whether that journey gave us the things we quickly grew to require from a special, which were spectacular and varied scenery, interesting things to see and do and ample chances to put the presenters into perilous and/or miserable situations.

The logic of the journey was important. The specials were always best when there was a clear instruction to get from point A to point B. It's what we forgot when planning the hopeless India special, which saw the presenters meandering about the country with no real sense of purpose beyond the tenuous 'trade mission' brief. Ideally, we'd have a better plan than that one and something that would present itself as a tough but achievable journey which could be undertaken in two weeks or so.

In parallel to this, we'd start thinking of a brief for the type of cars we'd use. For the original America special and Botswana the presenters were just told to buy normal cars, and this worked very well because their natural inclinations led them to models of very different sizes and shapes, giving the pack shots a brilliantly mismatched appearance, like the Bash Street Kids or Top Cat and his gang. For Vietnam they had to choose motorbikes of course, and that's one reason why I've never much liked this special. The machines weren't interesting and had no character, making the whole show entirely about the presenters. Plus, as one TV critic pointed out, the 'challenge' was to undertake a trip that ordinary Vietnamese people do all the time without making such a bloody fuss.

By the time we got to the Middle East we had a vague idea about mixing things up by making the trip in new cars, but getting car makers to donate three brand-new models in the certain knowledge they'd be ruined and dusty when they got them back was never going to be easy. We ended up with small sports cars simply because we'd never featured them in a special before. Likewise, the use of estate cars in the search for the source of the Nile. Luckily, the editorial was strong enough to gloss over that inexplicable choice. When we started these specials the cars were sourced in whatever place we were going to, either by getting a person on the ground to do the leg work or remotely from the UK, harnessing the local equivalent of *Auto Trader*. In more recent times, lack of choice and the inability to get whatever we bought checked out by trusted mechanics made it preferable to buy the cars in the UK and have them shipped overseas, even if that meant buying them well in advance.

Once we'd got a location nailed down and a type of car in mind, the real donkey work would begin. Especially if we needed an actual donkey. We'd bring in an additional producer, Chris Hale, who would lead the charge on the fine-grained research about the country or countries we wanted to visit, earning himself the nickname 'Diligent' for his admirable devotion to 't' crossing and 'i' dotting. A local fixer might be hired to get out there and start exploring the roads and trails we'd found on maps, reporting back on how passable they were, or otherwise, and sending in pictures of the land-scapes. A director would be assigned to start fretting about specific things like the precise location of the big meet-up that would start the film, while our production management team started the lengthy process of securing visas and filming permissions and all the other vast slews of paperwork that made each special a logistical minefield. And also a bit of a fire hazard. Their remit included tedious but vital details like finding suitable cars to use as tracking vehicles. In the UK and much of Europe, this was simply a case of unearthing a company that would hire us a Range Rover. Or when Land Rover announced the new Range Rover and somehow made the boot seem smaller and the wrong shape, a Discovery. But these sorts of 4x4s aren't always commonplace in other countries and something similar would have to be found with, crucially, a split tailgate to allow a camera to poke out but the person working it to stay in.

Once a mountain of research had been generated and many more maps had been stared at, the producer and the director would fly out to wherever we were going and undertake a recce, looking for things like a start point and a likely end location, assessing the possible routes and searching for interesting things along the way. Where there was good stuff, we could send the presenters towards it and something might happen. To my mind, this is where the India special went wrong as we became obsessed with topping what had gone before, leading to fatal over-worrying and then, in turn, to a series of painful set pieces, instead of letting the action unfold naturally.

Our advance party would return from their travels with reams of notes and hundreds of photos so we had as good an idea as possible of the types of terrain we'd be getting into. And the sorts of mud we'd be trying to get out of.

Then, finally, after three or four months' worth of solid work in the planning and detailed preparation, the time would come. A team some 20-odd strong, comprising our usual band of presenters, film crews and people from production, along with extra support from survival experts and a medic, would head off to film the damn thing. For two weeks or so, those of us left in the office would nervously await news of how it was going, hoping that all was well, that they'd get enough material, that they wouldn't get arrested, that the local rebels wouldn't start posting bits of them back to the office. And then the triumphant troops would return, stinking and dusty and wearing Ray Mears survival clothing, which was odd since they'd just got off a BA jumbo and caught a black cab from Heathrow, and they would entertain us with their tales of derring-do while the precious tapes and memory cards from the cameras would be whisked to the edit suite to begin the two or three long months of being diced and sliced and carefully finessed into the shimmering prize that would enliven the holiday season. Or, in the case of the India special, the glitter-wrapped turd that we plopped onto the post-Christmas dinner table.

Personally, I always had a strange relationship with the specials. There was plenty to get involved with at the planning stage but they were still weird for a script editor because they had almost no script. The team would go off into the field for two weeks and the whole thing would be made into some sort of sense back in the edit suite without once having troubled a Word document. For this reason, I didn't like the specials.

For many other reasons, however, I did. Mainly because after the many months of hard work, attention to detail and dedication that went into making them happen, they were usually really, really good. Apart from India, obviously. India wasn't good at all. Sorry.

# It's All Scripted

*Top Gear* generated a lot of noise on the internet, especially in its later years. A new episode would air and people would take to forums and message boards and Facebook groups to discuss it. It was very flattering. As Oscar Wilde said, there is only one thing in life worse than being talked about, and that is not being minutely dissected on Reddit by a man who wants to know why you haven't lapped the 2014 model Nissan GT-R. The show even enjoyed its own vibrant fan-centric forum, although this sometimes seemed like a website for people who actually disliked *Top Gear* and wanted to meet up in a virtual environment to discuss how much they hated this series and wished the programme could go back to being more like a previous series, which they also hated.

Reading online comments about your own show is a dangerous game. Richard couldn't bear it and stayed well away. James used to delight in winding Hammond up with a deliberately contrary approach which involved trying to find spiky criticism by typing his own name into Google followed by another, more robust and unbroadcastable word of his choosing. Jeremy used to insist that 'we can't do things based on what the internet thinks' but then read the forums anyway.

I found it hard to stay away too. It was interesting to get a flavour of what people thought of our efforts, even though very many online comments seemed to be critical. Still, you can't please all of the people all of the time, and other things that get said when you worry that the world thinks your show is shit. Only one thing really made my face itch with fury; repeated claims that *Top Gear* was 'scripted'. This was a pretty regular accusation: 'It's all too scripted,' someone would say; 'I just hope next week's show isn't as scripted,' someone else would join in; 'They need to lose the scripted stuff,' another person would add. The word 'scripted' was used as a synonym for 'set-up', which was fair enough. Sometimes we did things that were set up. But scripted, says the excessively defensive script editor, was not the way to describe it because I'll let you into a secret: *Top Gear* was scripted. Of course it was. All television is scripted.

Documentaries are scripted, nature programmes are scripted, the news is scripted, 'reality' shows are scripted, the weather forecast is scripted. And that's not a bad thing because a script isn't necessary a bulky document in which every word and deed is written down in advance. A script can be simply a rough guide that tells the performers, the director, the film crew and all the other people involved in the production where the story starts and where it hopes to get to. *Top Gear* used to embark on two whole weeks of filming for the hugely complicated, expensive and arduous Christmas specials with little more than a piece of paper that carried the opening link, justifying why we were there and what we hoped to do, and then a yawning void waiting to see what happened next. That still counted as a script, just as much as one for a track test, which would be pretty tightly written and in some detail. We never went out on location without a script, but a script could be many things from a carefully structured and fully formed road test to a flimsy statement of intent in which the most common word was 'whatever'.

The actual process of writing a script took several forms. If it was for a film presented by Richard or James and required some careful structuring and application of thought, the respective presenter might write out his basic ideas or talk them through on the phone and then Andy Wilman would ignore them and bash out a rough script in the office. Then the respective presenter would ring Wilman and shout at him, after which he would send his mess of a document over to me and I would shout at him too. From years spent in the edit, when it came to story structure Wilman was a maestro. Unfortunately, when it came to working with a Word document he was an utter buffoon. By some process of back-and-forth between Wilman, the presenter and me, and probably a bit more shouting, we would formulate a script. And then the presenter would go out into the field and probably say a load of new things that weren't in the script but had popped into their head on the day, and the entire story would be rethought and reassembled in the edit suite.

Scripts involving Jeremy were a bit different. Richard and James were writers but Jeremy was something beyond that. He was a connoisseur of words, a man who obsessed over them and who couldn't rest until they were right. TV directors tend to think in pictures and regard the visuals as the most important element of a film. Jeremy used to delight in antagonising them with the preposterous claim that *Top Gear* was '99 per cent words and one per cent pictures'. The directors would roll their eyes, and in doing so spot an especially interesting cloud they wanted to film. 'Yea!' I'd remind them unhelpfully while standing just behind Clarkson. 'It's all about the words!' I liked words too, so I liked this claim. Although obviously it was a bit bollocks.

If we needed a script for a track test or a single car review on the road, Jeremy might hammer out some words on his own to get the ball rolling and then send them over to me in an email with a familiar note attached which said, 'Add facts and gags'. Then I'd do my best to comply with this instruction, filling in my bits in italics and sending the document back so Jeremy could have another run through it, and we'd back-and-forth like this until the newly minted script was in a fit state to be released into the wild.

Sometimes, rather than working remotely, I'd go over to Jeremy's place. He'd drive the computer and I'd sit opposite or pace around behind him, throwing out metaphors and set-piece suggestions on demand as his rigid index fingers stabbed at the keyboard, like someone playing a tiny game of whack-a-mole with his laptop. His typing technique was inelegant but the speed at which he wrote was remarkable. I've never worked with someone so capable of coming up with words at such a rate; and of a quality, in draft one, that most writers couldn't hit on version 20. All I had to do was try to keep up, filling in the gaps whenever an extra brain was required.

'It's as minimal as . . .?' Jeremy would say.

Um, I dunno, I'd reply, pacing over to the window and back. Swedish prison? 'No, too modern, something older and more miserable . . .'

An Amish electronics shop?

'Not quite right. Simpler than that . . .'

A monk's underpants.

'Yep, that's it.'

And so it would go on. We could hammer out two or three scripts in quick succession working this way. For the three presenter films it was less about precise words and chunky analogies, more about getting an intro right. The studio introduction was vital, since that set the tone and established the question we would be answering or the challenge we would face. It had to have a simple yet stout line of logic to hook in the viewer and get things moving. Once you were up and running you could deviate from this theme, though I always felt the best of our big VTs stayed true to their core concept. Once the studio intro and the top of the film itself were in place, everything else should follow. Landmark elements would be filled in so that you could get some sense of structure and how the story would evolve. If there were challenges or tests coming up, it made sense to order them so that the most damaging and dramatic came at the end. The actual details of what would happen were always vague because we just didn't know. Hence the word 'whatever' featured a lot. Directors used to hate it. How could they know where to point their cameras if an entire set piece, one potentially lasting some ten minutes, was covered with one word, apparently written by a grumpily texting teenager?

Sometimes friends would remark on a 'really funny ad lib' or 'that thing James came up with' and you'd quietly admit that these spontaneous moments were confected in the office four weeks beforehand. Other times you'd hear complaints of how 'scripted' something was and you'd be desperate to prove that it really did just happen on the spur of the moment and Richard really did just come up with that funny thing that he said about it.

## It's All Scripted

In our world, a script wasn't a detailed prescription of everything that would happen. A script was a plan. Sometimes the plan was to drive a new car around the airfield and say some chewy and metaphorical things about it, in which case the plan could be quite carefully written out. Sometimes the plan was to drive across an entire continent in three old cars, in which case it was barely longer than this sentence. Either way, the plan was never set in stone. Things could and would change. It didn't matter. Whatever happened, it could be painstakingly pieced together in the edit with new lines of voice-over to smooth the story forwards.

In *Top Gear* world, scripts were vitally important to give a point and a purpose to any endeavour, but they weren't a rigid guide. We planned and we plotted but in many cases we accepted that the fates would guide us and three very quick-witted blokes would react accordingly in ways that would entertain and amuse, or something close to that. A few years ago, one of the big awards shows announced a fresh category for a new style of television as defined by *Made In Chelsea*, *The Only Way Is Essex* and so on. It was called 'scripted reality'. We were surprised by this in the *Top Gear* office. 'Scripted reality?' someone said, curiously. 'Haven't we been doing that for years?' We had, because though we let the cars break down and the calamities occur, the presenters wouldn't have been in the situations where those things happened without some sort of script. That was why *Top Gear* had to be scripted. It's not like they chose, for example, to buy three old Alfas and go to an Italian car show in their spare time. That was planned. The plan was written onto a script.

Of course, this slightly unravelled in 2005 when we won an International Emmy for best 'non-scripted entertainment' programme. Oh God, we thought. If we admit some parts of the show have a script, will they take it off us again? Given my job title, I was especially surprised to hear of this new honour. In fact, I wanted to go to the ceremony in New York and accept it on behalf of the programme, so that I could go up on stage and say, 'We're all very shocked to win this prestigious award, and none more so than me since I'M THE SODDING SCRIPT EDITOR.' We decided this was a bad, idea. Someone else went to America to accept it, just to be on the safe side. Probably for the best. Turning up with an idea written down in advance would have seemed like typical *Top Gear*. You know, far too scripted.

# As Not Seen on TV

Making television is time-consuming, fiddly and often quite expensive. Producing *Top Gear*, in which ambitions were high and production values higher, was especially long-winded. I've often heard websites and viral video makers say they want to shoot something 'like on *Top Gear*', but filmed in an afternoon and on a budget of about 30 quid. You'd have to quietly explain that *Top Gear* looked like *Top Gear* because of the time spent on it and that included the underrated factor of many, many weeks in the edit suite, fluffing and finessing to make everything as good as it could be.

Because of the considerable time and effort that went into making every item, nothing was written, filmed and edited lightly. It was all there to be part of the show and discarding films was considered to be A Bad Thing. Even so, sometimes a completed VT never saw the light of day. There were various reasons for this, one being that it was simply very boring. Jeremy's test of the Lotus Europa, for example. Even Lotus themselves seemed to be struggling to find a point to this car and when we track-tested it there really was very little to say about it. The finished film was passable but the phoned-in tediousness of the car itself seemed to have rubbed off on everyone around it; and when other contents of the series expanded to leave an excess of content, this was the natural casualty. It didn't really matter. After a very short shelf life, Lotus gave up on this car, having sold about four of them.

A similar lack of interest did for Clarkson's test of the Pontiac Solstice, which we shot in California at the same time as the item in which he attempted to beat his own PlayStation lap time around Laguna Seca. We thought this was being terribly efficient and cost-effective, filming two items on one trip to the US. We overlooked how dismal and crappy the Pontiac would be and how little our home audience would care about a car that, mercifully, wasn't going to blight British showrooms. When series 7 started to bulge at the seams, the Solstice went in the bin.

Dullness and dismalness were rare reasons for an item to get junked. A better reason was some kind of technical issue that derailed the whole thing during filming. Some time in 2007 the presenters decided that beach buggies were the coolest cars in the world. Or at least, Jeremy decided that and the other two humoured him by agreeing while not really listening properly. I wasn't really paying attention either and then found myself on the way to some rural part of East Anglia to meet a chap who made modern-day beach buggies, with a brief to drive one of his cars and see if it was up to much. Since it was like a mildly less vile VW Beetle and seemed quite well made, I went back to the office and reported that it was okay. Off the back of that, plans were hatched to film it on a beach in Wales, and since we needed more Hammond films to make the balance of the series work Richard would present it. This all seemed fine until the day of the shoot when we discovered

191

a fairly major problem: the beach buggy was hopeless on a beach. It was a detail I hadn't spotted in my test drive, since this took place on a road. On sand, which we naïvely assumed was its natural habitat, it wasn't happy at all. In fact, it got stuck almost constantly. And then it broke down. Plans to get it working and then put different tyres on it came to nowt and the half-hearted beach buggy test was dropped into the waste disposal.

This, however, was not our greatest technical hitch. Sometime in 2004 James took on a project to build a flying car. It was deeply ambitious and because of this we enlisted the help of some engineering students from a well-known university. And for reasons that I'm sure made sense at the time, the car to be made flyable was a Rover Metro. With very little time and almost no money, the students did a sterling job of grafting some wings and a tail onto it, stripping a load of weight out of it and getting it to an airfield in Gloucestershire ready to be filmed taking its maiden flight. There was just one problem. The thing powering the car down the runway was its normal engine. And its normal engine drove the front wheels. So every time it started to lift into the air the drive wheels lost contact with the ground, the car slowed down, and then it hadn't got the speed to take off. What we got that day was endless footage of a small car with wings on its roof doing tiny and rubbish wheelies. A new plan was hatched to sort this problem, possibly by making the Metro rear-wheel-drive, but it all started to sound like a very expensive way to kill James May and the entire item was scrapped.

As tech failures go, that was nothing to the problem that blighted an attempt to stage a race up the coast of Florida, with Jeremy in a high-tech nuclear submarine. Everyone flew out to the US and waited until the sub hove into view so that Clarkson could get on board. Except the massive vessel didn't hove into anything. It was out at sea. And it was stuck there because, suffering from the one fault you really don't want from a submarine, it had sprung a leak. The sub was stricken, the leak was not going to be fixed in a hurry, so the *Top Gear* team packed up and went home. Except, that is, for the chap who did our minicams. He was already on board, having been taken to it a few days early so he could rig the craft for filming. He ended up staying for a week, trapped on a leaky submarine with nothing to do except keep out of the way. After that, the stars of military logistics failed to realign and the sub race never happened.

The home-made armoured car, on the other hand, did happen and never got on air for a very different reason. The set-up was supposed to be based on some claim about the world getting more dangerous but the economy looking less prosperous, so top business people or politicians needed to obtain protection without spending hundreds of thousands on bespoke, armour-plated Mercs or Range Rovers. Naturally, *Top Gear* was here to help with a cut-price alternative. Not a terrible idea, all told.

So we got a Fiat Panda, subjected it to some ingenious bulletproofing and general toughening, and then put it through some tests. At one point it was hooked to a powerful winch system so it could ram headlong into the side of an old BMW. In another set piece it was taken to a firing range and peppered with bullets. Ideally, we wanted Hammond to be inside the car for this but the safety people won't let a person sit in a real armoured car just in case something goes wrong; let alone a Fiat Panda with home-made 'bullet-proof' windows, which were basically half a dozen sheets of normal glass glued together.

There was a basic rule for films like this which said that the tests and feats of strength should get more and more spectacular as the item went on. We were still learning stuff like that at this point and the tests did not go in an ascending order of spectacularness. That's no problem, said the director, I can move them around in the edit. Which would have been fine, but for the fact that each fate that had befallen the car had left a new and distinctive scar on the daftly modified Panda's skin. At one point the side window plainly became pockmarked with bullet holes, before the car had ever been to the rifle range. Dents appeared and disappeared, damage was magically there and then gone, the whole item turned into a sort of deranged, live-action spot-the-difference. It was a mess. Eventually, everyone lost the will to sort it out and the cheapo armoured-car story was scrubbed from the schedule while the car itself slowly rotted in the *Top Gear* boneyard.

Some time after this, we embarked on what would become my very favourite disaster from 22 series of *Top Gear*. It was, if memory serves, 2005 and London Transport was selling off its Routemaster buses after years of faithful service. They were going for surprisingly little money and this alone was enough to prompt *Top Gear* to buy one. But then what to do with it? We were a car show. We didn't do buses. But hang on a sec, what if we took inspiration from a familiar slogan usually used to sell lager: *Top Gear* doesn't do buses, but if we did they'd be the best buses in the world.

With that idea in mind, our new Routemaster was lightly modified to make it the greatest piece of public transport in history. It would have ways to improve the view from the windows, it would have a system to stop annoying yoofs playing their music too loudly, it would banish the curse of sweaty smells from the person sitting next to you and it would offer on-board entertainment systems, the like of which had never been seen before. This was all utterly tremendous and would make for a terrific item on the show.

Hammond and May would share presenting duties on this one and fetched up at Dunsfold one day to film our new creation. Unfortunately, what had seemed like brilliant ideas in the office didn't seem that great in real life. The view enhancer was a roller blind with a picture of a sunset on it. The annoying music stopper system was a pair of scissors behind breakable glass, which you used to cut the headphone cord of the teenager beside you. The banisher of bad smells was a can of deodorant on a string. It was all basically crap. Richard and James manfully attempted to show off these idiotically bad inventions in a way that made them seem like ingenious ideas rather than the weak rubbish we'd come up with in the office. They were having a hard time taking it all seriously, but that would change when the final flourish was revealed up on the top deck. A radical in-journey entertainment system had been rigged to the roof and would descend majestically to the floor upon demand. What actually happened is a small piece of board plopped gracelessly from the ceiling on four bits of string to reveal the world's smallest and most pathetic slot car track. At this point Hammond and May could keep it together no longer and were reduced to such a giggling mess they couldn't deliver any more pieces to camera. They got their breath back some time later, but only enough to christen our useless Routemaster reinvention 'The Unfunny Bus'. James even came up with a little song based around the refrain, 'Get on boaaaaaaaard', to which I later added some more lyrics. The only ones I can remember went like this:

*Get on board the funny bus*
*A comedy ship that is sinking*
*Get on board the unfunny bus*
*What the fuck were we thinking?*

The Unfunny Bus was far too pathetic to be shown and the footage was locked away so that no one would ever get to enjoy its awfulness. As a final kicker, we couldn't work out what to do with the bus itself and it sat down at Dunsfold for years, taunting us with how big and red and unfunny it was.

A while later I really wanted to dig out the bus footage, the bulletproof Panda, the Europa and whatever else was lying around, and package it all on a straight-to-DVD release called *Top Gear – Too Shit to Show*. For some reason no one was very keen.

The thing about *Top Gear* is, we didn't mind admitting to our mistakes. It's just that, usually, we liked to put them on television.

# The Student Bedsit

The original new *Top Gear* office wasn't really a home. The Beeb had found some spare space in their White City building, the silver one next to the A40 out of London that was once compared to a stack of sardine cans, and told everyone to work out of there until permanent accommodation was ready. We dug in among the detritus left by a previous production, seizing whatever essentials had been left behind and hurriedly rubbing off the writing that said, 'JANE'S STAPLER – HANDS OFF!!!!!!!!!'

Eventually, and with our first series rushing towards us, we were assigned some proper office space. It was a strange, L-shaped room and like most offices in that building the main part was also a corridor to somewhere else. Perhaps the architects of this layout thought it would be 'open' and 'inclusive', completely overlooking that it was also 'annoying' and 'No, I don't know where room 4726 is, please sod off, I'm on the phone.'

The building services people said they'd give it a lick of paint and a spruce up before we moved in. Andy Wilman was presented with a handy BBC chart showing possible colours for the walls, and suggested complementary colours for the dividers that went between the desks. There was also a section outlining the wall and divider colours which did NOT match and should NOT be paired together under any circumstances. Naturally, Wilman chose a combo from this list. It was wilful and silly disobedience on a minor matter involving authority and therefore a very *Top Gear* thing to do. It was also why we ended up working in an office with vibrantly blue walls and bright orange desk dividers.

We made that office our horribly decorated home, slowly filling it with the debris of ongoing TV productions and covering the walls with complaint letters, bad pictures of colleagues and the other ways by which a long-serving team bonds over its selection of impenetrable in-jokes.

The office was messy and scruffy and had a mouse that lived in a pot plant on top of the filing cabinet, coming out at night to gnaw through anything that had food inside. Every flat surface seemed to be covered in old newspapers, discarded magazines and car parts. When Hammond made a programme about germs for the BBC science department and got some experts to swab one of our desks, the lab came back with a list of several unappetising elements including actual poo and a note observing that, technically, our office was less hygienic than the lavatories at a music festival. We were very happy there.

Unfortunately, every few years the BBC likes to move everyone into a different building for reasons that are never very interesting or indeed clear. It's sort of like a very slow game of musical chairs and although there aren't any clear penalties, if your favourite programme suddenly isn't on air any more that could well be the reason. They simply lost their seat. Who knows, perhaps the production team behind *One Man and His Dog* are gamely plugging on with their endeavours from within an underpass on the outskirts of Shepherd's Bush. I suppose that would be quite appropriate.

In the case of *Top Gear*, we were being moved into the second floor of a strange building across the way, which had been built to house some kind of mini power station before someone had a change of mind. There was a clue to its original purpose in its name; it was called The BBC Energy Centre. If it had been full of generators, that would have made sense. Since it wasn't, the title sounded like some kind of sub-hippie creative space drivel.

We had one end, with a long low ceiling and a cruel devotion to blotting out natural light. *Top Gear* magazine and website had the other end, with more windows and a sort of mezzanine effect that left a big gap in the floor, open to the level below and the production office for *The One Show* where, despite having far fewer than 365 staff, they seemed to sing happy bloody birthday every single day. Eventually we assumed they were just doing it to be annoying.

When we moved in, the office was pristine. The desks gleamed with radiant greyness. The walls shimmered as fresh beams of fluorescent light danced off their freshly painted surfaces. The air-conditioning system had yet to embark on its ongoing project to assess outside weather conditions and then make the room either a bit too hot or a bit too cold, depending on what would be least pleasant for its occupants. There were bespoke graphics on the wall and an enormous mural of a detail from a Bugatti that from some angles looked a bit like a penis. From end to end it was a brand-new dedicated *Top Gear* workspace. And within a matter of months we had turned it into another scruffy, stinking hovel.

Desks became buried under a slew of books and magazines. Piles of tyres and crates of spares began to cover open bits of floor space. The unwashed tumbleweed of hi-vis vests, white coats and waterproofs began to gather in shambolic mountains outside the store cupboard. Hastily Blu-tacked maps and pictures of potential locations covered walls, as any thought of preserving the paintwork took a distant second place to the business of planning and preparing for filming.

Wilman and I sat on the far side of the room at a bank of three desks, me at one end, him at the other, a spare place between us. Andy was a one-man maelstrom of mess and his corner of the office set the shambolic tone. The unoccupied middle desk soon disappeared under a slow-moving glacier of shite that advanced towards me across no man's land, sucking in old newspapers, discarded tea bags and promotional T-shirts as it went.

Things got so bad, the BBC sent a lady from building services up to have a stern chat with us. The word 'hazard' was used quite a lot, often preceded by words like 'trip', 'fire' and 'health'. We held out for 'Dukes of' but it never came. She had a point. For the main office of a major television programme, it was a disgrace. For the main office of anything it would have been a disgrace. Unless you were a company that billed itself as the world's leading creator of botulism.

And yet the London production office was a pristine temple to the gods of cleanliness compared to the festering dustbin of the office down at the airfield. You might have seen this one on TV. It was the shabby green Portakabin which was our home whenever we filmed anything at the studio or the track and which maintained an extraordinarily low standard in the fields of appearance and odour.

If you approached this rank outhouse from the front you went up a set of disturbingly rickety stairs and then entered the main production office, a uniquely bleak room featuring a bank of desks up one wall and a range of things on the floor designed to make you trip and face-plant into the shelf with the pens and scissors on it. From here it was a swift right turn into the storeroom piled high with car parts and a simply enormous quantity of crisps, the kind of place in which you could find almost anything you wanted, as long as what you wanted was some jump leads, a porcelain leopard and an industrial amount of Quavers. From there it was another right turn into what was sometimes called 'the dining room', a title that rather oversells a bleak space with a big table in it which was the backdrop for, among other things, the opening links into the Patagonia special. From there it was a sharp left into another joyless antechamber, featuring a couple of horrible floral sofas and an unstylish white vinyl bench which few realised was a leftover from the unloved studio set used in the original pilot show. Off this area was the top celebrity guest green room, denoted by a torn piece of A4 gummed to the door which said 'TOP CELEBRITY GUEST GREEN ROOM' and pictures of previous star visitors covering its walls, giving the place the feel of a bad Italian restaurant. Next to that, a cramped make-up room, an unsettling chamber in which The Stig could hide, and a damp and mouldy kitchen which often reeked of whatever someone had used to mask the smell of damp and mould.

Then there was the presenters' room, off the back of the main office. That was a whole Petri dish of interesting things in its own right and best not entered unless you could remember when you last had a tetanus booster. At its heart were three unsettlingly stained sofas, arranged around a filthy coffee table, while off to one side was a constantly malfunctioning computer upon which words could be rewritten and the feeble internet connection used to look up things you wanted to know in three days' time. As befitted its former use in some sort of aviation-related role, the room had a wide view out onto the airfield from two crudely installed bay windows, the sills of which would fill up with old magazines and dead flies. There were a lot of dead flies. James became convinced that someone was popping in when we weren't there and adding more of them from a mythical and repugnant aerosol of his own invention called 'can o' flies'. During the day, the presenters' room would slowly fill up with smoke and old scripts so that by the time recording started it was sometimes hard to find the door. The room stank. The whole building stank. Once, when we hadn't been down there for a while, someone opened up the place to find an owl had got into the building, flapped about a bit and then died, and their first reaction was, 'Gosh, this place smells a bit nicer than normal.'

It didn't have to be like this. When we first moved to the airfield office from the much smaller and equally dismal Portakabin we'd occupied for the first few series, the people who owned the site offered to tart it up and make it more habitable. A good lick of paint, brand-new carpet throughout, we could make it nice, they said. Wilman had a simple message for them; 'Don't you fucking dare. Leave it exactly as it is,' he insisted. 'I want it to feel like a student bedsit.'

This wasn't because he was naturally slovenly. Well, it was a bit. But there was also an ingenious logic behind his desire to keep us working in moderately squalid surroundings. He thought it kept us honest, and focused our minds on the task in hand. Yes, we could have had lavish soft furnishings, table football and a drinks fridge that didn't smell like a dead mermaid. Once we started to experience true success on a global scale that's what you would have expected. We were, in our later days, one of the world's biggest television programmes. We should have operated out of premises lined with ermine and oak. But we had worked hard to get to that point and we had to keep working hard to stay there. Fripperies and fancies would have only distracted us. Working in rooms that appeared to have been vacated by an especially messy gang of smackheads kept our feet on the ground and our brains on the job. Also, it deterred BBC management from coming in and talking to us. Yes, it was sometimes unappealing and a little unhygienic, but it was a brilliant way to stop the collective minds of *Top Gear* getting ideas above their station.

Some weeks after the show ground to a halt, I went into the empty office in London. The place was eerie without people in it. A mountain of newspapers wobbled precariously on top of a filing cabinet. A stack of off-road tyres loomed ominously over my old desk. The malfunctioning back door from James's hearse ambulance was shoved up against one corner with a load of other left-over props and half-broken shards from long-distant shoots. I felt sorry for the person tasked with coming in and clearing up this place. If it was me, I would probably just call in the wrecking ball and be done with it. The place was an utter cesspit. But it was our cesspit. And it was, in its own small, sticky, oh-God-don't-touch-that kind of way, an important part of what made *Top Gear* what it was.

# The Game Show

Every so often, in the process of planning and plotting a new series, we would have a collective crisis of confidence about what we were doing. Was it too samey, was it too predictable, should we come up with something new to draw the viewers' attention lest we make a triumphant return to discover that everyone in Britain is watching *Call the Midwife* on the other side?

This brief flutter of worry would end in one of two ways. Either we'd get over it and crack on with what we'd got planned. Or we'd desperately think of something new, and since it was invariably born of mild panic, whatever it was would be bollocks. And that's how the game-show segment happened.

The idea came from Clarkson and Wilman, although I think it was based on a suggestion from a mutual friend. It was really very simple. A willing member of the audience would join Jeremy on stage and attempt to answer a series of questions. Every time they gave an incorrect answer we would cut to a live feed showing their car in the car park, which would then suffer some mishap at the hands of a

204

white-coated *Top Gear* producer. Fail to name the capital of Peru and your rear spoiler would be smashed off with a cricket bat. Misremember the year *Titanic* came out and watch with horror as your pride and joy took a hammer to the headlight. Drop the ball on the very final question and your inability to name three members of Girls Aloud would see your entire car crushed.

This rather brutal idea seemed to have pros and cons. On the plus side, the question element allowed viewers to play along at home and there was no doubt it contained an attractive amount of jeopardy. On the downside, it also seemed needlessly mean and, to my mind, it contained a fundamental flaw: We were a car show, we were supposed to love cars. It was bad enough that we often broke and bashed up stuff that we'd bought, but at least that was ours to do with as we pleased. Damaging or destroying another petrolhead's motor? That seemed beyond the pale. Also, game shows seemed to work best when there was a chance to win something new, not when you were playing just to stop something you already owned getting buggered.

I couldn't work out if the jeopardy and *Schadenfreude* outweighed the cruelty and oafishness. It was hard to know since we weren't game-show experts. Making a good game show is harder than it looks. You wouldn't expect the producers of *Countdown* to powerslide a Lamborghini the wrong way through Hammerhead, shouting clever metaphors and knowing the right moment to switch to the super slo-mo to make it look extra cool. I don't know why we thought it was a sensible idea to enter the game-show, um, game.

Jeremy knocked away these objections like a man taking a bat to someone else's door mirror. 'It's going to work,' he insisted. Just to be sure, it was decided that before the series proper we would head down to the studio and pilot the game show segment in front of a live studio audience. Since we were there, we'd also test out our other product of pre-series nerves, a revamped Star in a Reasonably Priced Car segment in which the celeb guest was followed by a camera crew for their whole time at the track and their entire 'day at *Top Gear*', edited into a VT package to go along with their lap.

Wobbly-voiced interior-design doyenne Linda Barker gamely agreed to be the star for the pilot; I grumpily started writing some questions for the game show while the production team worked on the actual mechanics of making the car-smashing sequences work. This was the tricky bit. You can't just pluck someone from the crowd and, for the sake of spectacle, hope they're a bit thick so you can begin to hack away at their car with a claw hammer. The contestant would have to know in advance what they were taking part in and what the consequences could be. Then it became clear that those consequences couldn't be as catastrophic as intended. In our minds, or at least in Jeremy's mind, the hapless punter would have fetched up for a nice day out, agreed to take part in some quiz and then found themselves walking home because they didn't know who played the fifth *Doctor Who* and now there was a skip on top of their car. Trouble is, you can't just smash someone's car until it's an ankle-high pancake in a pool of its own fluids. This would break several BBC rules, and probably some actual laws. Plus, to really destroy a car without risk of a mild explosion needs careful preparation. And once you start needing careful preparation, it sucks all the mad, freewheeling joy out of it. So the destructive ambition was wound back from the brink and now the contestant's car would merely get its lights, windows and mirrors damaged. But wait, said someone from the BBC sensibleness department. You can't break legally mandated parts of a car and give it back to the owner when they need to drive home. That would be dangerous. What you must do is find out in advance what car it is, decide what parts you're going to smash and then have replacement parts on hand to be fitted before the owner leaves the premises.

This was all getting quite complicated. And quite tedious. It was peril with all the peril taken out. Nevertheless, we'd committed to giving it a try and it was too late to pull out. Still under a sort of huffy teenager's duress, I made my one useful contribution by coming up with a name for the new segment. It would be called Deal or No Wheels. It's a terrible name, I know. Then off we went to Dunsfold to give these format changes a trial run with our prearranged punter and his prearranged car with a prearranged stash of spares while out on the track prearranged Linda Barker did her prearranged turn for a prearranged day at *Top Gear*.

We filmed everything and then whisked the footage into the edit so it could be cut together into a mock episode to see how everything worked. On watching it back, the answer seemed to be that it didn't. The new star feature wasn't terrible and there was nothing much wrong with seeing a guest's whole day at the show but it ate up time and added precious little. It was a DVD extra or online bonus feature which we'd confused with a useful addition to the show.

Then there was Deal or No Wheels. Between the question asking, the live linking to the car park and the actual smashing of car parts, it took bloody ages to film and this is never good when you've got a hot, tired audience on their feet and their level of enjoyment is conspicuously on the wane. But there were bigger problems with this new feature, which only became truly apparent when we saw the finished edit;

it was charmless and pointless and it didn't fit at all into the structure or tone of the show. It was, to use a very technical television term, shit.

Once again, we had tripped over our own attempts to rethink things that probably didn't need rethinking. This is why *Top Gear* was never asked to design skyscrapers. We reverted to the usual format for the stars and Deal or No Wheels was quietly shuffled away in the hope that no one ever mentioned it again. Sadly, Jeremy didn't get this memo and every so often the game show would rear its hammer-smashed head. We'd be talking about the next series and pondering if anything should change when suddenly Jeremy would remember it, although perhaps not the fine detail of how bad it was.

'We should do the game show,' he would exclaim. 'It was brilliant!'

Umm, not sure it was, I would mutter.

'It was,' he would insist. 'Get the DVD and watch it again, it was brilliant.'

Sadly, the DVD could never be found. In fact, I hope the DVD is never found. We should be okay on that score. I remember there was a copy on my desk for a while. And I remember the day I filed it in the correct place. Which was the bin.

# The Rage of James May

In the earlier days of *Top Gear*, each presenter had quite a different sort of fan base. Jeremy attracted shaven-headed blokes in tuned cars who believed the best way to draw someone's attention is by shouting, 'Oi Oi!' while Richard drew the female audience, largely made up of girls who thought he was doe-eyed and cute and should have websites set up in his honour. But James had the most specific fan group of all, which was nerdish men of a certain age who wanted to engage him in intense discussion about technical matters, ideally over a pint of brown beer.

During studio recordings you could get a brilliant overview of these remarkably different demographics. I had a seat at the back of the director's gallery which came with a set of headphones and a small control panel, allowing me to listen in to the presenters' personal microphones. The main reason for this was to pay attention during each link to ensure the words broadly made sense and someone hadn't said 'bum hole' by mistake instead of 'Fiat'. But during breaks in recording, while the cameras were being reset, you could also eavesdrop on each presenter as they idly chatted with the audience. Click on Clarkson's mike and you'd hear some bloke with a Sheffield accent insisting that his Calibra Turbo could do 200 mph. Prod the switch for Hammond's channel and you'd hear little more than coquettish giggling. If you tuned in to May's microphone, however, you'd invariably hear the sound of a slightly nasal gentleman talking at length about broad-gauge railways or fixed-pitch propellers or the Laycock overdrive on their Triumph Vitesse and then asking if he'd ever been to the Goose & Baboon at Little Grunting where they do a marvellous pint of Scrotley's Old Blindness.

As *Top Gear* became more popular these specific subgroups began to blur. There were lads who wanted to talk to Richard. They were girls who fancied Jeremy. But although James's fans became more varied too, one constant remained: for a lot of people May was their favourite *Top Gear* presenter because he seemed like the one you'd want to have a pint with.

I always suspected that in viewers' minds a drink with Jeremy seemed like an overbearing prospect, because he'd probably spend all evening talking at you and then the table would fall over and something would catch fire. Richard lived in the countryside and would probably take you to one of those weird rural pubs where everyone goes quiet as you walk in. But James seemed like the sort of chap who would meet you in a perfectly nice local boozer for a couple of pints of bitter and a lovely chat about Airfix models or canal boats or something.

Well I'm afraid it brings me no pleasure to tell you that in real life James May was a vile monster who hated pubs and used to burn down at least one a week in order to achieve some bizarre form of arousal.

Not really. James was and is a brilliant bloke to have a pint with. And maybe, if the mood takes you, a game of darts. If the *Top Gear* production team ever went out en masse for a few drinks, James was the presenter most likely to join us. This was partly because Jeremy and Richard both spent a lot of their time outside London whereas James lived just up the road from the office, and partly because James just liked being in pubs. And maybe, afterwards, a curry house.

The last time I remember this happening was when we piled into some west London boozer and occupied the big table in the back corner for the evening. May appeared, had a few pints and some food with us, then politely made his excuses and left. A short while later we asked for our sizeable food bill only to discover that on his way out James had quietly settled it. So yes, James May is a good bloke. Which brings us to the title of this chapter, and the one and only time in 13 years that I can remember him coming close to losing his temper.

The irony of growing fame and its attendant increased fortune is that you also get offered more free stuff. As *Top Gear* became more popular, the office was forever receiving advances from companies wanting to give the presenters things for nowt. Being the BBC, we were obliged to behave like good publicly funded servants of the nation and turn down these offers, no matter how tempting. Jeremy used to delight in recounting how, upon ordering a new car, he would baffle sales staff by demanding to pay full price and noisily rebuffing any attempt to give him money off, even if discounts were made available to every other punter. Such was our dedication to being good that sometimes when unsolicited free things arrived in the office, we would follow Beeb regulations and send them back. But that didn't apply the day we received a consignment of pies.

The pies arrived from A Well-Known Maker Of Pastry Items, addressed very clearly for the attention of well-known enjoyer of pastry items, Mr James May. Under normal rules, we should have put them back in the post with a note saying return to sender. But they were pies. Their monetary value was small, they'd have gone off before they'd even reached the sorting office and besides, they looked delicious. As a production team we made an executive decision to buck the usual BBC edicts and then eat the evidence. With very little effort and quite a lot of lip smacking, the pies were gone.

Not long afterwards, James popped into the office and someone happened to mention the pies in passing.

'Pies?' he said, his eyes lighting up.

Oh yea, we explained, someone sent in some pies for you but I'm afraid, erm, we ate them.

'What?' he spluttered. His brow furrowed and his natural bonhomie seemed to evaporate.

Yes, someone continued, but you see, you weren't around and they'd have gone off by the time you got here.

'I could have come in to get them,' May said flatly. He sounded genuinely irritated. 'But you've eaten them. You've eaten my pies.'

We shuffled awkwardly and looked at our feet. James seemed rather upset. We could have told him we'd nicked a consignment of gold Rolexes or Armani trousers sent for his attention and he wouldn't have given a stuff. But the pies, and the covert consumption of them when he wasn't around, this felt like a betrayal. 'I can't believe you ate my pies,' he said again, in an uncommonly stern tone. Then someone made him a cup of tea and no more was said on the matter.

I think *Top Gear* viewers liked James because he seemed like the normal one, the nice one, the one you'd take to the pub. And they'd be right. All the presenters were fun company, but James was the most at home simply talking shite over a decent pint. He was excellent company. A word to the wise, however. Don't ever steal his pies.

# Five Ways to Die in Bolivia

If a travel agent told you that your holiday destination included somewhere called The Death Road, you'd probably say sod this, we'll just go to Center Parcs. But with the heady combination of arrogance, optimism and idiocy which powered *Top Gear*, we thought it sounded like the kind of exciting, interesting, uncomfortably dangerous place that would make good material for a television programme. And that's how we ended up filming the 2009 Christmas special in Bolivia.

After discovering what was claimed to be the world's most dangerous road we worked backwards to find a good route, which was from the interior of Bolivia to the coast of Chile, and a hook for the cars we'd buy, which was to disprove a previous hypothesis that even over tough terrain you don't need a 4x4. Not our strongest editorial, but enough to get us going using the assumption that within 20 minutes viewers would have forgotten the original aim of the programme, having been distracted by James May's trousers falling down or, as it turned out, James May falling face first onto a gangplank.

Next thing you know we were all in Bolivia, ready for a date with The Death Road. Which turned out to be one of the many innovative ways in which this country will try to kill you. As far as I could work out, there are at least five of them. The first, reassuringly, is aviation. Flying into La Paz airport is a strange experience because your plane achieves its cruising height and then, with no apparent change in altitude, appears to drive straight onto the Bolivian runway. Our flight managed this without being turned into a terrible fireball but it soon became clear this was the exception not the rule. The helicopter that was going to drop the presenters into the rainforest at the top of the show? That had crashed. The plane we had chartered to fly everyone upcountry to the start location? That hadn't crashed. But its sister plane had, and now it was needed to fill in elsewhere (crashes permitting). Everyone you speak to in Bolivia has been in an aviation accident or knows someone who has, and speaks about it in the breezy, casual way the citizens of other nations would discuss dropping a dinner plate.

The problems affecting our travel upcountry meant that instead of flying we had to drive to our chosen starting point where the star cars were waiting. And this in turn gave us an exciting insight into the country's second effortless mechanism of doom; its roads. Forget the official *camino de la muerte* we'd gone there to find. It turns out that every street, every avenue, every highway in the entire nation is a potential tumbling cauldron of twisted metal, shattering glass and screaming victims. The roads themselves are loosely surfaced and badly laid out, which is exciting enough, but then they're also populated by an endless stream of lumbering lorries coming around blind corners, possibly on the wrong side of the road, and banzai taxis for which there are only two speeds, 80 mph or zero, the second often achieved rapidly upon misjudging how many lorries are around the next corner. You know that giddy, tingly, dry-throated feeling you get when you have a near-miss in the car? In Bolivia that lasts for the duration of any given trip.

Assuming you survive your journey you may awake the next morning, as we did, and discover that Bolivia has prepared a surprise in your hotel bathroom, where the metal shower head is connected directly to the mains by a piece of wire that sprouts from a crude crack in the wall, putting water and electricity into thrilling proximity. The alarming appearance of this apparent death apparatus led some crew members to forgo washing, while Jeremy was more resourceful and used the shabby outdoor swimming pool as a giant bath, rinsing his hair by swimming a single length, leaving a sudsy wake of shampoo behind him.

Still, at least the Electrocution Hotel was more comfortable than our accommodation for the following nights, which was camping. And this in turn introduced us to another solid way in which a man may die in Bolivia; at the hands of Mother Nature. Specifically, all the bitey, spitty, nasty things the vile cow has chosen to leave in the rainforest. Dump your shoes outside your tent and they'll become full of scorpions. Abandon your bag on the ground without zipping it up and by morning there'll be a snake in your washbag. Lie still for too long and you'll find a weird double-puncture bite on your arm which will be cheerily identified by the team medic as 'made by some kind of spider . . . but as long as you feel okay you're probably fine'. Camping in the rainforest sounds like a terribly interesting and romantic notion. In fact, it's hot and uncomfortable and your tent is permanently full of insects, most of which want to remove things from, or add them to, your blood. Also, and no one tells you this before you go, when night falls in the rainforest every single creature in it embarks on a sort of rhythmic shouting contest so that you're attempting to sleep in the middle of an animal rave. By the second night, I became so bored with my sweaty, noisy insect-o-drome that I decided to sleep in my Toyota Hilux crew truck, an ingenious plan that was foiled the following day when Clarkson 'borrowed' it in order to test the depth of a water crossing and promptly drove it into a river.

The days went on, long and hot and itchy. May's Suzuki kept breaking down. Hammond's Toyota decided it had no need for something as trivial as brakes on these mountain roads. Our search for The Death Road started to seem irrelevant. They were all death roads. We'd been camping for days. We'd been baked, we'd been soaked, we were behind schedule and we were tired. But one thing kept us going. After nights of clammy camping, we were heading towards one glorious night in a proper hotel.

You can't imagine the joy this brought when finally, after dark, our shambolic convoy spluttered to a halt outside our digs for the night. It was small, it was modest but still it promised a more luxurious experience than another evening of bedding down in David Attenborough's rucksack. I went straight up to my room and had a shower. I didn't care that there appeared to be an electricity substation wired directly into the pipework, to this day it remains the single nicest bathing experience I have ever had. After that, pop on some fresh clothes, maybe wander downstairs for a quick beer with the crew to celebrate another day of not being dead, and then into bed for a damn good night's sleep in a room that wasn't filled with moths and despair. If only someone outside wasn't playing extremely loud music.

I went downstairs. The loud music was coming from a building behind the hotel. It was a bar, and it was hosting a party. But not just any party. With the quivering smiles of people used to politely delivering bad news, the hotel staff told us it was a birthday party for the adult daughter of a local drug lord.

Wilman and I snuck into the middle of the hotel garden and like a sweaty and slightly scared outtake from *Shaun of the Dead* climbed a child's slide to see over the back wall into the bar. There were a lot of people and they were enjoying the pulsing tunes a great deal, as if something at a local drug lord's party was making them all very keen on deafening music and not going to bed. Conversely, silence and sleeping were all our tired and tortured crew were interested in.

'THIS IS RIDICULOUS,' shouted Jeremy over the pulsing bass. 'WHAT?' I replied.

'I'M GOING TO SLEEP OVER THE ROAD,' he yelled. And then he got up, dug out his wallet, and marched straight through our hotel, across the street and into the hotel opposite, brandishing his credit card in front of him like a tiny rectangular dagger. One minute later he walked back in exactly the same manner.

'THEY'RE FULLY BOOKED,' he bellowed.

'WHAT?' I replied.

Wilman decided this situation needed executive producing. He grabbed the hotel manager and instructed him go next door and tell the local drug lord to turn his bloody music down. The manager made the face of a man who didn't want to lose a finger, or maybe a head.

You can't really call yourself an Englishman unless you can do the special Talking To Foreigners In English voice and Andy Wilman has a spectacular Talking To Foreigners In

English voice, one which was only amplified by having to shout over the mighty sounds of Now That's What I Call Dancing While Off Your Face On Cocaine . . . 5! 'I. Understand,' he said carefully. 'Then. You. Must come. With me. To translate. And I. Will tell. Him.'

The hotel manager agreed and the pair left the hotel. The rest of us waited expectantly for what we predicted would be one of two sounds. Either the same music, but suddenly quieter. Or the same music at the same volume, with a single gunshot in the mix. In the event, we heard neither.

Next door, the conversation with the local drug lord, via the hotel manager, went like this:

'Tell. Him. To turn. His music. Down.' A brief flurry of Spanish.

'He says no.' A sigh from Wilman.

'Tell. Him. If he. Does not. Turn down. The music. I will. Turn it down. Myself.' A slightly longer rattle of Spanish.

'He says that if you try to turn down his music, he will kill you.' Wilman looked into the drug lord's eyes. They were the eyes of a man who would happily kill someone for messing with his stereo.

'Tell. Him. I understand.'

Wilman trudged back into the hotel. 'Yea, he's not going to turn the music down,' he said, and went to get a beer. No one got much sleep that night. But as I lay there listening to the thudding, repetitive sounds of Coke Party vol. 9 booming into the night I consoled myself with two thoughts. This was still better than camping. And at least, so far, no one had died.

# *Stigmacher*

When it came to having Formula 1 drivers as guests on the show, we chose very carefully. There are, sad to say, many dullards within motorsport and we wanted only F1 guests who would give us something interesting. Fortunately, there were those too. There was hyper-keen Lewis Hamilton, who loved the programme so much and cared so deeply about his lap time that he'd have been a guest on every series if we'd let him. There were chatty, honest, laid-back drivers like Jenson Button, Mark Webber and Daniel Ricciardo, who'd give decent chat and firmly file themselves into the folder marked 'good blokes'. There was Kimi Raikkonen, who was never going to be a blabbermouth and who appeared not to know or care where he was, but proved to be as dry and funny as you'd hope all the same.

There was, however, always one driver we really wanted on *Top Gear*. We knew he didn't need to do anything as tawdry as come on our crummy car programme. We knew if he did he'd polarise the audience. We knew Damon Hill would probably struggle to enjoy any episode he was on. But still, we wanted Michael Schumacher on that sofa. He was a seven-time world champion, he was a controversial figure, he was F1 driver big game. Andy Wilman was a massive fan and would have crawled through a box of vinegar-sodden razor blades to get Schumacher on the show. We were just getting the top off the Sarson's bottle when we received a call from a well-known booze company.

The well-known booze company had hired Schumacher to front its 'drink responsibly' campaign. It seemed like a strange logic. You make booze, but you want to remind people not to use too much of your product, and you'll do this by using someone who's famous for driving a car? It probably made sense in the meeting. As part of their deal, the well-known booze company got a few days of Schumacher's time during which he would do as they pleased. Within reason of course. I'm sure if they asked him to hover over Ipswich in a hot air balloon shouting 'baboon stools' through a trombone, questions might have been asked. Appearing on *Top Gear*, on the other hand, might be okay.

It became clear, however, that this wouldn't be a regular Star in a Reasonably Priced Car appearance. Because of his ongoing relationship with Ferrari and the wider Fiat Group, Schumacher could not be seen at the wheel of a Suzuki Liana but he could happily lap his own car, which was an 800 horsepower Ferrari FXX. Maybe he hoped we wouldn't notice this brazen attempt to get to the top of the F1 drivers' lap board. Normally we took a hard line on matters relating to the Reasonably Priced Car. Any guest who said they'd only come on the show if they didn't have to set a lap time was politely told to sod off. Rules were rules, after all. But this was different. This was Michael Schumacher, and he was bringing his personal, rare groove Ferrari instead. We just had to think of a clever way to deal with this break in protocol.

The internet was awash with rumours about the real identity of The Stig. People often tried to claim it was Schumacher. The papers were more canny, and were closing in on the real chap inside the white suit. What if we monkeyed with all of this by getting the bona fide motorsport legend to dress up as The Stig and then unmask himself? The well-known booze company people weren't sure about this. It seemed like a big ask and such a wheeze would have to go through Schumacher's people. It was suggested that we ask them in person. Producer Alex Renton and I flew to Frankfurt, stepped off the plane, walked through the airport, then into a tunnel that led to the hotel next door, had lunch with Schumacher's manager, walked back through the tunnel into the airport and got onto the BA Airbus home. We'd visited another country and not once gone outside. It gave a strange sense of what it would be like to be a business person.

The lunch seemed to go well. The Schumacher camp was not familiar with *Top Gear* and the idea of The Stig. Our insistence that Michael would be the perfect person to 'play' him took some delicate framing. It is always said on the show that he is the best and the fastest driver in the world, we said. That went down well. He has a weird personality and we give hints that perhaps he is a robot or an alien. That went down less well. Um, no, not a robot alien, more like an incredible superhero. That sounded better. This whole idea would be put to Michael and they would let us know.

Back in London we waited nervously for the verdict. Finally, from Switzerland via Germany and the well-known booze company came the answer – the multiple world champion, he say yes. We'd let him drive his FXX and show his don't drink too much booze please promotional film; he'd let us make him The Stig for a day. The most successful Formula 1 driver of all time was coming to our draughty, crappy track.

The day arrived. It was 17 June 2009, the first studio recording of the 13th series. The show contents had the hallmarks of a half-decent comeback. We had a majestic race from London to Edinburgh between a steam train, an old Jag and a raffishly named motorcycle called a Vincent Black Shadow. We had a toweringly infantile news item about Sir Ranulph Fiennes pooing out a mobile phone. And, unbeknownst to the studio audience, we had the most successful racing driver of his generation revealing himself to be The Stig.

Some time in the middle of the morning a warning went out to clear the airfield, the runway lights came on, and a silver private jet whistled in to land. He was here. One of the production team brought him from his plane to our crappy office and led him into the smoky, stinky presenters' room where we were running through the week's script. Clarkson, Hammond, May, Wilman and I greeted him with varying degrees of babbling obsequiousness and offered him a seat on the nearest tatty sofa. Schumacher looked impassively at the dubious mark on the cushions – I think it was badly scrubbed bird poo – and squeezed himself in between the arm and the revolting stain. I remember thinking he had an unusually smooth and flawless complexion, like a computer rendering of a real person. We slouched around on the other chairs. He sat bolt upright with perfect posture. Wilman did the talking, explaining that The Stig was a very important character on the show, we had never revealed his real identity, there was lots of speculation about who he might be, we wanted to make a big thing of him unmasking himself, we thought he should come into the hangar, walk through the crowd to the stage, and then Jeremy would ask him to take off his helmet, if that was okay, and then he might ask some odd questions because we had a running joke about the things The Stig got up to when he wasn't driving but don't worry about that, and then maybe you can talk about other things. Schumacher didn't say a word during any of this and his face remained an unreadable blank. When Wilman stopped, I think he might have muttered a single 'okay'. As soon as he had done so, someone arrived to usher him out to the track to drive his FXX and with that he was gone.

Oh dear, we said to each other when he'd left the room. He didn't seem very amused by any of this and he's definitely not interested in our daft gag. He's wondering why the hell anyone let him agree to this and he's not going to play along. We were wrong. Schumacher wasn't speaking because he was listening, taking in all the information, absorbing everything so that he could process it and act upon it in the way he would have done with data about his racing car on the way to another world championship. His silence and solemnity weren't signs of lack of interest. They were an indication of attentiveness from an unusually keen intellect.

We got another demonstration of how sharp his mind really was after he'd lapped the track a few times and come in so the Ferrari mechanics could check over the car. Wilman had taken himself over to the start line to make sure all was okay with our star Stig. Schumacher approached him with a question; 'Has a Formula 1 car ever lapped this track?' Wilman said we'd had a 2004 Renault F1 car here and it went round in 59 seconds. Schumacher thought for a moment, crunched that number in his head and ran it against his experience of this track he'd never seen before today. A 2004-spec car. Renault. 59 seconds. 'When the car did this time,' he said, 'was it damp but with a drying line?' He was exactly right. We found this pretty extraordinary.

Not as extraordinary, however, as what happened later that afternoon when we got to the studio recording. Schumacher was reminded of his role and listened to this brief with the same flat, impassive expression. Walk in through hangar doors, go up onto stage, take helmet off, chat. If he could manage that, the sheer surprise of the reveal should make this work. We weren't expecting to get much more than that. In the full Stig suit and lid combo he was led to the hangar. The presenters wrapped up the link out of a test of the Lotus Evora, James introduced the Ferrari FXX and we played in the VT of 'The Stig' lapping it at sensational pace. Jeremy slapped the time on the board and then the hangar doors opened. Break a leg Michael.

He stepped into the room and stood there, arms folded in a perfect Stig stance. It was a promising start. Now the walk to the stage. Unexpectedly slow. Brilliantly slow. Really making the most of the moment. Good stuff. He sat down. 'If you want to do it, on your head be it,' Jeremy said. 'Remove your helmet.' The Stig shook his head. In the gallery we looked at each other. Did you tell him to do that? No, did you? No. Well if no one did then . . . sweet mother of soddery, bloody Schumacher's padding his bloody part. He WAS listening, he was taking it in, he had understood the importance of this whole set-up and how to make the most of it. This was superb.

Jeremy asked him to be brave. The audience started clapping and chanting; 'OFF! OFF! OFF! OFF!' Slowly, perfectly and tantalisingly slowly, Schumacher started to remove the Stig lid. God, he was really milking it. It was amazing. Finally, the helmet was off. The crowd went wild as they saw the face of a seven-time world champion, a man who didn't need to be there, who could have said no to all this nonsense but was now right in the centre of it and handling it with a panache we couldn't have dreamt of. He sealed the deal by giving Jeremy a cheeky wink. We didn't do unseemly things like whooping and high-fiving in the *Top Gear* studio gallery, but if we did this would have been the moment for it. That Schumacher was also funny and clever and effortless in the subsequent interview just made things even better.

We'd been very pleased with ourselves for having the idea of making Schumacher reveal himself as The Stig but we never expected it to go so well, entirely thanks to the diligence and surprisingly superb comic timing of the man himself.

You'll know of course about the terrible skiing accident that befell Michael Schumacher in 2013. If you're a fan of the man, you might try to think of him in happier times, driving for Ferrari, putting in another virtuoso performance on the track, claiming another world title. But for those of us who worked on *Top Gear* in 2009, the happiest memory we could ever have isn't of Michael Schumacher as one of the greatest Formula 1 drivers in history. It's as the best Stig we ever had.

# The BBC

The BBC loomed large over *Top Gear*. Obviously it did, we were a BBC show and we worked out of a BBC office with its slightly patronising posters about toner recycling and its weird canteen with an entire counter labelled 'simply potato'. But the Beeb loomed larger in *Top Gear* world as a spectre and a spoiler, the monolithic corporation that was trying to ruin our fun. It would be referenced as such in scripts and sometimes Jeremy would write a newspaper column referring to something the BBC health and safety people had told us we couldn't do. Or, even worse, something that we *had* to do and at which we had huffed like teenagers and grunted, 'This is *SO* unfair.'

From hearing *Top Gear*'s moans and rants about the dear old BBC, you might have formed the impression that the show hated the corporation and vice versa. This was not true. Of course, in the long history of the programme there were problems. Every so often a small amount of interference would arrive on our doorstep which would have to be listened to, reasoned with and if all else failed told to sod off.

From time to time the question of a female presenter would be raised in management circles, not least when research showed that almost half of *Top Gear*'s audience was now made up of women. Some factions within the Beeb thought this clearly showed that we needed a woman on screen. It seemed an odd logic, like discovering that your band had strong appeal among porcelain owl collectors and so deciding to replace the guitarist with a person who sat there looking at porcelain owls. Would that make porcelain owl collectors like the band even more? Or would that ignore the fact that creative endeavours have a fragile chemistry beyond simple stats and to fiddle with them only risks ruining their appeal to all sectors of society? It's not like we were boorishly against having a woman on the show when we started. We screen-tested quite a few female presenters but none were quite what we were looking for. In the end, the two people who seemed right for the job happened to be chaps. And then, after finding another chap who was right for the job from series 2 onwards, we realised that these three men had a very natural and very funny way of talking to each other which we wanted to preserve. Popping a female presenter into the mix would have changed the dynamic because two men taking the piss out of a woman for choosing the wrong car/shoes/type of hare-brained limousine design would seem brutish and bullying. Whereas two men taking the piss out of James May just seems like the way that three male friends would talk to each other. So we fended off all attempts to change the gender split of the presenters, not because of deep-seated sexism but because we thought we had a line-up that worked. And the audience seemed to agree. Women, as well as men.

Small skirmishes such as these sometimes led to an uneasy relationship with management, but don't mistakenly believe that *Top Gear* was constantly bothered by interference from above, handed down via Chardonnay-sodden harpies and feckless yes men. There were only a few of those. There were rather more very clever, very talented and very supportive people. We got wonderful backup through the life of the show from editorial policy, from press and publicity, from all manner of other departments who aided and enhanced the production process. This is one reason why though it may have publicly whined and moaned, *Top Gear* didn't hate the BBC.

I don't think the BBC hated *Top Gear* either. I think it sometimes found the show irritating and obnoxious and perhaps even a little embarrassing, but we delivered strong viewing figures, we always polled way above average in audience satisfaction surveys and we provided a noisy, boorish counterpoint to BBC2's worthy, quietly reflective programmes about homeless turtles and the building of the Aswan High Dam.

Unfortunately, since there's no denying that we could be noisy and boorish, I'm convinced the wider BBC thought we were stupid. I was especially certain of this back in the days when we were part of the factual department and had been invited to take part in a departmental pub quiz. For no accountable reason this took place on HMS *Belfast* and some of the questions were read out by newsreaders. I know, it sounds like the kind of dream that would make you vow to give up eating cheese after 3 p.m. This really happened and a load of us shambled down to the river to put in a showing as Team Top Gear. Even before the quiz started a producer from another show came over and started trash-talking us, which would be normal if we were at a wrestling match in Kentucky but seemed odd coming from someone who lived in Islington. The thing is, the *Top Gear* team was not stupid and we demonstrated this by taking the lead and then holding it, all the way up to the mid-quiz break. People used this hiatus to go outside for some fresh air which, among television people, often comes in a Marlboro packet. Rather than smoking, however, half the people there seized upon *Top Gear*'s commanding lead and accused us of cheating. 'You can't be in the lead,' said one woman, furiously. 'I mean, you're *Top Gear*.' Refreshed by this invigorating round of cruel character assassination on the deck of a warship, we went back indoors and continued to lead up until the final round, which was about the BBC itself. On this, we let ourselves down. In fact, I think out of ten questions we got one right. In the final reckoning, this piss-poor showing dropped us to second overall but still we went away happy. It was a very *Top Gear* result. We knew about the news, sport, literature, the theatre and geography. We just didn't know a damn thing about the internal structures and processes of the very place where we worked. And we were proud of that. Even if colleagues from other programmes thought we were thick. Actually the *Top Gear* production team in all its forms has always been the brightest, most dedicated and most thoughtful group of people you could hope to meet. Apart from me. I failed GCSE maths and I think the word 'poo' is hilarious. But the rest of them were great.

Weird floating pub quiz cheating allegations aside, *Top Gear* rubbed along with the BBC, even if the rubbing was sometimes in the wrong direction. It was important to push our luck, but also important not to push it too far because, in truth, there are several reasons why *Top Gear* couldn't have been made with any other broadcaster in the world. Without wishing to be vulgar, one of those reasons was money. *Top Gear* was an expensive show to make. A lot of broadcasters couldn't stomach that. Sometimes even the BBC couldn't either. When a round of hefty budget cuts arrived a few years ago, it was decided with perverse logic to slash the cash given to the most successful programmes first. Wilman manoeuvred his way around management and got them to agree that, since they didn't want us to reduce our production values, the only solution was for less money to equal fewer shows, thereby maintaining the budget per show at a level that would allow us to do what we did. That's why the number of *Top Gear*s per year started to fall.

On the cashflow front, it also helped to be part of a large organisation that could soften the blow of overspending. Sometimes *Top Gear* used to go over budget. At which point we'd have to go cap in hand to the BBC, look at our shoes, mumble a few words about not letting it happen again, and they would find a few quid more to help us out. Try that at a small, independent production company and you might get the money, but you'd come in the next day to find they'd sold your computer.

Another great thing about making the programme for the BBC was the lack of ad breaks. It's amazing how much the flow and rhythm of a TV show gets disrupted and ruined by a sudden break, so the viewer can be sold breakfast cereal and incontipants. Whereas having a full 59 minutes in which to allow VTs to run and studio items to ebb and flow was a luxury a commercial broadcaster wouldn't have allowed us.

And another benefit was that we rarely ran at the prescribed time, taking advantage of BBC2's unusually relaxed attitude to Sunday evening timings to ask in advance for what they called an 'overrun', which would allow a programme to go on for a little longer. That's why sometimes you'd look at your watch on a Sunday evening and notice it was past

9 o'clock yet *Top Gear* still seemed to be on. If we couldn't cram all of that week's contents into the usual time slot, we'd beg the channel for a little more. The powers at the channel were usually very accommodating and we loved them for it.

And since we're still on things that made us love being at the BBC, it's important not to overlook the billowing enormity of the corporation's music licence, put in place to permit their radio stations to function but freely available to programme makers who had (almost) any choice of music to put on their films. That brought the joyful freedom to pair great visuals with the perfect piece of music without worrying that it was going to bankrupt the production.

There were, then, many reasons why we liked being part of the BBC. But I'd go further and say that being part of the Beeb was vital. It was rarely acknowledged or spoken about but the truth is that the BBC made *Top Gear* what it was, having a subtle but vital effect on the entire show. The Beeb was the piece of grit in the *Top Gear* oyster that enabled pearls to be made. Without something to push back against, without a corporate machine to moan about, without the feeling that we had to sneak things past the grown-ups, *Top Gear* would not have been what it was. Making *Top Gear* felt like being at school. We were the naughty kids and the BBC was the staff. Every time we sneaked a rude word or a saucy joke into the show, we were shouting 'ballbags' from the back of class while the teacher's back was turned.

Andy Wilman was brilliant at hiring people who fitted in with this classroom attitude. If presented with two candidates for a job, he might hire the one who seemed less impressive on paper, simply because in person they seemed more likely to gel with the team. I always thought our recruitment process should have included a school bus parked outside the office, with candidates being invited to get onto it one at a time. If they went straight to the back seat, they were probably *Top Gear* sort of people. It's what the presenters would have done. Although Jeremy, Richard and James were very different characters, they all had something in common, as did Andy. They were bright kids who got told off more than average at school. And they had grown up to be bright men who got told off more than average at work.

That's why we needed the BBC. We needed to skirt as close as possible to the almighty bollocking in the headmaster's office. We needed to feel like the rebellious class in a school full of sensible high achievers. It just wouldn't have worked as well in a broadcaster that said do what you like. After all, where's the fun in that?

That's why *Top Gear* owes the BBC an enormous debt of gratitude. Without the Beeb and its occasional meddling and form filling and probable belief that we were morons, there would have been nothing to kick against. Without the BBC I'm sure there would have been *Top Gear*. It just wouldn't have been the same.

# The Bollocks Hour

We had several small traditions in the *Top Gear* office. One of them was that at the end of a long Tuesday working on the script, James would leave the building with the words, 'What time do we get to the studio tomorrow?' It was hard to know if he was joking or not.

The answer, since he always asked, was 9 o'clock, when five of us, the three presenters plus Andy Wilman and me, would assemble in the grotty back room of our production office and await the unmissable arrival of studio director Brian Klein, one of the nicest men in television, but also one of the clumsiest. Brian would turn up, hoof someone's cup of tea across the floor and sit down on half of Richard's bacon sandwich; and then, once everything was mopped up, we'd begin read-through of the script and a quick canter through the news stories.

After this, Andy would cannon out of the room to go and bark at his troops, Brian would march over to the studio to begin briefing his crew and the rest of us would be hanging around until we were called to the studio for rehearsals. There was little to do but sit around and talk rubbish. I called this period The Bollocks Hour. It was a pleasant period of idle distraction before we resumed the serious business of making the show. Also, there are few more amusing people to talk bollocks with than Clarkson, Hammond and May.

A typical Bollocks Hour would contain some or all of these elements. James would disappear from the room and return with a bag of chicken crisps, sitting down on the sofa to eat them with mechanical precision and visible delight. Jeremy would rummage through the current day's papers on the coffee table and begin avidly digesting the news, reading out passages he found interesting or amusing. Richard and I would engage in a brief but enthusiastic chat about Land Rovers, which would be interrupted by noisy complaints about '1940s farm equipment' (May) or 'murderer's cars' (Clarkson).

James would announce that he fancied another cup of tea. Richard would agree. James would open the door, attract the attention of one of the production team and loudly proclaim:

'Richard Hammond would like a cup of tea.'

Richard would sigh, 'You utter bastard.'

'He's very insistent,' James would add, his head still out of the door. 'Oh, and if you're making one, could I have one too, please?'

Richard would fume with mock indignation at being made to look like a prima donna.

James would fetch his small suitcase, pull from it a pair of shoes and a shoe-cleaning kit and begin a very precise routine of polishing the shoes to an agreeable shine. Richard would announce that he needed to urinate and that having given it some thought his best course of action was to take this matter to the lavatory. While he was gone James would steal the label maker from the office next door and use it to create a small sticker for Hammond's bag, which would read 'Bellend'. Jeremy would give up on the papers and begin to thumb through the nearest car magazine looking for pictures of its writers engaged in hard cornering for the camera while wearing a steely-eyed, po-faced, joyless expression we called 'oversteer face'.

Richard would return from the loo and pull up a picture of some clattery old car on his phone, announcing with barely concealed excitement that he was thinking of buying it. 'Why don't you just get a proper car?' Jeremy would say from behind his magazine. James would explain how and why he was one day going to open a shoe shop with the express intention of allowing no customers onto the premises.

Jeremy would find nothing else of interest to read and would sit for a moment looking bored and making an inexplicable whistling noise. James would thumb idly through a stack of press releases and announce with a heavy heart that it was 'all bollocks'. Richard would ask aloud if it was acceptable to have another bag of crisps. 'Yes,' James would say, emphatically.

Richard and James would embark on an in-depth conversation about air traffic control, based on their respective helicopter and aeroplane experiences. Jeremy would declare that this was 'literally not interesting'.

James would receive a phone call from a man attempting to mend his existing old car or a man attempting to sell him another one. Either way the man would appear to be called Nigel.

Jeremy would begin a short lecture on the shortcomings of the test car he was driving that week.

One of the production assistants would stick their head round the door and ask if anyone wanted a hot drink.

'Well I don't, but I think you'd better make Richard Hammond another cup of tea,' James would say.

'You twat,' Hammond would hiss.

'Yes, you should hear some of the things he's being saying about you,' May would conclude. 'Oh actually, if you're making Richard Hammond one, I'll have one too.'

Jeremy would suddenly remember something good he'd seen on YouTube and plonk himself in front of the computer at the side of the room in order to find it. Richard would find a photograph of an American muscle car in a magazine and hold it up with the wide-eyed, open-mouthed expression of a very excited cartoon character.

Jeremy would demand to know why the computer wasn't working. James would ask Richard if he was planning to do the recording dressed as a 1980s new romantic again. Richard would robustly tell James to go away and remind him that his recent run of shirt and jacket combinations appeared to have been selected while wearing a blindfold. Jeremy would find the clip he'd seen on YouTube and invite everyone to gather round to watch it only for the internet connection to fail.

James would wonder out loud if dogs got sad, or if they sometimes just looked sad. Richard would suddenly remember another piece of livestock that had been added to his collection at home. There would be a short argument about the countryside.

Jeremy would tell an anecdote about an evening out which might or might include a new restaurant, an obscure foodstuff and a chance encounter with a middle-ranking actor. Richard would discuss the many and varied reasons why the greatest food in the world is cottage pie. James would open another bag of crisps.

The star guest would be ushered in to say hello and then be taken off to the track.

'Of course, I know this but I want to check that you lot do,' Jeremy would begin. 'What's that new Toyota called?'

One of the production team would creep in and ask if anyone would like a drink.

'Richard Hammond would like a cup of tea,' James would say.

'Oh come on,' Richard would cry.

'Yes, he's been getting quite angry about it,' May would continue. 'Oh, and if you're making one, could I have one too, please?'

Finally, the assistant floor manager would appear in the doorway and announce that it was time for rehearsals on set.

'I'm afraid we've had a change of plan,' Hammond would say gravely.

'Yes, we're very busy here,' Clarkson would add, flicking idly through an old copy of *evo* magazine.

'Could you get someone else to do it?' James would ask, helpfully.

Then they'd get up and head to the studio. And that would be the end of The Bollocks Hour. I liked The Bollocks Hour. If there was one thing we were good at on *Top Gear*, it was talking utter bollocks.

# *Being Sensible*

There's an ongoing dilemma that affects all car magazines and programmes, *Top Gear* included. Feature lots of ordinary cars and some of your audience will complain that you're boring. Feature lots of supercars and another section of your audience will claim you don't feature enough things that 'normal people can afford'. We used to get more of the latter, especially when we reached a point where we felt we didn't have to review a car just because it was new and on the cover of *Autocar*. New Mondeo? New Astra? New whatever that medium-sized Toyota is called? Well we could . . . but sod it, there's another version of the Pagani Zonda just been announced so let's cover that instead. Then we'd brace ourselves for another flurry of letters and emails complaining that we had our head in the clouds. And the clouds were made of V12s and carbon fibre.

In 2008, Jeremy came up with an idea to address the section of the audience that wanted to see normal cars for normal people. We would do a sensible road test of the brand-new Ford Fiesta. Of course, this was *Top Gear* at the very height of its pomp. We couldn't very well do an actual straight and bone dry road test full of earnest talk about boot space and running costs and then expect it to sit alongside other series contents like a lorry smashing through a brick wall and a V8-powered blender. A big chunk of our regular audience would yawn themselves inside out. But that was okay, because while our sensible road test would impart actual information and show you stuff like rear legroom to appease the people of Sta Prest trouser town, these things would be dressed up in an increasingly silly and dramatic way.

The starting point was a studio link involving a letter from a Mr Needham in the accepted 'Why oh why oh why . . .' manner people use when writing to television programmes, which sounds like an obsessive compulsive struggling to spell yo-yo. From here the VT package started in sedate style, only to use tissue-thin 'rigorous' testing procedures as an excuse to ramp up the action, with a chase around a shopping centre and then a full-on Royal Marines beach assault. The formula of providing actual information about the car in a moderately daft way seemed to work. Obviously, it took a mighty amount of work behind the scenes in a way that bumbling around the Cotswolds doing an actual road test wouldn't, but the main thing is, it was interesting. The Fiesta test left two legacies in the office. Firstly, a large bill for cleaning tyre marks off a shopping centre floor. And secondly, a desire to do more of these 'sensible' reports.

The following year we had a Renaultsport Twingo kicking around at the track and in a strangely out-of-character move James May took it for a quick lap, coming back to declare it 'marvellous'. That was all the encouragement we needed to cue up another way of appeasing Mr Needham, especially since Renault offered up a preproduction car to do with as we pleased. When you said 'as you pleased', we asked, did you mean take it to Belfast, bang it into a few things and then fire it into the docks? Um, yeeees, replied Renault, cautiously. So that's what we decided to do. The only bit we were stuck on was a practical yet also utterly stupid demonstration of boot capacity. Half seriously, I suggested that it could be the actor Ross Kemp. 'That's it!' exclaimed Clarkson. As luck would have it, Jeremy was quite matey with the man who used to be Grant Mitchell and the next thing you know we were in the park near his house, inserting the BAFTA-winning actor and presenter into the back of a small French car. Kemp proved to be a tremendously nice chap and very game for being shut in the boot with a camera in his face, ad libbing veiled threats about what he'd do to Jeremy when he escaped. Another great victory for sensibleness.

So in series 16 we did it all again with a Skoda Yeti and this time – as well as tests involving dug-up race tracks, teams of firemen and hyperactive dogs – we found a man who was happy to receive a tattoo in a moving car even though the results would almost certainly look like he'd been scrawled on by a toddler and a man who was able to land a helicopter on the Skoda's roof, which is a lot more dangerous than it looks. All we needed to complete the very sensible series of very sensible tests was the return of Ross Kemp, this time demonstrating the ample size of the glovebox. Now, in truth, the Skoda Yeti does not have a glove compartment capable of accommodating the presenter of *Ross Kemp on Gangs*. But no matter, because Skoda very helpfully agreed to modify a Yeti with a second dashboard installed across the middle of the car and with careful framing Jeremy could sit on the back seat and appear to be behind the wheel of a normal car. There was just one problem: Ross Kemp was busy. Or at least, too busy to lend himself once more to *Top Gear* as a comedy prop. Happily, the delightful actress Sienna Miller agreed to step, quite literally, into the void between the real dash and the dummy one, then poke her head into the glovebox. This was cutting-edge consumer journalism.

There was often talk in the *Top Gear* office about the 'rule of three' which said that many things – jokes, metaphors, presenters – worked best when there were more than two but fewer than four. It's a pretty standard rule of writing and it seems to work, to be effective, to have some substance. And, since we'd done three 'sensible' road tests perhaps it was a good time to lay Mr Needham's complaints to rest.

Then, in summer 2012, we got a call from Twickenham stadium saying that they were about to replace their pitch and did we have any interest in giving the old one a send-off by utterly ruining it? As luck would have it, around the same time Kia announced a new Cee'd and said they could let us have a load of cars to do with as we pleased, if we were interested. When you said 'as you pleased', we asked, did you mean take them to a legendary sporting venue and attempt to play rugby with them? Um, yeeees, replied Kia, cautiously. So that's what we decided to do. For what end, we didn't know. Technically, *Top Gear* was in some downtime between series, we weren't scheduled to shoot anything for weeks, but there was just a narrow window between the last game on the old turf and the people arriving to tear it up. Jeremy was free, James was free, the cars were ready. It was time to play rugby. And, despite the obvious problem that cars can't catch, the match went rather well. Now we just had to decide what to do with it. We could, perhaps, have transmitted it in the next series as a stand-alone game. But perhaps it would be more fun as the finale to another sensible road test.

We started to think of other tests we might do, perhaps involving Ross Kemp or Sienna Miller or both. Then we got a call from Hollywood. Would *Top Gear* like to come to Budapest to report on the making of the new *Die Hard* movie? Visiting film sets to see other people at work wasn't really the sort of thing we did. We'd love to come over, we replied. But we don't want to see you doing some car stunts and stuff. We just want Bruce Willis to get into a medium-sized Korean car and honk the horn. Amazingly, they said yes. They were probably a bit confused, but the main thing is they said yes. We got a Cee'd over to Hungary, we turned up on the set, we waited around a bit, the A-list talent arrived in full John McClane get-up, obligingly beeped the horn, and within five minutes he was gone. It was well worth it. *Top Gear* had been offered some time with Bruce Willis and we had turned it into an utterly throwaway moment.

Inspired by this, we decided to try another blink-and-you'll-miss-it Kia moment with 'a local guitarist'. The local guitarist was called Eric Clapton, but we somehow forgot to mention this. 'He'll do it, but don't ask him to play "Layla",' warned his people. 'He *won't* do "Layla",' they insisted. A day later we turned up at his house with the Cee'd. The affable axe legend picked up his instrument, already plumbed into the car. 'What would you like?' he asked breezily. As one, the crew shared the same thought: Don't say 'Layla', don't say 'Layla'. 'What about this?' Clapton suggested. And then he played 'Layla'. What a top man.

Giddy with the success of our star-studded sensibleness we came up with one more test which involved asking current Cee'd-driving celeb lap board topper Matt LeBlanc to set a lap time in the new model to compare against his efforts in the old one. The only problem was, Matt LeBlanc lives in Los

Angeles. But that was to overlook what a fan he was of the show and when we suggested he make a cameo appearance as a test driver he offered to make a special trip to Dunsfold. This was the power of sensibleness.

After treating such an A-list cavalcade with such casualness in the name of consumer journalism, it really was time to rest the 'factual' road tests unless we could find some way to top that. Which we probably couldn't. This would have been sad news for sensible reporting and for Mr Needham, but for one thing. The sensible reports were very real but, between you and me, Mr Needham didn't really exist.

# The Naan Bread

There was an unwritten rule on *Top Gear* that the further away from cars we got, the worse an item was going to be. As a general guide, if you didn't see a car moving on screen for over two minutes, the film was probably crap. Unfortunately, we sometimes forgot about this rule. Which is how come we ended up making an idiotic thing in which we took over an art gallery and filled it with motoring-themed things. If memory serves, it came about because of some bet Jeremy had made with a mate who ran a real art gallery, but casual bets aren't necessarily a good basis for actual television programmes. Otherwise we could have filled 40 minutes watching Hammond trying to fit six Creme Eggs into his mouth.

Before anyone realised this, some very nice people at a gallery in Middlesbrough had agreed to let us take over their building and James May and I were on a train to the North East in cheery mood. I think we spent most of the journey looking at Triumph Dolomites for sale on the internet. We'd had this idea to record a real-time audio guide to our exhibition, the kind you listen to on a little rented headset when you visit a proper gallery. Except ours would be a gag based on the gallery's many rooms and James's on-screen persona, which had a poor sense of direction, inspired by James's real-life persona, which also had a poor sense of direction. We thought the headset idea sounded hilarious. Then we realised that for it to work (which is to say, to send baffled members of the public blithering about into walls and down fire escapes and into the disabled loo), we'd have to record a full-length commentary for real. Hence we were sent up to the location early and James spent the afternoon wandering about the gallery, describing left and right turns in excessive and baffling detail while I sat in the café downstairs and occasionally rang him to ask how he was getting on, which would prompt him to tell me to sod off, and this too would be recorded onto the commentary along with, if I remember correctly, a part where he broke off a speech about sculpture to go for an actual wee. Eventually, the idiotic commentary was recorded and we went to the hotel for a drink.

The next morning there was some co-ordinated grand plan which involved Hammond going off to plug our terrible art show on local radio, Jeremy driving his rubbish 'art car' to the location and James hanging some more pictures or something. This is where it went a bit wrong. May and I loafed around the hotel with our film crew for ages having an agreeable breakfast and then someone couldn't find some car keys and someone else had lost their phone. There was a general bit of dithering about before, finally, we headed towards the gallery. We all had a lot to do and everyone else had been busily filming for ages, except us. Jeremy rang me to see how we were getting on and I had to explain that we were still in the back of a crew van, bumbling out of the hotel car park.

The thing about Jeremy is that he likes exaggeration. Also, he's very good at it. So his reaction was quite hyperbolic.

'You're *WHAT*?' he boomed. 'This is a *complete* DISASTER.' I was tired and possibly a bit hung over and not in the mood for overstatement.

'It's *not* a complete disaster,' I snapped. 'If you want a fucking disaster . . .'

At this point the line went dead. In retrospect, this was almost certainly because we were on mobile phones and one of them had dropped the connection. But at the time, I didn't think of that. I thought Jeremy had hung up on me. And I was very cross about this. How rude, I thought. How bloody sodding rude. And this put me in a foul mood that somehow lasted all day and into the evening, right up to the point when the director said he had quite enough footage with Clarkson and May in it and perhaps I would like to get them out of his way by taking them for a curry. 'Ooh, a curry,' said James. I struggle to think of a moment when James May would turn down the offer of a curry. Unless of course he was already consuming a curry, and even then he'd have to think twice before turning down another. So the three of us went into Middlesbrough to get a curry.

The curry house we were recommended didn't, I would guess, get a lot of stars walking into its premises. As a consequence, Jeremy and James were treated like royalty and immediately ushered to the 'VIP area', which was a table at the back, up a couple of steps. Ironic really, since a lot of very famous people notoriously don't 'do' stairs. Unfortunately, although a tiny set of steps might have repelled Mariah Carey, it did not hold back the Indian food connoisseurs of 'Boro, all of whom wanted to come up to the VI table and get autographs from the unexpected Ps sitting at it. The restaurant realised this might become a bit annoying and, without being asked, brought forth a solution. Which was to get a member of their staff to stand in front of our table as 'security'. And to make his role clear, he was wearing a high-visibility vest. Ironically, this only drew more attention to us. Oh look, people probably said to each other, there are two blokes off the telly, over there behind that lone man standing motionless inside a dimly lit restaurant wearing a bright yellow tabard.

Of more concern to me was that as soon as we sat down James's phone rang and he started a lengthy conversation with his girlfriend. This meant that Jeremy and I were left to make conversation. Which was a problem since, as you might remember, I was still in a petulant piss of a mood, specifically with him, and didn't want to talk.

The thing about giving someone the cold shoulder is that it often helps if they're at least dimly aware of what you're doing and why. Jeremy wasn't. And I wasn't about to tell him, because we were men in a curry house in Middlesbrough on a Friday night, trying to ignore the hi-vis-wearing waiter's arse that hovered above our tray of dips. We weren't about to start talking about emotions. So instead I sat there furiously texting people, like a narky teenager.

'Are you alright?' asked Jeremy in a personable way that only made me more furious with his inability to understand my huffiness.

'Yes, I'm fine,' I hissed, staring intently at my mobile in the manner of a surly youth on a bus.

In 13 years I can remember only two other proper arguments with Clarkson. One was about the MG ZT 260 track test and my insistence that the silly music was setting the wrong tone. 'I know why you're saying this,' said Jeremy. 'It's because you like that car.' And one was over his insistence on calling the Ferrari Enzo the F60.

'But it's not called that!'

'It is now.'

The frustrating difference with this argument was that Jeremy appeared to be unaware of it. Finally, May wrapped up his interminable phone conversation. At last. James was here to save us from conversational awkwardness with some erudite observations about the quality of the chutney. Unfortunately for me, he'd been talking for so long that our food was turning up. And this is when the naan bread arrived.

This wasn't a naan in the sense you might imagine. It was not a loose ellipse of doughy goodness that could fit on a small silver plate with only a little overhang. What they had brought us that evening was a sheer sheet of bread, a thing so vast it could be used as a metric for how much rainforest had been destroyed that week, and which hung vertically like a schooner's sail from its own intricate tower of scaffolding. As two or three waiters lowered it into position, I realised with dread it was cutting my one lifeline out of this terrible evening, shutting down all lines of communication with James May. A naan curtain had descended across the table.

'Are you okay?' Clarkson asked. 'You seem distant.'

'I'm fine,' I insisted grumpily.

For a brief moment it seemed we were on the world's worst first date, stuck between a bouncer's back and a vast wall of ghee-sodden bread in a cosy cubicle of our own conversational awkwardness. I tore at the western edge of the epic bread in a frantic attempt to eat my way through to James on the other side but it was useless. I would need help. I raised my voice and exhorted May to eat some bread. 'What?' he said from somewhere deep within naania. I sent another five texts to other members of the team, imploring them to join us and help me scoff my way to May. They didn't reply. Jeremy and I ate in silence.

The next morning no more was said. The air was clear and we got on with filming baffled Middlesbroughians looking at car art. We had quite a nice time up there. The curry, I'm certain, was particularly good. The art gallery film, I'm equally certain, was not.

# Secrets of Success

If you want an in-depth explanation of how and why *Top Gear* became so successful, I'm afraid I have no idea. Not in any way that could be written down and then synthesised in a laboratory. I don't think that would work. You'd just end up with a strange and confusing programme in which every other voice-over line started with the word 'meanwhile'.

If you boiled *Top Gear* down to its basics, it was a show in which a man standing in an aircraft hangar introduced a car which he then skidded about a bit, and then a mute man in a crash helmet drove around in a circle, and then the man and two other men would talk about cars for six minutes, and then the three men would be on a wet airfield somewhere and they would attempt to make something but they would disagree about how to do it, and then someone you vaguely recognised would be in the aircraft hangar talking about their new film, and then they would drive a hatchback around in a circle, and then the three men would be on the wet airfield again and their attempt to build something would be completely terrible, and then the programme would end.

Would you watch that? Or would you think, *Oh Jesus, I wonder if* Game of Thrones *is on yet?*

*Top Gear* seemed to work because there was more to it than that, some of it science and some of it whatever the opposite of science would be in this context. I don't know. Perhaps double art and then a free period. Obviously a great deal of *Top Gear*'s appeal came from the three presenters and their obvious enthusiasm for their subject matter. Television executives have a strange take on car shows and who should present them. They'd never allow a food programme to be fronted by someone whose favourite dish was chicken nuggets or let someone lead a fashion show simply because they owned a pair of trousers, yet automotive programming was sometimes handed to clueless know-nothings whose claim to be interested in cars was largely because they'd got one. Conversely, Jeremy could deliver lengthy office-bound lectures on electronic brake force distribution, Richard would delay delivering a piece to camera because he simply had to look up the price of second-hand Maserati Quattroportes and James might lose an easy 20 minutes discussing the finer points of the Austin Montego. They were the real deal. More than that, they had a passion for the subject and passion, as proven by everyone from David Attenborough to Peter Snow, is a very watchable thing.

If you're a keen student of film and television writing you may also recognise the presenters as conforming to the personality types of a classic comic trio. You have the power-crazed, headstrong leader. You have the excitable action man who's a bit stupid. And you have the level-headed one who gets ignored. It's pretty much textbook stuff, although it was never engineered to be that way. If you want to get really serious about it, you could argue that the *Top Gear* presenters made up a typical Freudian trio of the ego (Richard), the superego (James) and the id (Jeremy). But let's save that for BBC4. The main thing is, they had enough in common to get along but enough that was different to find each other annoying, frustrating and ridiculous. Yet fundamentally they looked like they were having fun and I suspect a large part of their appeal, especially for men, was that they reminded you of your own bunch of friends or seemed like the group of mates you wished you had. Either way, that made them compelling to watch. Also, in their buffoonery, the presenters provided a strange window into the stubborn, stupid, very occasionally ingenious workings of the male mind which I suspect men related to and women found revealing, if also depressing and annoying.

Of course, that theory only applied to adults. I suspect children didn't overthink it. They just liked the three presenters because they were a rare case of grown-ups on television acting like kids. Not hyperactively talking down, like children's TV presenters, just naturally behaving in a childish way. They were best friends that bickered, they tried to fib their way out of their own mistakes and they got to play with toys all day. These were all relatable things, if you were seven.

This childlike glee and silliness was very important, and it relates to a very sage observation about the show from a former editor of *Top Gear* magazine. Stupid people doing stupid things isn't funny, he said. It's just slightly pitiful. Clever people doing clever things isn't funny either, because it's probably quite boring. But clever people doing stupid things, that's where comedy lies. The loss of dignity, the pig-headed pride, the feeble insistence upon things going wrong that actually this was exactly what they intended. That was another part of *Top Gear*'s appeal; watching the failings of bright, articulate people who should know better. The failings were all part of it. In fact, we used to have an unofficial slogan on the show which said, 'Failure is funny'.

Every so often we'd get approached by one of those outtake shows and be asked if we had any sweepings from the cutting-room floor which could prove amusing. Whenever this happened we'd have to explain that *Top Gear* was one of the few TV shows where we prayed for something to go wrong and that when it did it was not ruthlessly edited out but placed front and centre in the show. Someone falling over, someone stalling a car, someone trying to claim all was well as smoke poured from their engine behind them; the things other shows would hide away were the bedrocks of *Top Gear*'s ongoing lust for disaster.

We enjoyed feeling like the only programme that celebrated cockups. We also liked being the only programme that would, say, visit Transylvania and not once mention Dracula, and we very much enjoyed being the only show that, if required to put the presenters in special clothing, would inevitably leave on all the shop labels to show that the stuff was brand-new and the presenters were out of their depth. Basically, we liked being silly. It's no coincidence that Jeremy was a huge Monty Python fan and his sense of humour erred towards that sort of daftness. We also shared a love of nineties news spoof *The Day Today*, which reared its head in his strung-out, absurd delivery of certain lines on the show (and also in the office; whenever a press release was mislaid Jeremy would shout, 'You've lost the neeeeeeeews!'). Few viewers probably spotted it, but hopefully those who did enjoyed the reference. It seemed important to put in that sort of little detail, to reward those who got it without alienating those who didn't.

As the audience got broader, there were probably more who didn't get references than did. It was hard to know really. Who was the typical *Top Gear* viewer? Empirical evidence suggested that *Top Gear* became one of those programmes a whole family could watch together. Dad might like the show for the cars, the kids would like it for the mucking about, mum would find the presenters amusing and secretly fancy Richard a bit. Or James. Or maybe even Jeremy. He did have a bit of an alpha male thing going on.

Beyond the mythical family unit of 1974, the show's audience was harder to pin down. A very demure female doctor friend of mine, a woman with extremely refined tastes, was one of the biggest fans of the show I knew. I also met some oafish petrolheads who didn't like it at all. All sorts of people enjoyed the show. All sorts of people hated the show too. You just couldn't be certain who was in which camp. All we knew is that our audience was a broad church and we'd try to make sure there was something for everyone across a whole series. Three new cars driven on a road trip to keep the nerdier end of the audience happy; some sort of build film in which there was lots of arguing and falling over to amuse the more casual viewer who didn't give a toss about crankshafts. Wilman used to defend daft things like smash-and-bash bus racing with the insistence that it was 'for the kids'. Sometimes I'd counter with my personal benchmark for the other end of the spectrum, which was Rowan Atkinson. He was famously quiet, thoughtful and erudite in real life. He was also a bona fide fan of the show. Whenever we were in the office and a rough cut of some really moronic new item was flickering across the screen, I'd imagine the man who played Blackadder quietly sighing and going off to make a cup of tea.

I hoped that Rowan Atkinson, and indeed anyone with a brain, would forgive our stupidest moments and respect that a lot of the show had more thought and craft put into it than we would care to let on. If you wanted another secret of *Top Gear*'s success, hard work would be it, incorporating a relentless attention to detail and a refusal to do things the easy way. A phrase I never heard in our production office was, 'Oh, that'll do'. Working on *Top Gear* was a completely immersive and intensely full-time job. I once went on holiday and stepped off the plane to find several messages from Jeremy on my mobile.

'Porter, can you call me.' Beep.

'Porter, Clarkson, call me. Urgent.' Beep.

'Porter, Clarkson, really need to speak to you ASAP.'

My phone ran out of battery before I could ring him back. There were more messages on the machine at home.

'Porter, it's Clarkson, give me a ring as soon as you can.' Beep.

'Porter, it's Wilman. Jezza really needs to speak to you, give him a call as soon as you can mate.' Beep.

'Porter, Clarkson. Where are you? Call me. It's urgent.'

*Oh God*, I thought. *Someone's died*. I rang Jeremy straight away.

'Got your messages, been on holiday, what's going on?'

'Oh, don't worry,' he said. 'It's nothing.' I never did find out what he wanted.

Over the years I worked from time to time on various other programmes and some of them were quite astonishingly wishy-washy in ways that wouldn't stand up on *Top Gear*. I'd go so far as to claim we had the hardest-working and most dedicated team in all of television, and I'm not just saying that because I'm still friends with many of them and hope they'll buy me a drink.

If another show wanted to copy our work ethic I'm sure they could and did. What they'd find harder to replicate was another vital part of what made *Top Gear* work, which was the relationship between Clarkson and Wilman. It's rare to find a presenter and an executive producer who are best mates as well as colleagues. They knew each other inside out so they could short-circuit a lot of normal blather in their conversations and ring each other at any time of the day or night to discuss an idea or concern without the usual social niceties that say you shouldn't bother someone with work stuff at 9 p.m. on a Saturday. That sort of tight bond between the on- and off-screen big cheeses shouldn't be underestimated, as it was the vital heart of the show's production.

The viewer had no idea of all this, of course, and probably wouldn't even be interested. They just wanted an hour of amusing television on a Sunday evening, though I'd say this too was a part of *Top Gear*'s success. Sunday nights were traditionally barren times for TV scheduling. As a kid, you'd hear the music to something boring like *Songs of Praise* and it would only remind you with a crushing certainty that the weekend was over and tomorrow you had to go back to school. When, in 2002, they told us *Top Gear* was getting a Sunday night slot rather than the Thursday evening scheduling the show used to enjoy, we were initially despondent. Sunday night? That's like being shown exclusively in an old people's home. Actually, it was good for us because it meant we could make the timing our own and, though it took us a while to realise this, provide a noisy hour of unthinking entertainment before you had to iron the kids or put your work shirts to bed. We were once involved in an ill-fated football show project that would have occupied the same slot on a Sunday evening and for which we came up with the slogan, 'the weekend's not over until we say it is'. I think we could just as well have used that for *Top Gear*. Except it sounds a bit self-important. But it had a ring of truth too. Unless you were watching a rerun on Dave. In which case, Wednesday afternoon is not over until we say . . . oh, there's another one on straight afterwards. But having an original transmission slot that became a little piece of escapism before the reality of an incoming Monday sank in was definitely to our advantage and a little thing that helped us along.

In truth, however, I think the success of *Top Gear* came from many things aligning in a unique way. Three presenters who naturally got on, backed by a great team thinking of unusual ideas and carrying them out with an attention to detail that extended from the beautiful way they were filmed to the precise manner in which they were edited, and the whole thing broadcast at a time when people were at home as a family and just wanted to be entertained. It's all that, and it's more than that too, like wondering why the Rolling Stones were enduring and successful when some other bands weren't. It's really just some blokes playing instruments and singing. But at the same time, it's not just that. Sometimes it's best not to overthink these things. Oh look, James May has just fallen over! Ha ha!

# *Jumping the Shark*

You probably know the expression 'jump the shark', used to define the moment when a TV show passes its peak and resorts to silly gimmicks from which it can never recover. It comes from the US sitcom *Happy Days* in which motorcycle-loving coolness enthusiast The Fonz put on some water skis and literally jumped over a shark. After this bizarre sequence (written to showcase actor Henry Winkler's real-life water-skiing skills, fact fans) *Happy Days* continued to top American ratings and lasted for another six series, so it's not like it killed the show. But jumping the shark is about something more subtle and insidious than that. It's the moment when fans begin to lose trust in their beloved show, fearing that the producers will come up with ever more elaborate ways to insult their intelligence.

Jumping the shark, not literally, was always in the back of my mind on *Top Gear*. Whenever an idea started to get silly or bloated or had a needless flash fire written into it, the fear would rise again. 'Instead of this,' someone would mutter. 'Why don't we get a car, and a ramp, and a shark . . .'

Jumping the shark seems to happen when the makers of a programme become desperate to top what's gone before and do so with some cack-handed stunt or gimmick. In *Top Gear*'s case, it led to moments when we couldn't trust that funny things might happen naturally, as they had in the past. We had to make sure they happened by planning them in advance. Hence the 'accidental' fire in the caravan holiday film of series 8. The camp-site owners thought, not unreasonably, that a burning caravan on their property would be bad for business, so it wasn't even shot in the same location as the rest of the sequence, the whole set-up being filmed in a field up the road with a broadly matching backdrop. We were faking it, and we got busted for it.

The problem with fakery is that once it's been exposed viewers start to look for it in everything. There develops an assumption that everything you're doing is fake, which undermines the many real things seen on screen. This led us, in a long-winded way, to the Nile special in which Hammond was almost constantly leaving things on his stove which looked as if they could cause a fire at any moment, but then didn't. It was a knowing nod to the expectation of synthesised calamity. We'd reached a point where we couldn't surprise viewers with what we did, but hopefully we could surprise them with what we didn't do.

Of course, sometimes a potential shark-jump moment came not from an engineered disaster but just from the item being a bit rubbish. Usually, this was when we got too far away from cars themselves and entered realms we had no business occupying. The art gallery film, for example. Or the time we took over a radio station. That one was absurdly complicated to set up, what with finding a radio station that would let Clarkson, Hammond and May take over their drive-time show and the technical difficulties of setting up a video link to the traffic camera control room and yet, when it came down to it, most of the film was about the presenters being shut in a room and trying to be funny. It had its moments, my favourite being when Richard visibly angered the sports presenter by wilfully misunderstanding his tetchy remarks about cricket, but in general it was a bit pointless, a bit self-indulgent and had the whiff of water skis scudding lightly up a ramp. It's easy to say this now, of course. At the time, it seemed like a great idea. Why wouldn't *Top Gear* take over a commuter-centric radio show and revamp it with some brilliant new ideas? That sounded like just the sort of thing we would do. We'd spend a long time thinking over ideas, but sometimes you couldn't see how duff they were until you'd filmed them, edited them, put them on television and let nine years pass before writing a book about them.

This isn't to say, by the way, that everything *Top Gear* did that was silly and set up had to be an utter clunker that sent our leather-jacketed heroes sailing gracefully over the head of a big bitey fish. The Reliant Robin film, for example, was one of my very favourite things we ever did and provided a perfect example of how we could cock about without insulting the intelligence of the audience by making it very clear from the off that we weren't asking anyone to believe this was real. This could have been the shark jump to end all shark jumps, especially if we'd filmed as originally scripted. Jeremy and I wrote the Robin film up at his place in Oxfordshire and based it around a set-up in which all three presenters were instructed to live as Northerners in the 1970s. There they were in a terraced house, with Hammond in a tin bath in front of the fire and James stroking a whippet and various other bits of clichéd stupidity. Then off they went in their funny little three-wheeled cars, which inevitably fell over all the time. We howled with laughter in Jeremy's office as we came up with lines like a phone call which ended, 'That were Eunice at number 14. Our Richard's gone o'er agin'. Sometimes two blokes in a room can get wrapped up in their own little world and forget that what they're writing is basically shite. Triumphantly, we finished the script and I headed back to London. By the time I got there, I'd gone right off this idea. It was too set-up, it required too much acting and it made very little sense. Thankfully, when I got to my computer there was an email from Jeremy, who'd realised the exact same thing. He gave it a complete rethink, stripped it back, took out the gratuitous arsing about and put in some actual facts about Robins. The crucial thing that remained was an unspoken invitation to the viewer which said sit back, relax, pop your brain out for a few minutes and just enjoy the silliness. We know this isn't real, you know this isn't real, but we hope it amuses you. As long as you don't ask the audience to believe something that's clearly unbelievable, you're probably okay.

I thought the Reliant Robin film showed that *Top Gear* could do silly and set-up films as long as we didn't try to pretend they were anything but. It felt like we'd found a nice formula for that. And then we went and completely forgot this with what I think could be our closest attempt to leap over a Great White's back – *The Sweeney*.

How we ended up with this one is simple: a new movie of the seventies cop show was being made and the producers approached *Top Gear* to ask if we would take care of their car chase, reasoning that no one in Britain knew more about making cars look cool and exciting on camera. This was very flattering. It sounded like the makings of a good item. Trouble is, to show us doing it properly sounded a bit boring.

To leave Jeremy and Richard to do it and make a right cock of things seemed like the more *Top Gear* thing to do, even if it risked contrivance and calamity you could see coming from 20 miles away.

From then on the entire thing became a total pain in the underparts. For one thing, the BBC were nervous about what they saw as free promotion for someone else's movie and pored over every element of our plans. The Sweeney people had their baddies driving a Range Rover which we argued would be too tall and wobbly to do any plausible driving high jinks, so we set about finding a sportier car which carried the whiff of no good. Naturally, this was a Jaaaag. Then the Beeb started worrying about product placement. The original script contained a short chase through a caravan park which I rewrote into something much longer and more complicated and using several locations only to find there was no money in the movie budget to do any of the stuff I'd come up with. We definitely couldn't help on that score because we couldn't be allowed to fund a private enterprise. Between the BBC editorial policy and the scouting of locations for a chase that couldn't be paid for and the finding of cars and tracking vehicles and so on, this item gradually began to consume the entire team. It was an unwelcome distraction. We were busy preparing for the 18th series, we had many, many things to do but now we had an entire production wrapped up in just one thing. It wouldn't have been a surprise to find that James May, who had nothing to do with this, had popped into the office for a cup of tea and somehow become roped in to finding a static caravan supplier.

To my mind, the situation was out of hand. We were compromising other items in development just to get this thing made, all because of the foolish pride of proving to the movie people that yes, we were the best in the world at filming cars. Really, the right answer should have been, that's very kind of you but we're a bit busy. I made this clear in the office in a huffy teenage manner but no one was listening. They were all on the phone trying to find exploding trees or slow-motion doves or something.

Maintaining a grumpy stance on all this, I ducked out of going on the shoot itself. Then the night before it started, I got a message from Andy Wilman that I should get myself down to the location in Kent tomorrow. I rang Wilman straight away and shouted at him. This is all self-indulgent bullshit I ranted, and you can shove your shoot up your arse. Yes, that's right, I'm exceedingly professional.

I got up early the next morning and drove to Kent. Well, you know what those motivational speaker types say; there's no 'I' in 'team'. Although there are several in 'completely twatting pointless *Top Gear* item'. Still, I did my bit and showed up for day one of the shoot. And day two. And day three. The movie people were very nice. So were the actors. And while Clarkson and Hammond clowned around, our other film unit with a proper director and state-of-the-art tracking car got some great shots for the real movie. But that didn't stop the finished item being forced and pointless and a steaming puddle of runny turd on your telly.

In the office, I didn't disguise my dislike for *The Sweeney* film. Just to be contrary, Jeremy felt duty bound to defend it. We got stuck in a stubborn man cycle of trashing and defending it.

'It was terrible,' I'd spit.

'It was brilliant,' Jeremy would insist.

'It was the worst thing we've ever done.'

'It was literally the best item I can ever remember.'

'I heard people watching it actually died of disgust.'

'Watching that item actually cured some children of their diseases.' And so on.

On reflection, the bit with Ray Winstone and Plan B in the car pretending to do a jump is genuinely funny. Maybe *The Sweeney* film isn't that bad. Mind you, I don't think Jeremy thinks it's that good either. But obviously neither of us could admit that.

The biggest problem with *The Sweeney* VT is that it came hot on the hopeless heels of the underperforming India special and this run of contrived silliness wasn't good for our shark-jumping record. But then in the following series we made the P45 micro car, rallied a Bentley Continental GT and played rugby with Kias, proving that we could be exceptionally daft without completely insulting the viewers' intelligence.

I don't know if we ever truly jumped the shark, since it's quite a hard thing to define. We definitely owned the ramps but I hope they rarely felt the desperate caress of the water skis.

# Plan of Hope and Glory

In the first few series of new *Top Gear* each programme had a theme. One week it would be luxury, another it might be Lamborghini. Sometimes the theme would be obvious, other times we might barely mention it until at some point it was decided that the themes were too restrictive and viewers probably didn't give a flying monkey's bum about them anyway. So they were dropped. But at the end of series 20 the themed show made a one-off reappearance for an episode we called Best of British.

There were a few reasons for this. Firstly, in among all the mucking about and saying things were crap, it was nice to end on a programme that had a more positive tone. Secondly, on the mysterious Rubik's Cube of the *Top Gear* office programme contents whiteboard, we could stick Jeremy's Jaguar F-type review along with Richard's Range Rover Sport test and send James off to look at the new London bus, which we'd been toying with featuring for ages. And to cap it all, the star in the Reasonably Priced Car would be that proud Briton, Australia's Mark Webber. Well, no one said the theme had to be all-encompassing.

All we needed to cap off this festival of chest-puffing national pride was a memorable finale in which flags could be waved and tubs could be thumped. And so it was decided that we'd gather together one example of every single motorised, wheeled thing made on British soil and line them up on the runway at Dunsfold. But hang on a sec, the whole point of this feature was to turn the jingoism up to the max. A line-up on an airfield, that was at the patriotic fervour level of a Princess Diana tea towel. We needed to go further. We needed the full Nigel Farage's Union Flag underpants. We would do this on The Mall. It was one of those times when *Top Gear* was unbowed by the weight of its own ambition. Only this time we couldn't be rubbish.

You might think getting dozens of machines lined up on one of London's most recognisable roads would be a simple job. It's not. But it speaks volumes about the skill and dedication of the *Top Gear* production team that it was made to look like something effortless and not, as is actually the case, the product of many months of extremely hard work.

Shutting down The Mall, for example, takes some doing. Obviously it's possible, but just getting the permission requires endless meetings, a great pile of paperwork, many kind words and a small pile of cash. And then, just when you think it's all sorted, you casually mention that you'd like to fly a drone over the proceedings and somewhere in the distance you hear nine trees being felled to make enough paper for the permission forms.

Then there are the machines themselves. How many powered, wheeled devices do you think are built in Britain? Whatever your answer, it's actually five times that number. Unless you were being silly and said a million. There are cars, there are lorries, there are motorcycles, there are earth movers, there are racers, there are lawnmowers; the breadth of stuff screwed together on one large island is pretty breathtaking. And we wanted one of each.

It was remarkable the stuff that started coming out of the woodwork once the team started digging. I mean, I pride myself on being the kind of encyclopaedic car geek other people avoid at parties, but there was stuff I'd never heard of in my life, and lots of it.

Managing this massive list took immense dedication. It's all well and good ringing some tiny sports car company or enthusiastic hearse maker and sounding them out on the possibility of fetching up on The Mall one weekend for a spot of filming, but it takes more work, more follow-up phone calls and constant reassurance to make sure everyone actually turns up when asked.

Nothing was as straightforward as it might have seemed. When it was decided that the presenters would arrive on The Mall in red, white and blue F-types, Jaguar said yes, absolutely, no problem at all. Apart from the blue one. So that became another job for someone; to stay on top of this, to pester regularly, to turn on the charm, to become a right royal pain in the arse in the knowledge that the alternative might be to let it slide, allow others to assume it wasn't important and then end up with a patriotic finale in which a fleet of Jags cruised down The Mall in those classic British colours of red, white and bright orange. I suppose we could have turned it into a joke about Bhutan. But this wasn't really the time or the place for flag-based high jinks. In the end, Jag found a preproduction F-type in the right colour and just one of many problems was solved.

The logistical mind-frig didn't end with simply getting the location and the cars, however, because with that many vehicles the mechanics of getting everything in the right place at the right time involved a load of extra head scratching until a perfect plan of action had been refined.

On the evening of Saturday 22 June 2013 we assembled at sundown. Half the team milled around on The Mall itself, killing time and watching slightly pissed tourists totter past. The other half occupied our designated staging area on Constitution Hill, up the side of Buckingham Palace, and waved in the endless line of lorries dropping off cars and other machines. Finally, at midnight, The Mall was ours.

A meticulous floor plan had been worked out so we knew exactly where each thing was supposed to be, and vehicles would be released according to how far forward they were in the line-up with communications maintained by mobile phone, by walkie-talkie and by people waving a hi-vis vest over their heads and shouting 'OI! OVER HERE!'.

If you've ever tried to park a car in a very precise spot, you'll know how annoyingly hard it can be. Now imagine trying to do that with dozens of cars. The varying widths of various machines flattered to deceive, which made absolute alignment easier, and also enabled us to fudge our way around a pedestrian crossing in the middle of The Mall that wasn't on the paper plan. The gap between the back of one car and the front of the next was more important and had been decided at precisely one metre. Any less and everything would look too bunched. Any more and the ruddy huge trucks, coaches and diggers at the back end would have spilled straight off the end of The Mall and found themselves poking into Her Majesty's pantry. To achieve this accurate vehicle spacing we used a computer-designed, laser-calibrated, GPS-compatible, metre-long piece of wood. It was only when the cars kept on coming and we were lining them up in parallel that we realised we should have bought two.

All through the early hours of the morning we worked, calling in the next batch of wheeled things, lining them up, and then the next and the next and the next until The Mall was full. The final row of machines slotted into place just as dawn broke over London. The presenters arrived shortly afterwards, their mouths agape at the sight of a daft idea in the office made real and on a scale they hadn't quite imagined. We were very proud of what Britain built and also, if we were allowed such things, a little bit proud of ourselves. I could have cried, although that might have been the immense tiredness brought on by spending all night shouting 'LEFT HAND DOWN A BIT' at an endless series of machines.

We shot an ending for the entire sequence in which Jeremy remembered one British-made machine not represented in the line-up and returned in his P45 microcar. Then Hammond said he was a total . . . and there was a rude word, obscured by a cannon going off. But the sight of all the vehicles stretching off up The Mall seemed to be enough and a heavy-handed attempt at comedy would only undermine it. The scene was cut from the final edit. You can tell as much from Jeremy's final 'goodnight', which is clearly dubbed on afterwards in voice-over.

We were very pleased with this film. It took a lot of effort and organisation for the sake of one stirring scene but it was all worth it. Although the mad, sleepless night on The Mall is only my second-favourite memory from the Best of British ending to series 20.

Weeks later we were in the studio recording the links for this final show and, it being the end of the run, it would have been nice to celebrate with an adult drink. Normally this isn't possible because Dunsfold is in the middle of nowhere and many people are driving. But on this occasion, there was a solution. The nice chap who brought down the new London bus for the studio said he would drive us all back to the city where we could carry on our merrymaking at a handy pub. We were delighted. Once the director called a wrap some drink was taken, a few nibbles were scoffed and then we grabbed a smorgasbord of booze and piled onto the top deck, dragging James May along for good measure. As it turns out, buses aren't very fast on the motorway but it didn't matter because we were cheery and squiffy and in no hurry.

As we pulled into London we stopped at some traffic lights next to another double-decker bus. The occupants of this normal bus were the expected Wednesday night mid-evening, late-working commuters. They looked miserable. I caught the eye of an especially deflated chap up against the window as he looked over at our bus, which was ostensibly just the same as his. Except his bus was muggy and sweaty and probably had a single empty can rolling up and down the floor, whereas our bus had 15 people dancing around swigging wine from the bottle in the company of that bloke with shaggy hair from off the telly. The man's expression never changed, but his eyes said I wonder what area that bus goes to, and if there's any way I can move there.

*Top Gear* didn't do big series finales very often. It didn't get on a bus very often either. But it worked out surprisingly well when we did.

# Drunk on Television

Some time in 2009 we accidentally hit upon a new occasional strand for the show in which two of the presenters were sent away to make a nostalgia-sodden film about a well-known car maker. It began with Lancia, which Jeremy and Richard claimed had made more great cars than anyone else, and moved on to Saab. We were going to paint a picture of a bafflingly contrary company that completely lost the plot until Jeremy, James and I spent an afternoon at Clarkson's flat reading up about them and concluded that actually they were brilliant. Mad, but brilliant. These films were gentle and, unusually for *Top Gear*, they had facts in them. As such, they provided a nice change in pace and they had a certain kind-hearted charm to them.

In the run-up to series 22 we decided to make another and Jeremy reckoned it should be about Jaguar. But there was a problem. Everyone is pretty familiar with Jag's greatest hits and there aren't many obscure or unusual artefacts in their history cupboard. Also, Jeremy kept erring towards a rant in which he decried the modern Jaguar range for losing the soft-riding suspension and trad styling found among Jags of old, even though the latest more dynamic and modern-looking cars were selling better than ever before. With this in mind, it felt like Clarkson and May would simply sound like two sad old farts reading out a disgruntled letter to the *Daily Telegraph*. Oh, and there was a plan to make a skit in the style of The Interceptors spoof from series 17, but about a mythical and disreputable character called Jaaaaaaag Man, which could have been hi-hi-hilarious or an achingly feeble stab at sketch comedy. All signs pointed to a Jag retrospective teetering between brilliance and utter horse plop, and about to fall onto the smelly side. This plan was put to one side while we thought about other car companies we could look at instead.

One day Jeremy suggested Peugeot. This seemed like an excellent idea. We liked Peugeots from the 1960s and 1970s when they were simple and rugged, we liked Peugeots from the 1980s and 1990s when they were sporty and pretty, and then we didn't like Peugeots from the 2000s when they became lumpen and ugly, something we'd often pointed out on the show. As we looked into the wider history of the company, it became clear that they were prone to sudden changes of direction on a grand scale and this formed the solid backbone of the film, combining a proper history lesson with a chunk of warped *Top Gear* logic that used their colourful history as an explanation for why they'd become a bit rubbish. This would then lurch into an extended sequence in which Jeremy and James pretended to be the typical Peugeot drivers much talked about on the show, which is to say befuddled, incompetent and uninterested in driving. To my mind, this bit was a worry. The viewer knew that Jeremy and James could drive perfectly well, and without hunching over the wheel in the manner of a myopic mouth-breather. But the plan here was for them to do all of those things. I thought you should always be able to turn on halfway through an item and get the gist of what was going on but with this plan you could be left confused. Were they themselves or were they acting? Had they lost their marbles or were they pretending to have misplaced them? There was an impurity to this idea that bothered me. Clarkson, however, was convinced it would make the point and sometimes you have to accept that slightly wonky concepts can turn out well if the flaws are steamrollered by stuff that is simply funny. The only thing we needed, as we planned this item, was a bridge between the history lesson, which was quite serious, and the pretend Peugeot driving, which was very silly. That's when we came up with the idea of the meeting.

What we'd do is mock-up a scene purporting to be the Peugeot board meeting at which they decided to make only bad cars in future. Obviously we couldn't claim to be recreating an actual meeting unless we wanted to get sued to next Sunday so it had to be preposterous. There would be outrageous accents, there would be fake moustaches, there would be an accordion player in a stripy jersey and the Eiffel Tower would be visible through the window in the accepted Hollywood movie style for any action taking place in Paris. It had to be deliberately absurd and the kind of cartoonish depiction of Frenchness seen on something like *The Simpsons*. Although it was harder for us to get away with such things on account of not being an actual cartoon.

Filming took place in Oxfordshire since Jeremy wanted to shoot a scene of dithering driving on the infamously idiot-unfriendly double mini-roundabout in Chipping Norton. This was a delight to all concerned since it was about the only shoot around this time that didn't seem to happen in Kent. It's hard to explain why *Top Gear* suddenly became magnetically drawn to the Garden of England, especially since we mostly ended up shooting in what appeared to be its compost heap and its flower bed where the dog goes to wee. The thing about Kent is that it's extremely easy to get to if you live in southeast London or another part of Kent. If you don't live in either of these places, it manages the incredible feat of seeming to be quite near and yet actually taking ages to reach, possibly on account of the vast capital city that stands in your way. Not that this troubled us on the Peugeots shoot since we were in the Cotswolds, the weather was beautiful, we got to zoom about in some lovely old cars, and then at the end of the day we'd shoot the meeting scene.

The amount of work put into this stupid, throwaway scene gives an indicator of the general level of detail that went into the average *Top Gear* shoot. A conference room had been found at a country hotel which had the right amount of grand, wood-panelledness to give the feeling of a boardroom at a long-established company. The only problem being that it didn't look out over the Eiffel Tower and wasn't likely to any time soon on account of being between Witney and Long Hanborough. To address this problem, a large frame bearing a vast green canvas was erected against the outside of the window, which would allow a Parisian view to be dropped onto the shots in the edit suite. Then the room itself was dressed, with pictures of old Peugeots on the walls and the table covered with plates of snails, bowls of onions and other edible clichés.

A few of us volunteered to put on black roll-necks and paint on comically thin moustaches in order to make up the numbers in the scene. We sat at the conference table groaning with xenophobia in front of the strange green window and waited for the film crew to finish their final tweaks to lights and camera positions and so on. I forgot to mention, there was one other prop that appeared in large quantities on the table. It was wine. Not pretend television wine. Just wine. It was the end of the day and I didn't have to drive anywhere afterwards so I took a swig. It wasn't bad. I had another swig. There was a bit of a delay while the cameramen worked out how to deal with the green backcloth reflecting in the table. This could cause terrible problems when they tried to superimpose the Parisian skyline in post-production. A small debate broke out as to how best to sort this. I took another swig of wine. The sound recordist wanted to check the microphones. One of them wasn't right and needed adjusting. I took another swig of wine. Finally, we were ready to shoot. No, wait, we weren't. One of the wine glasses on the table was empty. It was mine. I refilled it in a generous manner and off we went. There was a lot of silliness and ad libbing and several pauses while cameras were repositioned. I kept on drinking the wine. Still not prop wine. Just real wine. The room seemed to become very hot. I got very into my small part as a mythical member of the made-up Peugeot management team, mugging for the camera, delivering faux French lines with gusto and drinking the wine in a realistic manner. Still the filming went on. We'd been in the hot, packed, wine-filled room for over an hour. There's no other way of saying this, I was a bit pissed. Goodness, I thought. Here I am, with a gallon of lard in my hair and a small moustache drawn on my face with eyeliner borrowed from a hotel receptionist, swigging wine and shouting 'MALHEUREUSEMENT!' And this, the last time I checked, is my job. Sweaty, slick-haired and drunk on television. This was tremendous. Another bottle of wine was opened. James started banging the table. I think he was a bit squiffy too. Jeremy began speaking in increasingly

276

mangled French sentences. 'Hey! You should claim thishisish likc a breakfasht meeting,' I spluttered. Jeremy did. Everything seemed hilarious.

It wasn't. Most of it was drivel. Wilman used his typical deft touch in the edit suite to cut out all the bollocks from the Peugeot boardroom scene and reduce it to its salient point. I think it worked out in the end, serving a purpose as a short piece of silliness to telegraph the sudden change in tone from straight-faced history lesson to idiotic slapstick. Some people loved the finished product, others not so much. Personally, I was quite fond of it, especially the way it blended actual information and a serious point with utter stupidity and brainless entertainment. This was what *Top Gear* did. Also, I'm a bit biased about this VT since I'm in it.

The funny thing about briefly appearing on television is that you get lots of messages from friends saying they saw you on telly, some expressing this in the manner of a concerned tip-off as if you may have been kidnapped, drugged and forced to perform as an unconvincing Frenchman without memory of it afterwards. Strangely, the only people I didn't hear from were Hollywood casting agents desperate to bag the subtle and highly nuanced skills that had really brought that faux French person to life. I was quite surprised about that. It was such a complex and multilayered performance. At least, I think it was. I'm not entirely sure. I think I might have been a bit drunk.

# *A Bad Year*

On reflection, 2014 wasn't a good year for *Top Gear*. It started with the fallout from an idiotic and indefensible thing that was said during the Burma special.

Then there was the N-word controversy, introduced and enthusiastically stoked by one of the tabloids. Given that this was based on some footage stolen from an edit suite rather than broadcast material, given that Jeremy didn't actually say the word in question, and given that in all the time I'd worked with him I'd never heard him say that word nor anything close and knew it wasn't the sort of thing he would do, I thought this would fizzle out very quickly. Instead, it just seemed to get bigger and bigger, to the extent that it pushed the news of Gerry Adams getting arrested off the front pages. It seemed strange. The leader of a political party was arrested for alleged involvement in the kidnapping, murder and secret burial of a woman, and that was deemed not as interesting or important as a fat old TV presenter mumbling something that sounded a bit like a bad word. Shortly afterwards Adams was released without charge. Things dragged on rather longer for Clarkson.

Normally Jeremy rode out controversy without giving it the oxygen of further publicity but on this occasion he was mortified and made a short video insisting he would never use the word in question and had censored himself in the broadcast version of the scene so there could be no suggestion that he would or did. It reminded me of that bit in Father Ted when the titular priest gives a slide show to the local Chinese community in which he repeatedly flashes up a picture of himself followed by the words, NOT A RACIST. Still, I suppose he felt he had to do something to make it clear that he wasn't a habitual user of such a terrible word.

The story rumbled on. Questions were being asked at the BBC. I imagine there were a lot of meetings. Within management, there seemed to be those who respected Jeremy as a supremely talented broadcaster and those who found him an oaf and an embarrassment. The second faction seemed to see this new controversy as a chance to take him down a peg, or perhaps even remove the peg altogether. After years of despairing at things Jeremy had said on television, now they were trying to take him down for something he hadn't. More meetings took place. Eventually, they decided not to sack a TV presenter for something he didn't say on TV.

Meanwhile, we were concerned that raw footage, 'rushes' in telly speak, could have been stolen from our edit suite in the first place. If nothing else, there was a principle at stake here. The unvarnished footage from any programme would contain all manner of mistakes and mishaps and beloved stars showing an inability to walk and talk at the same time, or having small meltdowns over an incorrectly ordered latte. It would be in any broadcaster's interests to make sure leaks like this weren't allowed to happen.

Sure enough, the BBC machine swung into action. There would be an investigation. But not into the edit suite leak. It would be an investigation into the workings of our team. Not because of leaking but because they seemed to think we weren't working properly. Except the investigation wouldn't be called an investigation, it would be deemed a 'health check'. Well now hang on, we said. We never broadcast this footage, our presenter re-recorded his own piece to camera to avoid any risk of confusion over the bad word, we didn't do anything wrong, so why are we being investigated? No one could say.

It was hard to avoid the feeling that some members of management hoped the not-an-investigation would turn up tales of rampant racism within the office or expose a browbeaten and utterly miserable production team, desperately stretching the chains of their shackles far enough to carve 'HELP' into the walls of the office. Of course, it didn't. One of our long-serving cameramen, and one of the most decent human beings you could hope to meet, summed it up best when he exercised his freelancer's right not to waste half a day being interviewed. I've worked on this show for a long time, he said. If I didn't like it or agree with it, then I wouldn't. It summed up the feelings of the team, I think. Telly is a fickle business and people move around a lot. But *Top Gear* kept staff a long time, and there had to be something in that. We were a loyal band and a lot of us found this meddling off the back of a newspaper story rather than an actual transgression of corporation code rather insulting. Even so, one by one we all trooped in to see a very nice producer chap who'd been landed with the job of investigating us without calling it an investigation. And at the end of it, management read his report, refused to show us the findings, and decided that what *Top Gear* needed was a second executive producer. The existing executive producer told them to sod off. A little more politely than that, but not much. We were a tightknit gang, we were generally a happy bunch, and we liked the show as it was. Another chief would just make things more complicated. Also, who on earth would want that job, coming into a team that didn't want or need their presence? You might as well offer to put a blob of snot in your own tea, to save anyone else the bother of having to find one. Wilman fought like mad to protect his turf and his team until the BBC agreed that there would be another producer, but they would review our efforts from afar rather than coming into our domain and wondering why their tea always tasted weird. It was a small victory, but the damage was done. Our edit suite had been robbed and a newspaper had used a tenuous story to attack one of our presenters, but somehow we felt under suspicion. Still, we thought, at least we've got that trip to Argentina coming up, that should take our minds off things.

That didn't go very well either. You might have heard. The number plate of Jeremy's Porsche 928 caused a storm of controversy we couldn't have seen coming and inspired some extraordinary conspiracy theories. One said that we'd been planning to visit Argentina and had searched the country to find a car with a plate that could rile the locals. Yet the Porsche had been registered with that sequence of letters and numbers since it was new in 1991. To have found it we'd have needed to hack the DVLA computer system illegally and then hope that the car still existed, that it wasn't a tractor or a lorry or something we didn't want, and that it was for sale. Ah no, said another conspiracy theory, it's the other way around. They found this Porsche for sale, realised the plate said something that could be offensive to Argentinians and decided to shoot their next special in South America, causing trouble wherever they went. This ignores the amount of long-term planning that goes into a *Top Gear* special, planning that had been ongoing for months before the Porsche was bought.

As the newspapers and the websites turned themselves frothy with indignation at another stupid *Top Gear* stunt, our desperate attempts to provide the calm and logical proof that the plate was a pure coincidence sounded like a squeak drowned out by the roar of outrage. The trouble was, we were hoisted by our own petard. To an outsider, this sounded like exactly the sort of idiotic thing *Top Gear* would do. Personally, I thought it seemed too subtle to be one of our daft endeavours. We'd have daubed things down the sides of the cars, as we did in North America all those years ago. And there was no way we were going to do that or anything like it because we already had the extensive research and warnings from local fixers which told us that the Falklands situation was a hot topic in Argentina, it was being raised again by a sabre-rattling government and we should not make light of it if we wanted to come home alive. We had no idea that our best intentions would be betrayed by a horrible quirk of fate.

We'd decided in early spring that South America was the destination for the next special after plans to follow the Silk Road across to China had dissolved due to concerns about the length of the journey. Instead, we would go to the end of the world. It seemed like headline enough to get us rolling. After choosing the location, deciding what cars to take was the next thing we had to sort out, and we mulled on this for a long time before deciding that with a general shift away from big, thirsty V8s in everything from F1 to BMW M-cars, we could give this much-loved engine format a good send-off. The presenters were asked to pick a V8-engined car they liked. We were sitting round in the office with Jeremy one day, looking at various cars online, when he announced that he wanted a Porsche 928. Someone starting tapping in a search. 'No, wait,' he interrupted. '928 GT. That was an epic car. Find me a 928 *GT*.'

Porsche nerds will note that this model bridged the gap between the lounge-lizard S4 and the track-hardened GTS. Many years ago, Jeremy declared it his favourite 928 of all. The problem is, it wasn't a massive success when new and a look round the internet turned up just two for sale. One of our researchers called the numbers in both ads and left messages asking to inspect the cars as soon as possible. Only one of the sellers called back. Since the star cars needed to be on a boat across the Atlantic as soon as possible or they wouldn't make the scheduled start of shooting, a Porsche mechanic was dispatched to have a look at the car. He declared that it was good, and on that basis it was bought remotely, collected from the seller by a shipping company and crated up for its long trip to South America. No one from our team ever physically saw the car and when we checked back we discovered that the plates had been blanked out in the ad.

The three V8s made it to the start point in Bariloche and were stashed at a local hotel. It's here that an Argentinian website, tipped off that *Top Gear* was coming to town, papped the cars and put the pics online. This was slightly annoying for us and warranted a spoiler alert but there was nothing we could do. The presenters and the crew fetched up shortly afterwards and their road trip began. No one read anything into the plate on the 928. If you're from Britain you don't look too hard at British plates since they're a functional fact of life and the start of a shoot is always fraught with many other concerns, leaving precious little time to see hidden messages where none exist. Back in London, however, a keen-eyed person in the office happened to read the comments section underneath the Argentinian car pap's pics and noticed that someone had spotted what they thought was a sly reference to the Falklands War. It was a hell of a leap of logic, but we were concerned that it was getting attention. By the time we got hold of the crew on the ground they'd discovered the growing internet conspiracy too. There were alternative plates in the car, left over from its brief time on a private registration, but to stick them on now would be weird and it would knacker continuity. Instead, we had some 'comedy' plates bearing swear words made up in the UK and planned for Richard and James to affix them to Jeremy's car as an on-camera prank, once they'd been delivered by a crew member joining the group later in the trip. Unfortunately, they got there too late.

You'll have seen what happened next on the show. It wasn't pleasant. Our friends and colleagues had to make an impromptu break for the border and back in the office we could only wait for intermittent reports of their progress. Never had the safety of our team been under such threat and the radio silence as they plunged cross-country was agonising. Mercifully they made it out alive but the star cars weren't so lucky, being ditched at the roadside still full of recording equipment and eventually impounded at a local police station.

The sad thing is, we could have had an upbeat and good-natured ending to this adventure. Our intended The End of the World Cup item could have been great, featuring our three plucky cars against a specially sourced squad of locally made Fiats decked out in national colours and driven by the finest car footballers the region could supply. When everything went to cock, a whole stadium made of shipping containers was almost complete down at the docks in Ushuaia. Better yet, Team Top Gear had a star substitute on his way in the form of England legend Gary Lineker. In fact, when things went sour and our plan went awry, the former footballer was moments away from getting on the plane at Heathrow and only a frantic phone call stopped him flying all the way to Argentina for nothing; except, we must presume, a pretty frosty reception. As an aside, Lineker was later booked to be our studio guest for the eighth show of series 22, just before everything went wrong. If you're a car show hoping for smooth running, my advice is don't book Gary Lineker.

We never got to see our finished stadium, never got to enjoy our plucky lads in their battered cars taking on the local titans in their slick new saloons, never got to enjoy the triumphant moment when the star of England's 1986 World Cup took to the pitch to settle an old score.

The main thing was, our team got out alive. But our best-laid plans had been spoilt and we found ourselves at the centre of a controversy that, for once, wasn't our fault.

It was, all told, the perfectly crappy ending to a pretty bad year. But still, we had 2015 to look forward to. Oh.

# The End

Anyone who ever worked on *Top Gear* was frequently asked two questions. The first was, Who is The Stig? The usual response was to release a smoke grenade, use the ensuing confusion to torch the place and then wait for the extraction blimp in the agreed manner. The second question was, What's Jeremy Clarkson like? I used to answer this one the same way every time; you know what he's like on telly? Well, pretty much that.

It was true. All three of the presenters' television personas were their normal personalities, cranked up a couple of notches. That was particularly true of Jeremy. In real life he was more nuanced and more layered, a fiercely intelligent man with a broader range of interests and sensitivities than he showed off on screen, but the fundamentals were the same. He had, over time, honed a perfect TV version of his most extreme characteristics without seeming self-conscious.

People used to like hearing that Jeremy was basically the same as he appeared on telly. That sounds like fun, they would say. Yes, it is, I would confirm. And it was. Jeremy was funny and clever and he led our merry band from the front. No one cared more about the show than he did. I always got the feeling that Richard and James were capable of giving their all on *Top Gear* duty but were also able to switch off, disappearing home to tinker with old motorbikes and think about other things. With Jeremy, it was a full-time job. Even after 13 years of the new format, he retained a boundless enthusiasm for making the programme and he never stopped thinking of ways to make it better.

The flip side of working with someone so totally dedicated was that he expected the same devotion from those around him. It could make him very demanding. Researchers would work long hours trying to find answers to new questions he'd just thought of the night before a shoot. Producers would reorganise best-laid plans at short notice because he'd come up with a fresh way to approach a subject or arrange a sequence. It was hard work, but the team accepted it because we knew that even the most outlandish last-minute request was made not out of petulant diva-ishness but because he wanted the show to be as good as it could be. Almost without exception, Jeremy's demands were for the good of *Top Gear*. Anything peripheral to that wasn't an issue. He ate damp supermarket sandwiches from the back of a van on shoots, just like the rest of us. As long as someone could rustle up a can of Diet Coke and he could palm a runner a £20 note in return for some Marlboro Lights, he was no trouble. Moreover, in lighter moments he would tacitly acknowledge the talent and dedication of the team that turned his ideas into reality. In 2003, during a throwaway item in which the presenters picked their favourite British car, we shot a scene outside a fast-food lorry parked on the tarmac at Dunsfold.

'Where did this burger van come from?' James asked during a break in recording. He was told one of the researchers had organised it.

'I wouldn't be able to do that,' Jeremy observed. 'I wouldn't know where to start.'

James looked at the sizzling onion steam floating away across the airfield. 'No, me neither,' he said, wistfully.

From then on, whenever the team had arranged something especially brilliant or ambitious with their usual care and attention, the presenters would gaze upon the scene and declare that it would have been beyond them.

'I couldn't have done this,' Clarkson would say.

'No,' May would agree. 'We'd still be trying to book that burger van.'

Jeremy was the engine room of ideas and there's no doubt his demands drove everyone to work harder, but he wasn't beyond admitting that he needed a good and loyal team around him. It's what made the events of that evening in March 2015 all the more disappointing.

It was a Wednesday and we were in the studio recording the seventh show of the 22nd series. Superficially, all was going well. The VTs that week were solid; celebrity guest Nicholas Hoult was charmingly excited to be on the show; we were over the hump in our punishing ten-programme run and the end was in sight. In the production office, however, the mood was less than cheerful. Films for the remaining three shows were running late and Andy Wilman had stayed in the edit that day to oversee their completion. There was still one work in progress, nominally titled 'The Fizz', in which each presenter would pick a favourite current model and then zoom about North Yorkshire on some excellent roads in beautiful landscape celebrating all that we loved about cars and driving. This had

yet to be filmed. It was very short notice, there wasn't a real
script and the weather was looking iffy for the shoot, which
was to take place the next day. Within the tired team, tempers
were getting short.

We got through the studio recording without much trouble
and everyone retired to our crappy production office for a dry
pork pie and a glass of something tepid. Normally, Jeremy,
Richard and James would be driving home but in an unusually lavish move the production had paid for a helicopter to
fly them straight up to Yorkshire that night so they'd be fresh
and ready to start filming the next day. Relieved of their car
keys, the presenters seized this rare opportunity by settling
down in their room at the back of the building and opening
some booze. Jeremy poured himself a hearty glass of rosé.
In the popular perception of Jeremy Clarkson as the king of
classic rock 'n' raw steak ultrablokes he'd have been drinking
a pint of beer. Or Scotch. I can't remember the last time I saw
him enjoying either of those things because his long-standing
booze of choice was delicate hen-do fuel, earning him the
secret office nickname Axl Rosé. That night, Jeremy sloshed
himself another glass of pink wine and told our production
manager in quite robust terms that he was not getting on the
helicopter until he had enjoyed a few more. Shortly afterwards
I made my excuses and headed home.

What happened over the course of that evening is pretty
well recorded, the headline being that Jeremy had punched
our producer Oisin. When most of the team found out on
the Friday of that week I don't think we could believe it.
It was so stupid and so unnecessary. We were a tight team,
and Oisin was a long-serving and popular member of that
team. Whatever else is going on, you don't turn on one of
your own. That's especially true when you're reacting to a

problem brought on by your own insistence on getting pissed in a Portakabin rather than shipping out on time.

My wife got home that Friday evening to find me slumped on the sofa, staring into space. I told her this thing with Jeremy was really bothering me. 'I know,' she said. 'He's let you down.' That was exactly it. Jeremy had let us down. We'd happily work long and late, trying to find a unicorn, a Talbot Samba and a cat that looked like Kylie Minogue if that's what Jeremy wanted. But when the reward for the team's hard work was a smack in the chops, that suggested a lack of respect for the people who worked so tirelessly to make his vision a reality. Over the years all of us on the show had bickered and bitched and behaved as a close-knit group of people does, but we'd never started lamping each other.

The weekend after it happened, Jeremy tried without success to get hold of Oisin so that he could apologise. On the following Monday morning Andy was in the office early, still hoping that the two could sit down together and sort this out. It felt less like a well-meaning attempt to make things right and more like a hasty attempt to get out of trouble and it just wouldn't wash. For 13 years we'd been pretending we were at school. Now, sadly, it was time to behave like grown-ups. Jeremy must have realised this too. By late morning, he'd told BBC management what he'd done.

After handing himself in, Jeremy came over to the *Top Gear* office to apologise to the team. He didn't sit down or even take his jacket off. He just told us he'd made a confession to management and that he was sorry to all of us. With that, he left the office for what would be the very last time. I was furious. Properly, knee-jigglingly, teeth-grindingly furious. His apology seemed half-hearted and feeble, like a child saying the word sorry because they know it's what the adults want to hear, rather than a sincere reflection of remorse.

The next day, he was officially suspended and that week's *Top Gear* put on hold. For the following two weeks we continued to prepare for upcoming episodes on the basis that the series might be allowed to continue, but our efforts were without any joy or energy. Eventually we were told not to bother coming into the office. In the meantime, the world around us had gone mad. The news seemed consumed with Jeremy's fate, little caring that the relentless stalking of their photographers and reporters had driven our blameless colleague Oisin into hiding. A petition was started to demand Clarkson's reinstatement, eagerly signed by people who thought it was okay for a colleague to smack you in the mouth as long as some strangers reckoned he was a good bloke. The final document, some million signatures strong, was delivered to the BBC in a tank, by a buffoon from a right-wing website, accompanied by a man in white overalls with a foam tea cosy on his head pretending to be The Stig. As one online journalist said at the time, if you can manage to source a tank but you can't find a plain white crash helmet, you probably need to sort yourself out.

The following Wednesday the news came through. As befits a man with not much to do, I was having lunch with a friend when I got the text. The BBC wasn't renewing Jeremy's contract. That was it. *Top Gear* as we knew it was over. I thought I'd feel angry about this, but actually it brought a strange sense of relief. At least the matter was resolved. And anyway, what else were the Beeb going to do? Cheerily endorse assault in the workplace, as long as you were famous? They knew they had to punish Jeremy and this was a punishment greater than they could possibly imagine. He'd worked harder

and longer than anyone on *Top Gear*. It had consumed him.
It was his life. And they were taking it away from him.

After the news came through I got the Tube over to the
office. The whole production team was there. We didn't need
to be, but clearly no one could think of anywhere else to be.
We'd been through a lot as a gang, not least this last ridiculous instalment of our strange and unpredictable adventure.
As we sat around in the usual scruffy office it struck me
that though there was no programme to make and nothing
more to do, no one wanted to leave. We were a team. We
were friends. We didn't want to go our separate ways. It
was all very sad.

In the following weeks, I was filled with a strange and
melancholic feeling, as if someone had died. This shouldn't
have been a surprise. *Top Gear* had been a huge and all-
consuming presence in my life. It had occupied my late twen-
ties and all of my thirties. It had given me the most incredible
opportunities to drive amazing cars, meet interesting people
and go to unusual places. I mucked around in Porsches,
Astons and Lamborghinis or clung on to their passenger grab
handles while The Stig showed me what they could really do.
I went to Murray Walker's house, met my favourite member
of Blur and had my picture taken with Jack Bauer. I drove
The Death Road, helped a dwarf up a Majorcan mountain,
twisted my ankle on a nuclear missile silo in Berkshire and
played beach cricket with AC/DC. I got to work with three
of the best and funniest writers in the world and enjoyed
the ultimate writer's ego trip of hearing a room full of 700
people laughing at a joke I'd written.

*Top Gear* gave you the satisfaction of making a programme
that millions around the world seemed to watch and enjoy.
*Top Gear* made you more interesting to people at parties,

even if they just wanted to tell you how much they hated it. *Top Gear* kept you in touch with old friends, especially when they wanted signed pictures and studio tickets. *Top Gear* introduced me to colleagues I hope I'll remain friends with until I die. *Top Gear* was the reason I met the woman who became my wife. *Top Gear* was a massive part of my life.

The truly sad thing is, it was never meant to end this way. But actually, in the silly, feckless, childish, calamitous stupid world we had created, it's really no surprise that it did.

# *Thanks*

The team standing on the deck when the ship went down: Al, Alice, Becks, Brian, Chenoa, Claire, Emma L, Emma T, Greg, Hannah, JT, Jay, Katie, Kit, Krupes, Lauren, Liz, Nick, Osh, Phil, Polly and Wilman.

Andrew, Ben, Casper, Dan, Iain, Jay, Jon, Kiff, Ren, Rob, Russ, Toby, and all the location and studio crews.

Dan, Jim, Joe and everyone in the edit.

Andy B-F, Brycey, Captain Pat, Chris H, Chris R, Elena, Gary B, Gary H, Gavin, Grant, Jason D, Jim, John W, Jon B, Kate S, Katy H, Lakey, Nigel, Potter, Quentin, Rileino, Rowly, Sara, Stig Ben, Stig Perry, Stig 3, Su, Tara, Tiff, Vicki, Woodroffe.

Mikey, Charlie, Adam, Duncan and all the team on the 'other' side of the office.

Alan and Lucinda at Orion, Luigi at LBA.

Jeremy, Richard and James.

My wife for putting up with a man who was also married to a television programme.

And anyone reading this thinking, you missed out my name you utter bastard.